FAULT LINES

Cultural Memory and
Japanese Surrealism

Cultural Memory
in
the
Present

Mieke Bal and Hent de Vries, Editors

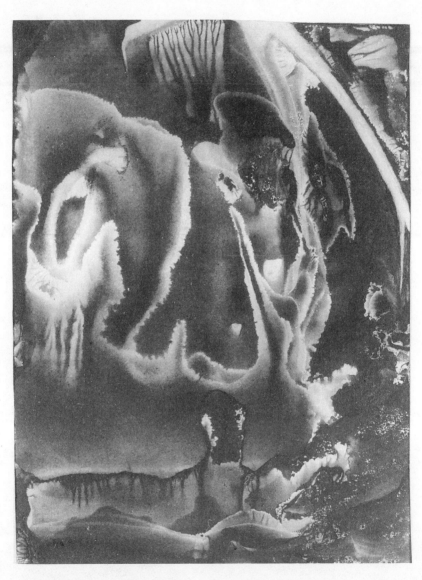

Takiguchi Shūzō, *Décalcomanie*, no. 70, 1962.

FAULT LINES

Cultural Memory and Japanese Surrealism

Miryam Sas

STANFORD UNIVERSITY PRESS

STANFORD, CALIFORNIA

Stanford University Press
Stanford, California
© 1999 by the Board of Trustees of the
Leland Stanford Junior University

Printed in the United States of America
on acid-free, archival-quality paper.

Sas, Miryam.
    Fault Lines : cultural memory and Japanese surrealism / Miryam Sas.
        p.   cm. — (Cultural memory in the present)
    Includes bibliographical references and index.
    ISBN 0-8047-3413-5 (cloth : alk. paper). — ISBN 0-8047-3649-9
(paper : alk. paper)
        1. Japanese literature—1868—History and criticism.
    2. Surrealism (Literature)—Japan.   I. Title.   II. Series.
PL726.55.S269   2001
895.6′ 144091163—dc21   99-24371

Original Printing 2001
Last figure below indicates year of this printing:
09 08 07 06 05 04 03 02 01 00

Typeset by James P. Brommer in 11/13.5 Garamond

Frontispiece and illustration facing half title from
the series Watashi no shinzō wa toki o kizamu
(Tick-tack, my heart—the watch; Takiguchi's trans.).
Courtesy of the Museum of Modern Art, Toyama,
by permission of Takiguchi Ayako.

Cover and chapter opening art by Yoshizumi Higashi.

*For Nira and Joel Silverman
and Sharon*

ACKNOWLEDGMENTS

In the writing of this book I have benefited immeasurably from the help, advice, and support of many professors, colleagues, and friends. First and foremost, I would like to thank my advisor, Edwin McClellan, for his unfailing support and kindness, for his many insightful suggestions, and for his encouragement throughout the research and writing of this book. I would like to thank Shoshana Felman for her continued support, inspiring presence, and thoughtful reading of this work from its earliest stages; and Edward Kamens, for his careful reading and ideas as well as for introducing me to the subtleties of allusion and intertextuality in Japanese premodern poetry, allowing me more fully to understand the radicality of the Surrealists' poetic projects. Geoffrey Hartman has also encouraged my explorations of memory within and beyond the field of this project.

My research in Japan, as a visiting researcher at Keio University, would not have been possible without the generous help of the late Etō Jun. His insights into the history of Japanese poetry and his comparative approach gave me a new perspective on my research and contributed in essential ways to my thinking about these works. Although those whom I interviewed in Japan or who helped with my archival research are too numerous to mention here, I would like to acknowledge the contributions of the following people, in many different areas: Uchibori Hiroshi, Abe Yoshio, Inoue Teruo, Okada Takahiko, Nakanishi Susumu, Katō Yasuo, Kudō Miyoko, Yagi Hiromasa, Yori Hiroko, Onzō Noboru, Toyoizumi Takeshi, Satani Kazuhiko, Ohno Kazuo, Shigeta Mariko, Ema Shōko, John Solt, Lucy Lower, Komuro Midori, and Kishida Asao as well as, in the later stages, Takiguchi Ayako, Nishiwaki Jun'ichi, Hashimoto Akio, Shimōkobe Michiko, Momokawa Takahito, Jay Rubin, Hosea Hirata, and Dan O'Neill. Because of the advanced age of those involved in prewar

Surrealism, when I returned to Japan in final preparation of this manuscript, I found that many whose work I consider here had died since my initial research trip. I would like to acknowledge the generous contributions of Satō Saku and Kawamura Yōichi and the work of Kanbara Tai and Okamoto Tarō.

My gratitude also goes to my colleagues in comparative literature and Japanese literature and my excellent students at Harvard and Berkeley. Noell Howell and John Tain provided incomparable research assistance and helped to compile the chronology and index. My research in Japan was supported by a fellowship from the Japan Foundation; a year of writing was made possible by a Mellon Fellowship. Final revisions were accomplished with the help of a grant from the Center for Asian and Pacific Studies at Seikei University. John Treat and an anonymous reader provided numerous useful suggestions and ideas for revision of the manuscript, for which I thank them. Many thanks to John Ziemer for choosing this book, and to Helen Tartar, Xavier Callahan, and Patricia Draher for their help in bringing it to completion.

I would also like to express my appreciation to Elizabeth Bernstein, Theresa Schwartzmann, Frédéric Maurin, Dan Rosenberg, Amy Greenstadt, Shannon Jackson, 57, Neil Mayle, Melissa Milgram, Sumi Shin, Josine Shapiro, Terry Hong, Mia Fineman, Naoko Kishigami, Eric Selland, and Montgomery Carlough for their inspiration, encouragement, and friendship from near and far. Three people in particular kept me going during the writing process: Michiko Tsushima, Takeyoshi Nishiuchi, and Yoshizumi Higashi. Their advice and close readings provided confirmation and variations on my own understanding of Surrealist poetic language in Japanese as well as philosophical reflections on the links between Japanese and European thought and aesthetics. Lewis Bangham supported this project in inestimable ways throughout. While this project owes debts to many people, any flaws or errors it still contains are mine alone.

Finally, I would like to thank my parents, Nira and Joel Silverman, and my sister Sharon for their love and support, from long before I ever wrote a single word.

M. S.

CONTENTS

ILLUSTRATIONS

A NOTE ON JAPANESE NAMES

Japanese words are romanized according to the modified Hepburn system used in the standard Kenkyūsha *New Japanese-English Dictionary*. Macrons are not used for well-known Japanese place names. Names of Japanese persons are given in the Japanese order, surname first.

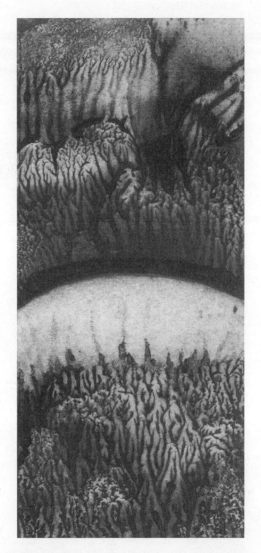

Takiguchi Shūzō, *Décalcomanie*, no. 38, 1962.

FAULT LINES

Cultural Memory and
Japanese Surrealism

WHAT IS CALLED SURREALISM

Some artists and critics write of Surrealism as a practice or process that, even today, has not been fully achieved, as a movement we are still on our way toward: when reduced to mere method or history, it loses all that makes it what it is, irreducible. Surrealism would thus be mapped as the site where a certain leap occurs. We do not yet know what, or where, Surrealism is. Still less, perhaps, do we know what is Surrealism in Japan.

Yet Surrealism is also a movement that is written of in the past tense: what it was, and what it failed to be. Still more, Surrealism in Japan is written into literary history as a movement that never was, or trivialized as a movement that hardly was, invisible to the canonical, educated eye (visible only, perhaps, to the savage eye that it invoked). It never coalesced. But part of what makes Japanese Surrealism fascinating is this impossibility of its coalescing into a single ideological force, a clarity that would appear singular, true, authentic. The anger with which certain factions attack the Japanese cultural imitation of things Western vented itself in force upon the

Surrealists, who went so far as to lace their poems with French idioms, aesthetic terminology, bad puns, and playfulness. Meanwhile Surrealism remained alive on the fault lines of its foundation, founded nonetheless, overturning the simplicity of oppositions like superficiality and depth, false imitation and true creation. Lack of closure, undecidability, the interest in process: all of these things are sighted daily in the world of theory. And yet the stops and starts of meaning and syntax make a difference, in ways that shall be examined below, and these are part of the daily grammar (or antigrammar), the dreamlike idiom, of the Surrealist view of experience.

Japanese Surrealism is striking and important both for the specific questions it raises and for its exemplary place as an encounter between cultures, literary movements, and languages. As a movement that challenges and breaks apart, explicitly and at its initiating moment, clear and bounded conceptions of language, poetry, and the transmissibility of meaning, Japanese Surrealism (as well as Dada) reframes the relation between content and consciousness and is thus a particularly strong and revealing case of cultural interaction. This avant-garde encounter makes apparent the inherent discontinuities and fragmentations within individual cultures that can become crucial opportunities for creative intersections between distant realities, distant cultures.

The specific historical development of Japanese modern poetry has received some scholarly attention outside of Japan. Věra Linhartová's *Dada et surréalisme au Japon* (in French) is the crucial work of translation and explication that comes closest, in taking on the broad movements and literary currents, to providing a literary history of this period in its avant-garde aspects. On the Japanese avant-garde writers, one of the most important works in English published by the time of this writing is Hosea Hirata's *The Poetry and Poetics of Nishiwaki Junzaburō*, which contains translations of some of Nishiwaki's most important writings, including part of his *Surrealist Poetics*. Hirata opens an original approach to Nishiwaki, discussed in the chapters below, along with a brief contextual history of the period. John Solt's intensively researched *Shredding the Tapestry of Meaning: The Poetry and Poetics of Kitasono Katue (1902–1978)*, to which I probably owe more than I know, will for many years remain the definitive work on Kitasono Katsue and his associates. The study combines literary biography and careful historical and poetic readings that reveal Kitasono's centrality in a complex web of poetic associations stretching from Ezra Pound to Ema

Shōko to contemporary poets like Shiraishi Kazuko. Through a critical analysis of the work of ten poets and their poetics, Makoto Ueda's *Modern Japanese Poets and the Nature of Literature* comes closest among works in English to tracing a trajectory for the development of modern Japanese poetry as a whole. Each of the above works, along with many others on related topics that are mentioned in this book, provides a part of the literary historical picture that nonetheless remains to be elaborated in its full contextual complexity.

While my work does not aim to provide a comprehensive literary history, this project (in addition to providing part of the story) engages crucial questions that any literary history needs to take into account if it is to go beyond a determinist causal narrative in order to understand the ways traditions and movements are formed and reconfigured from one culture to another, one language to another. The Selected Chronology provides basic facts related to the development of Dada and Surrealism in Japan as well as historical landmarks that marked the 1920s and 1930s in Japan and in Europe. These selected facts are meant to open up the contextual space for further exploration of the various cultural and ideological "shocks" and incongruities in Japanese cultural life during the prewar period. One might note the Great Kanto Earthquake of September 1, 1923, which, along with the fires that followed it, destroyed most of the structures of old Tokyo, as a coincident (and resonant) moment for the entry into Japan of these poetics of shock, these literary "fault lines." I would hope the Surrealists will be considered an important example among the many ruptures and reconfigurations that took place in Japan during this time. They can be seen both as a "symptom" of larger cultural phenomena and, more crucially, as a paradigmatic moment that can help to reconfigure our understanding of these cultural changes and this period as a whole.[1]

According to the writers of Surrealism in both Japan and France, the creative force of a poetic image comes from the juxtaposition of incongruous or contrasting elements, "distant realities." These words, traced to Pierre Reverdy, are cited by André Breton, Nishiwaki Junzaburō, and others. This reading of the poetic image (and its precedents), which I explore in Chapter 2, serves as a model in this book for my analysis of the productive encounter between cultural and literary movements, which I posit (through a series of close readings) as another kind of creative juxtaposition and transversal of "distant realities."

Freud's understanding of psychic functioning and experience, which fascinated the Surrealists, suggests for the critic a mode of reading of the Surrealist encounter in which the interactions between literary movements are no longer described as a simple transfer of elements from one culture to another, or even a fully conscious adoption. While a writer might choose to incorporate into a given work certain elements encountered in texts from another culture, this kind of influence is of less pressing interest than the aspects of the interaction that slip beyond conscious control or selection and constitute a kind of fault line or interval opened within a work by the encounter that is enacted there. In Chapter 3, I reframe the problem of influence, positing a cultural interaction linked closely with a figure of shock and consciousness: the elements of the encounter that endure may not seem the most important at the moment of the encounter, but may appear only later and at that time make themselves felt as the most crucial elements of the exchange.

Throughout this book I develop and explore a mode of reading of these avant-garde texts that illuminates their tension over the notion of meaning, what poetic or linguistic or cultural meaning is, and how it is constituted. These are problems that French and Japanese writers investigated in their new use of language and in breaking apart and challenging notions of poetic meaningfulness. In this sense they reveal a new level or new kind of "meaning" that explicitly evokes (and invokes) rifts and disruptions in the very process of its conception. At the same time we come to see the desire for, and indeed the necessity of following or constructing, some kind of meaning to be able to read the poems at all. Critiques of Japanese modernist importation of European ideas ignore this crucial aspect of the poetry that, I claim, is constitutive of the creative (and destructive) force of Surrealist poetic language.

Recent studies have also raised the question of war-time nativism and its relation to poetic constructions and interpretation. Readers of these texts judge the "reality" (or "authenticity") of the incorporation of Surrealist ideas in terms of metaphors of blood: pierced to the core by the reality of Surrealism, poets of a true avant-garde should not show a connection to a "traditional" lyricism that later critics would link with latent (and politically insidious) nativism. In Chapter 1 I analyze this problem in terms of both pre- and post-war interpretations of the Surrealist encounter, and I unveil some of the inherent complexities, hesitations, and ambiguities that preclude such simplistic and conclusive ethical judgments of purity or impurity, complicity or resistance.

The place of the visual, of sight, is central for Surrealism ("The eye exists in its savage state," wrote Breton in the famous opening lines of *Surrealism and Painting*), although it is at times overturned by a priority of representation or a priority of writing. This writing may then paradoxically be seen as a direct (nonrepresentational, present) transcription from the unconscious. The oppositions between visuality and writing, presence and sign, create a confusion within French Surrealist thought that at times reiterates the Platonic hierarchy of "thing" and representation and at other times reverses this hierarchy, or attempts to dissolve the barriers between the two poles. This central ambivalence toward the visual takes another turn in the works of the Japanese Surrealists, playing itself out through the distinct poetic dilemmas of modern Japanese language and in the individual projects of the Japanese writers.

Takiguchi Shūzō was the Japanese Surrealist whose work maintained the most intimate and lasting link with that of André Breton. Reflecting his struggle to translate and explain Surrealist thought in Japanese, Takiguchi's work embodies the difficulties of rearticulating, or rather, breaking down and then reconfiguring as possibility (through Surrealist experiments) the syntax and conventions of Japanese language and poetics. In the last section of Chapter 4, through an exploration of Takiguchi's concepts of "dream" and "actuality" in relation to poetic composition, I examine his intricate theories of poetry, his ideals of poetic community and communication, and at the same time his deep recognition (accompanied by regret) of the very "specific difficulty" of translation, the materiality of languages.

Chapter 5 deals most explicitly with the future of Surrealist poetics and its legacy. I trace the path through and beyond Surrealism first in Nishiwaki Junzaburō's changing ideas of eternity; in the pressing question and persistent images of the "void" and eternity I read his evolving relation to Surrealist notions of language and temporality. The chapter reopens and reconfigures questions of memory and nostalgia, particularly in terms of the work of Tomotani Shizue and Ema Shōko, two women Surrealists whose writings have not received the full recognition they deserve in the criticisms and analysis of the Japanese avant-garde. A reading of Tomotani's and Ema's works might be considered a partial revision of

Surrealism's legacy, as we reconsider the prewar avant-garde in light of their early writings which, even more than the rest, seemed to have vanished from the scene. In the last section of the chapter I trace the impact of Surrealism in the artistic and avant-garde movements of the postwar period.

The Epilogue opens one more route for exploration—the avant-garde artists' transfer of their quests from the realm of the literary to the field of performance. I propose the possibility that the search for "actuality" initiated by Surrealist writers—an actuality that transcends the boundaries of habit and convention—may continue in an engagement with the physical in the realm of avant-garde dance. I explore thoughts on avant-garde dance put forth by practitioners and collaborators in the Butoh movement, ideas that can at times challenge conventions of language and imagination as well as ideas of physical motion. In the rhetoric surrounding Butoh, images of memory and tradition are transformed and reiterated within a physical quest for actuality. This nostalgic quest, however, is often misread as representing or realizing national or traditional essences. A closer look reveals a more paradoxical structure inherent in the nostalgias and recollections that Butoh embodies, and a broader significance to be found in the projects of avant-garde dance as it takes the impulses of Surrealist experiments into the physical realm.

In reconsidering the definitions of avant-garde literary movements in the context of their Japanese transplantation, it is necessary to trace the specific usage of these terms both as personal guidelines within the corpus of individual writers and as literary and ideological boundaries for the formation of avant-garde groups and associations. Exploring the reinvention and repositioning of Surrealist terms and ideas within the specific vocabulary and projects of the Japanese writers, I argue that a vision of alterity, a foreign space located somewhere "beyond," plays a crucial role in formulations of avant-garde praxis for both the Japanese and French contexts. An exploration of Japanese notions of the surreal, calling for a rereading of received understandings and presuppositions about French avant-garde movements, may lead to a reconfiguration of this period written less in terms of a narrative history of literature than as the nonlinear route of a multivalent dialogue.

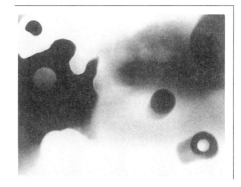

INTRODUCTION

> The air is a beautiful princess without bones.
> —Takiguchi Shūzō, "Documents d'oiseaux"

> Write subjectively. People who study Japanese Surrealism are too careful.
> They are afraid of making mistakes. But this is not a school textbook.
> —Satō Saku, editor of *Fukuikutaru kafu yo* (Ah, fragrant stoker)

In contemporary Japanese popular speech, heard in the streets or in TV commercials, one frequently notes the use of the prefix *chō-*. Encompassing the meanings "super-" or "ultra-," *chō-* can denote emphasis or excess: going beyond, surpassing a limit, crossing a boundary, as in *chō-bikkuri*, "shocking"; *chō-sugoi*, "ultra-cool"; or *chō-bijin*, "gorgeous." This is no longer, presumably, on the same level as an ordinary shock, an everyday cool, a run-of-the-mill beauty. This "ultra-" can be understood to convey the contemporary excitement (constructed at least in part by the mass media) implicit in the idea of progress, of speed, of convenience (*chō-kakuyasu*, ultra-cheap; *chō-kōsoku*, superhighway). The same *chō-*, however, marks the place of "sur-" in "Surrealist"; with it, we enter a world of early twentieth-century avant-garde poetics that may appear frail, ephemeral to our contemporary gaze. The thin, leafletlike magazines, with reproductions of drawings and photos imported from France and England on delicate newsprint[1]—it is within such artifacts that one hears the summons of that period. The journals become steadily thinner and more delicate as the war approaches. In their most idealistic moments, the ideas they purvey may on first encounter sound lyrical, whimsical, even romantic. Nonetheless their questioning of the poetic process, of the conventions and possibilities of language, contains at its core the force of a deep shock.

With the prefix *chō-* of *chō-genjitsushugi* (Surrealism) one has entered the realm of the strange, even the grotesque. Baudelaire writes in his journals (and his words are echoed by Nishiwaki Junzaburō in his *Surrealist Poetics* [*Chōgenjitsushugi shiron*]) that "the mingling of the grotesque and the tragic is pleasing to the mind."[2] This *chō-*, banalized in contemporary everyday speech, devoid of its radical power, may nonetheless recall a trace of Baudelaire's tragic realm. At its origins *chō-* signifies transcendence as well as transgression—something that moves beyond the everyday, breaks the mold of the category it modifies, and, taken to the extreme, might at any moment approach the point of disappearance.

Peter Bürger explores the paradox of what he terms the "historical avant-garde" in his *Theory of the Avant-Garde.* He describes the process by which the radicalism of an avant-garde movement is "consumed" by a given society over time by its very acceptance, "since now the protest of the historical avant-garde against art as an institution is accepted as art."[3] The same acts of protest, seen from the point of view of a later period, take on a changed meaning; Bürger explores the way the works of the European "historical avant-gardes" (early twentieth century) become transformed in the process of their reception (though one might add that their meanings were already divided, multiple from the start). He examines the reasons why the force of avant-garde acts as protest has been "consumed" by/ within the institutions of art.

Examining the interactions between Japanese and French avant-garde movements, focusing in particular on Surrealist and Dada literary works and manifestos, I consider in this book the ways these movements are transferred, transplanted, or transported from one place to another, one language to another. Questioning and reconsidering metaphors of influence that have been used to discuss the interactions between Japanese and

French literature, I work with alternative models of memory, and citation, to examine the process by which a movement from one culture is recalled, cited, and—not without a shock—transplanted into another.

By choosing to explore the paths of a literary movement through disjunctions in time and place, inconsistencies, and dissolutions, I aim to formulate alternative metaphors and models that can also be relevant to the analysis of cultural and literary interactions outside of the realms designated explicitly as "avant-garde." Taking the avant-garde as paradigm allows for a specific focus on the transfer/translation of literary ideas that specifically resist their own reification as a "corpus" and that undergo dramatic divisions and reconfigurations over time. Rather than positing similarity as the point of departure for a comparison, this study chooses to focus explicitly on areas riddled with disjunctions and inconsistencies from within (even before the process of translation or transfer from one culture to another has begun). This resistance to what one might term "consumption" in identity, is, however, inextricably bound up with restrictions and conventions specific to each particular national language and the particular situation of their production. Perhaps one might imagine the following figure in the transfer of Surrealist thought from one culture to another: one notices that the contents of a package are different at the time of their opening from the time of their packing—what we seek, then, are hints about the process of change undergone by the contents of the package during its transit. At the same time, the process itself unsettles the certainty about the point of origin, any reifiable or certain content even at the point of packing. It leads us to bring both ends of the transfer into question.

The analysis of the transfer, transplantation, or translingual adaptation of cultural movements can also illuminate the change undergone by avant-garde movements in their reception over time (as theorized by Bürger), and the effects of the distance between producer and recipient. As Bürger points out, "The avant-garde not only negates the category of individual production but also that of individual reception. . . . Given the avant-gardiste intention to do away with art as a sphere that is separate from the praxis of life, it is logical to eliminate the antithesis between producer and recipient."[4] It remains to be seen whether these definitions of the avant-gardiste's intention (to negate the category of individual production and to eliminate the division between artist and recipient) hold true outside of the sphere of Bürger's study, which focuses on European manifestations.

Among the large number of writers whose work was associated explicitly with the movements of Surrealism and Dada in Japan, those primarily responsible for the leadership of these movements include Takiguchi Shūzō (1903–1979), Nishiwaki Junzaburō (1894–1982), Kitasono Katsue (1902–1978), Haruyama Yukio (1902–), and (for Dada) Takahashi Shinkichi (1901–1987). Many critics trace the Surrealist movement in Japan to the group of students who studied with Nishiwaki at Keio University in Tokyo after his return from England in 1925. That group included Takiguchi, Satō Saku (1905–1996), the brothers Ueda Toshio (1900–1982) and Ueda Tamotsu (1906–1973), and several others. It is clear that Nishiwaki brought back ideas about Surrealism and news of other recent literary trends from England, and that the group met at cafés like the Hakujūji and at Nishiwaki's home to discuss these new ideas about art and literature. Alternative narratives of the movement's history, however, place Takiguchi or Kitasono closer to the center, or point to the work of painter-poets such as Koga Harue (1895–1933). In fact the seeds of interest in European avant-garde movements had begun much earlier.

Certain events and publications are often cited as founding moments for the avant-garde literary movements in Japan. In 1921, the year before his death at the age of twenty-nine, Hirato Renkichi distributed to passersby in Hibiya Park the pamphlet "Manifesto of the Japanese Futurist Movement" (*Nihon miraiha sengen undō*—Mouvement futuriste japonais). Takahashi Shinkichi published "Three Dada Poems" (Dada no shi mittsu) in the journal *Kaizō: Reconstruo* in October 1922, inspired by articles about Dada in the August 15, 1920, issue of the newspaper *Yorozuchōhō,* which contained excerpts from Tristan Tzara's Dada manifestos. In 1923, Takahashi published *Dadaisuto Shinkichi no shi* (The poems of Dadaist Shinkichi), edited by Tsuji Jun (1884–1944). Tsuji published his own introduction to Dada, "Dada no hanashi," in a September 1922 issue of *Kaizō: Reconstruo.* In that issue, one finds the piece side by side with such a well-remembered and canonical work as Shiga Naoya's *An'ya koro* (A dark night's passing), which was being serialized in the journal.

Often Surrealism in Japan is considered as a branch or offshoot of what is still called *modanizumu,* prewar Japanese modernism, which included self-designations in Japan of movements as diverse as Futurism, Dadaism, Constructivism, Imagism, and Neue Sachlichkeit. While the names were often directly cited from European movements, the meanings and connotations and strategic impact of the use of these names remain to be debated. Many coterie journals were founded—some destined to last longer, like *Shi to shiron* (Poetry and poetics), edited by Haruyama Yukio, and others, like *Le Surréalisme international*, to produce only one issue. Many of the same poets and writers branched off and reconfigured to form new journals, and scholars have carefully documented the genealogies of these small magazines and poetic associations and dissociations.[5] Writers such as Hagiwara Sakutarō (1886–1942), the poet and playwright Miyoshi Jūrō (1902–1958), Kitagawa Fuyuhiko (1900–1990), and the Futurist Kanbara Tai (1898–1997) criticized the Surrealists for having "lost touch with reality" and in 1930 split off from the journal *Shi to shiron* to form their own alternative poetic journal, *Shi: Genjitsu* (Poetry: Reality). In the chapters below, the stakes in some of these debates will be analyzed and considered in their rhetorical intricacy and depth. Many resonate strongly with dilemmas that still concern contemporary literary and cultural criticisms.

While Takiguchi maintained his explicit allegiance to Surrealism longer than Kitasono or Nishiwaki, all three were recognized literary and artistic mentors before and after the war. Yet many poets whose work we find in the pages of these literary journals have been all but forgotten—two discussed later are Asuka Tōru and Tomotani Shizue. There is still much room for a reconsideration of these movements and their legacies, and many more discoveries to be made beyond the bounds of this book, which touches just the tip of an enormous territory. The energy and strength as well as the frequent sophistication and subtlety of the work leave this writer surprised that more scholarly research has not recognized the contributions of these poets and artists. Artists and poets in Japan have been quick to attest that these early and idiosyncratic avant-garde works and journals were crucial in inspiring them to pursue literary interests and in enabling them to perform their own artistic experiments.

In "Tomorrow at Stake," an essay written shortly after the death of the Surrealist leader André Breton, Maurice Blanchot, French philosopher and critic, writes of the difficulties inherent in speaking of Surrealism and its history:

One cannot speak of what was neither a system or a school, nor a movement of art or literature, but rather a pure practice of existence (a practice of the whole bearing its own knowledge, a practical theory) in a determinate temporal modality. In the past tense, it would constitute a history, a fine story (the history of surrealism

is only of scholarly interest, particularly if the conception of history is not modified by its subject, and nothing up to now has appeared to justify evoking such a
possibility). And as for the present or the future, just as one cannot claim that surrealism has been realized (thus losing more than half of what names it: everything
in it that goes out ahead of it), neither can one say that it is half real or on the way
to realization, in becoming. What constitutes surrealism as an absolute summa-
tion, and a summons of such urgency that through it (be it in a most fortuitous
manner) waiting opens itself to the unexpected, also prohibits us from trusting
solely to the future for it to be accomplished or take form.[6]

Surrealism, according to Blanchot, calls for a temporal mode beyond
the simple retrospective. He suggests the need for a conception of history
that would be "modified by its subject," the invention of a new mode beyond the simple past or speculative future that can incorporate the historicity of Surrealism and at the same time evoke the urgency of its call to
the unexpected. His dismissal of "scholarly interest" implies a form of
scholarship that seeks and demands closure, identity, or a determinate and
final temporal mode. "Scholarship" would function here as an institution
in a way that recalls Peter Bürger's notion of the avant-garde "consumed"
by the institution of art: reified, closed, and thereby silenced. Blanchot's
tone in this text may be read as elegiac (in homage to Breton) or as a rearticulation of the ending represented by Breton's death, which although
unspoken is very present in this text. Blanchot suggests such a reading as
he questions in a footnote: "Why then, in the face of the 'absolute impropriety' of this death that filled us with grief, evoke 'the future of surrealism'?"[7] Because, in part, of its "absolute impropriety" and the desire to
evoke, while recognizing in some form the unjustifiability of this evocation, a possible future.

In the attempt to sketch out what have been considered the crucial
facts and events in the transplantation of Dada and Surrealism into the
Japanese context and their subsequent interpretation, one must confront a
temporal difficulty as articulated by Blanchot. One confronts along with it
the absence of a moment of origin and a moment of ending. Rather than
positing an arbitrary origin, this study opens by exploring a paradigmatic
moment of displacement, the path and implications of a specific node of
contact between French and Japanese Surrealist poetics. The notion that
the creative force of a poetic image comes from its bringing together "distant realities" (or distant worlds), and that this bringing together of incongruous or contrasting elements is a fundamental source of poetic creativity

(although similar ideas can be traced to poetic traditions long before these movements), plays a primary role in certain theoretical formulations of Surrealist practice. Without speculating on the reasons yet, let us trace the path of this particular vision of the poetic image with the hope that it can provide a clue in the search for a dialogic encounter with history.

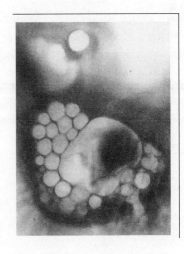

2

DISTANT REALITIES

The poet Pierre Reverdy (1889–1960) writes in the March 1918 issue of the journal *Nord-Sud* (North-South):

The image is a pure creation of the mind. It is born not of comparison, but rather by the bringing together of two more or less distant realities. The more distant and true [*juste*] the two realities brought together, the stronger the image—and the more emotional power and poetic reality it will have.[1]

THE POWER OF THE IMAGE

Reverdy's theoretical essay "On Images" defines the strength of an image through its "emotional power" and "poetic reality." His "bringing together of two . . . distant realities" is not to be read as a process "of comparison": it refers, rather, to a previously unknown form of *rapport* (relation) between the elements, a new invention. Reverdy's term *comparaison* may be taken to refer to other traditional tropes of poetry—not merely analogy, but "given conventions of language" in the broader sense (according to the dictionary, an "established relation between an object and another term, in language. See: allusion, image, metaphor").[2] Reverdy suggests the transcendence of fixed modes of contrast in favor of a more mysterious balance of distance and truth. It is this suggestion that Surrealist writers adopt in the quest for a method of departure from the conventions of poetic imagery.

André Breton (1896–1966), citing Reverdy's words in the "First Manifesto of Surrealism" (1924), adds: "These words, however sibylline for the uninitiated, were extremely revealing, and I pondered them for a long time."[3] Though Reverdy has generally been considered a symbolist poet, later in the manifesto Breton calls him a Surrealist at home (*surréaliste chez lui*). He comments ironically, "The image eluded me. Reverdy's aesthetic, a completely *a posteriori* aesthetic, led me to mistake the effects for the causes."[4] This note that "the image eluded me" serves also to mark the fact that it would not be conscious "meditations" that would come to represent the source of poetic images for Breton ("The absence of any control exercised by reason" was to become one of his requirements for Surrealist writing in this manifesto). Nonetheless, in defining Surrealism Breton states, "Surrealism is based on the belief in the superior reality of certain forms of previously neglected associations," terms that can be seen to take Reverdy's words as their basis.[5]

In the section entitled "Profanus" of *Surrealist Poetics* (*Chōgenjitsushugi shiron*), Nishiwaki Junzaburō, tracing this view of the image back to earlier European theories of poetry (e.g., Coleridge), cites Reverdy's and Breton's theories of the image. His translation of Reverdy's words might be rendered as follows: "The farther the two realities are from one another, and the more true [*heikin suru*, also balanced, in equilibrium] they are, the stronger the image [*shinzō*] will be." He seems to separate the question or aspect of the "distance" of the two realities from the adjoining problem of the "truth," "rightness," or "balance" (*justesse*) of the image.

For Nishiwaki, distance, especially the distance or disjunction of language, becomes a fundamental concern to which he consistently returns in his poetry and in his theoretical writings. In tracing the path of his biography (his moves from Ojiya in Niigata Prefecture to England and to Tokyo) and in reading the place of translation in his work (for example, his transcriptions of the Latin poetry of Catullus, unmarked, directly into his own poetic writings), both admirers and critics tend to center their analysis around this issue of distance, as well as around the related problem of translation.[6]

In 1954, at a time when Nishiwaki had long since dissociated himself from the Surrealist movement, he wrote a new preface for a reprint edition of the 1929 *Surrealist Poetics*. Here he points out that the word *chōgenjitsushugi* was used in the title only at the suggestion of the editor (Haruyama Yukio); Nishiwaki had originally intended to use the term *chōshizenshugi* (supernaturalism). Yet in the statement that directly follows his explanation, Nishiwaki continues to locate the central tenet of his poetics in a principle closely reminiscent of Reverdy's theory of the image: "[In this book] I attempted to introduce the theory that 'the fundamental nature of poetry is that it brings together contradictory elements and makes [them] harmonious.' I still believe in this principle."[7] The contradictory elements named by Nishiwaki correspond to the principle that, within the body of the text of *Surrealist Poetics*, he terms "two realities" (*futatsu no genjitsu*), in a direct translation of Reverdy's words. The critical terms of "distance" (in preface, *aihan*, "opposing"; in body of text, *hanarereba hanareru hodo*, "as distant as possible") and "balance," "harmony," *justesse* (in preface, *chōwa*, "harmony"; in text, *heikin suru*, "balance") are present in both versions. The distinction he makes in the preface with relation to his original poetic theory, then, concerns the term *chōgenjitsushugi* (Surrealism) rather than the explicit content of the poetic principles articulated in the text.

"Surrealism" was, he explains, a "term of recent invention" at the time he wrote *Surrealist Poetics*. When he wrote this text he had just heard the names of Pierre Reverdy and Ivan Goll for the first time; by the second printing, Surrealism had "caught on" and its political valence had changed. In 1954, "Surrealism" had long since become a familiar term in popular speech and, as such, may have been seen by Nishiwaki as "consumed" in the waves of artistic trend. Nonetheless, he would claim an eternal or achronic status for his theories. In Chapter 4, I explore further the problematic nature of the "eternity" Nishiwaki names and evokes in his poetry and in theoretical writings, and the way this "eternity" itself paradoxically changes and evolves over time.

"Poetry," that elusive entity, has slipped out while the door was open to admit the throng; or so one may interpret the images with which Nishiwaki continues his explication and renunciation of Surrealism in the second edition preface:

The way of poetry is long. It [would be like] seeking a flamboyantly attractive woman when one is wandering around a hedge in the country. Or, again, it [would be] as difficult to find as a man who can weep at a festival.[8]

These incongruous statements concluding the preface recall Nishiwaki's technique of switching suddenly, in the middle of a piece of expository prose, into the metaphoric or poetic mode. His images of the "way of poetry" emphasize the solitary and unexpected nature of the poetic encounter, the difficulty of gaining a grasp on it through conscious effort. Thus the preface seems to carry and perform a double message: both a denial or rejection of Surrealism and an evocation of an "eternal" mode of poetry that has, nonetheless, recognizable affiliations with Surrealist poetics. Stretching beyond the determinate modes of history, he attempts to make his Surrealist poetics transcend the circumstances of its own writing.[9]

As Nishiwaki (as well as Breton and Reverdy) describes, a poetics based on juxtaposition and harmonizing of incongruous elements had been the subject of experimentation long before these avant-garde poets adopted them for their own uses. Critic Amagasaki Akira, for example, employs terms very close to these in his description of the linking of unrelated meanings performed by *kakekotoba* ("pivot words" with multiple meanings) in classical Japanese poetics, although here it is often a question of a conventionalized doubling of the meaning of a single word (*furi*, "to grow old," and "to fall," as snow; *miyuki*, "deep snow" and "imperial visit").[10] Other recent critics, such as Nakanishi Susumu,[11] have claimed that a highly compelling "surreality" is already explored in the poetic images and contrasts of the Man'yōshū, the earliest extant anthology of Japanese poetry. At times such claims—if not necessarily as advanced by Nakanishi on this occasion—can risk dismissing the specificity and cultural effects of the Surrealists' project, and often retain a strong ideological valence in reclaiming an original effect that had been thought to result from interactions with Europe as "already present" in Japanese traditions.

This ideological tendency is stronger in some formulations—Man'yōshū Japanese poets did it better—than in others: Surrealists and premodern poets are interested in the relation between spontaneity or immediacy and language, thus representing another kind of literary critical cross-fertilization. Nonetheless, within the problem of translingual influence and translation, and within the context of the complex revolution in Japanese poetic language beginning in the late nineteenth century with the impact of translations of Western poetry (by writers such as Mori Ōgai, Ueda Bin, Horiguchi Daigaku, Kobayashi Hideo, and Nagai Kafū), one finds a wide range of poetic activity that mobilizes the effects of distancings and ruptures, estrangements and disjunctions. One might also consider the poetic experiments (and some translations) by Taishō-period poets such as Kitahara Hakushū or Satō Haruo, who worked side by side with the Surrealists, or earlier poets such as Kitamura Tōkoku, Shimazaki Tōson, Ueda Bin, or Ishikawa Takuboku, all of whom were engaged in an important (and, again, relatively canonically recognized) questioning of the poetic process.

I would not claim that this kind of effect is unique to the Surrealist poets or belongs exclusively to the consideration of their work. On the contrary, I am convinced that an analysis of these effects within the work of the Surrealists can serve to open a method or a model for the considerations of the problem of influence across the range of modern Japanese poetics and literary writings, and for cultural interactions and intercultural effects beyond these bounds as well. Within this range of concerns, the Japanese Surrealists provide a highly charged and intensely illuminating— and, to me, fascinating—test case and point of departure.

THE ARTICULATION OF DISTANCE

Rather than trace the broad history of the poetics of juxtapositions in Japan (itself a highly charged and often reconfigured tradition), here I would like to remain within the limits of modern Japanese experimental poetics, and for the moment focus on one example, a text by the symbolist poet Yamamura Bochō (1884–1924). Bochō is known to have studied Baudelaire in English, and this may be implicated in the proximity of his poetics to the ideas of Reverdy, also closely linked to Baudelaire. Only slightly preceding Reverdy's publication in *Nord-Sud*, the poem "Geigo" takes an important place in the history of experimentation in modern Japanese poetry. Yamamura Bochō, a Catholic priest as well as a poet, published the experimental poetry collection *Sei sanryō hari* (Sacred prisms) in 1915. The poem "Geigo" strikingly exemplifies a contrastive mode of poetic composition close to the above theoretical formulations of the Surrealist writers. Composed in 1913, "Geigo" is said to have influenced the early writings of Hagiwara Sakutarō, who read the poem before its publication;

its echoes can be detected in early versions of the poems in Hagiwara's *Tsuki ni hoeru* (Howling at the moon, 1917). (Hagiwara's famous anthology, Nishiwaki often claimed, inspired him to write poetry in Japanese for the first time, rather than only in French or English, and it exercised a profound effect on a generation of Taishō-period writers.) Hagiwara later wrote a detailed essay in defense of Bochō's "Geigo."[12]

The kanji (Chinese character) for *geigo* could be translated as "foolish talk," "nonsense," "jargon," "talking in one's sleep," or "delirious utterances." I use all capital letters in the translation to evoke (obliquely) the effect of the high concentration of kanji in the original:

Geigo

ABDUCTION SPONGE-CAKE

THEFT GOLDFISH

ROBBERY TRUMPET

BLACKMAIL SITAR

GAMBLING CAT

FRAUD CALICO

BRIBERY VELVET

ADULTERY APPLE

ASSAULT SKYLARK

MURDER TULIP

ABORTION SHADOW

RIOT SNOW

ARSON QUINCE

Each line of the poem consists of two nominal elements, not explicitly related. Bochō has eliminated all grammatical particles linking the elements of phrases, so the poem consists solely of the juxtaposition (or association) of contrasting nouns. Each line begins with the name of a criminal act; the nouns that follow these acts seem to compose an atmosphere of Baudelairean "luxury," perhaps to cite the objects that would appear in a "decadent" poem. The text, however, refuses to explain—nor does it allow for any closed interpretation of—the links between the elements. One recalls Reverdy's description of the poetic image as the linking of two elements distant and true; Bochō's thirteen-line poem inspired numerous imitations, but the later poems generally fail to reproduce the odd harmony of its lines.

Abe Yoshio, a scholar well known for his work on Baudelaire and on Japanese avant-garde poetry,[13] focuses on the absence of the particle *wa*, which might have been placed, in more standard nominal usage, between the two nouns (he notes precedents for such a form of isolated nominal use). *Wa* would connote a relation of equivalence between the nouns in question ("A *wa* B" or "A = B") and would thus have transformed their juxtaposition (or association) into a form of metaphor. "Bochō understood that Baudelairean poetics consisted not solely in the articulation of *correspondances* to be perceived as natural or immanent," writes Abe (in French). "More important, the poet was to construct associations in which the contrast, or even the rupture, between the two terms placed together would leave a forceful impression on the mind of the reader."[14] Abe traces the role of this poetics of incongruity and contrast rather than of association ("not of comparison," writes Reverdy), as it influenced the work of Hagiwara Sakutarō.[15] "Geigo" may be considered a forerunner of the kind of poetics developed and expanded in Surrealism.

One criticism frequently leveled against Japanese Surrealism, or against individual Surrealist works, is that the movement hedged too closely on "formalism." The Japanese poets are accused of adopting the techniques of European Surrealism in order to fulfill solely aesthetic aims, without sharing the political commitment considered such an important part of the European Surrealist movement. Yet often such factional critique leads to tautological or predetermined readings of poetry: "This poet is a formalist; therefore his poetry is apolitical."[16] The poets' attack on logical reasoning and conventional poetics produced many works that were difficult to interpret in the traditional sense. Although clearly these works do not aspire to function in the same manner as political polemic, or even as the explicitly politicized literary works of the time, to dismiss them as simply apolitical would constitute an oversimplification. The question of the political implications of projects that claim an aesthetic status, but which nonetheless reformulate discursive practices and reconstitute aspects of cultural traditions, is a matter of heated debate in Japanese and European cases: many critics trace the implications of both sides of this argument in their rereading of prewar cultural projects in light of the imperialistic militarism and nationalist projects of World War II that followed them (if not followed from them).[17]

We may recall the radical assertion in 1916 by the Surrealist Paul Eluard (1895–1952): "Let us not talk of war. It is through words that it is kept alive." Or we could consider the stand taken by André Breton and Louis

Aragon (1897–1982) at about this time, that to speak of war, "even if it was in order to curse it, was yet another way of advertising it."[18] Although the attitudes of French Surrealists toward open political engagement passed through various stages, their opinions of this time may cast light on the Japanese Surrealists' attitude toward politics: to choose to speak of European poetics and not of war, in Japan in the late 1920s and 1930s, can be construed as a self-conscious stance (whose nuances in both directions will be interpreted and debated below) in relation to the issues capturing public attention at the time. Further, to produce small, limited-edition texts constituted not only a reflection on the limited funds for poetry but also a resistance to the rise of a form of mass-appeal literature. (In an era when poetic composition was influenced by the medium of radio, some argue that the possibility for mass popular appeal encouraged the composition of easily understood or sentimental works.) Mass-produced literature and literary collections in this period, such as the one-yen books sold in series, would stand in striking contrast to the production of coterie journals of Surrealist poetry and theory.

Continual splits in Surrealist groups—European and Japanese—reflect heated arguments about this relation between reality and the surreal, and the production of journals appears to have been a continual struggle.[19] One could focus on the political reactions to Surrealist activities in Japan: the questioning of avant-garde writers by the special secret service police (*tokkō*) in the years just before World War II; the jailing of Takiguchi Shūzō for approximately nine months in 1941 for his Surrealist poetic activities; the arrest and time in jail imposed on a group of poets in Kobe in 1940. Turning the pages of Yamanaka Chirū's 1936 translation of André Breton's *L'Immaculée Conception* (The immaculate conception; Bon shoten), one finds that an eight-page section, "Romantic Love," has been excised by a rough pair of censor's shears. These facts are important to recognize. It would be an altogether different project, however, to shift the focus from Surrealist production to political repression by those who often had only a vague and superficial (or often mistaken) notion of the political implications of the works they censored. More relevant would be an exploration of the Surrealists' attack on what, for them, constituted conventionalized forms of language and sentiment as expressed in institutionalized literary and cultural forms, as well as their creative reappropriations of positive poetic and artistic projects.[20]

One might take Kitasono Katsue's well-known work *Kigōsetsu* (Semiotic theory, or Theory of signs) as an example of the difficulties inherent in this interpretative debate. Kitasono's work as a poet, editor, and theorist, along with his vast correspondence within Japan and abroad, was instrumental in spreading word of Surrealism in Japan, and of Japanese poetic innovations in Europe. *Kigōsetsu*, first published in *Bungei tanbi* under the title *Hakushoku shishū* (Collection of white poems) was reworked for publication in the 1929 anthology *Shiro no arubamu* (White album).[21] Published when the Japanese Surrealist movement was well under way, *Kigōsetsu* has been cited as an example of the formalism of Japanese Surrealism, in particular because of its repeated use of the word "white" and because of the "painterly" images of its first few lines. The poem commences:

> *Semiotic Theory*
>
> white tableware
> flower
> spoon
> 3PM in springtime
> white
> white
> red
>
> prism architecture
> white animal
> space
>
> blue flag
> apple and noblewoman
> white landscape
> . . .

Although the length of the poem generally prevents its citation in full,[22] the abridgment found in most critiques restructures (and thus transforms) the effect of the repeated word "white," making it appear merely "aesthetic" or "pretty" in intent, ineffectual and harmless. I would argue, however, that by the time a reader has encountered the persistent repetition of "white" in twenty-three of fifty-three lines, within a text consisting solely of juxtaposed, repeated nouns and adjectives (with verbs used rarely and only as parts of descriptive clauses), this relentless repetition across the horizontal visual expanse of the poem creates an effect more complex than merely "pretty."

More than halfway into the poem one encounters the lines "white socks / aesthetics / white aesthetics." The marked term "aesthetics" in relation to "theory of signs" changes the way one reads the "whiteness" of the long empty lines. Within the awareness of the poem's reference to its own poetic technique, to the process of its composition, the concept of "emptiness" has entered quotation marks. The ironic tone of the poem is subtle but persistent. The repeated words "silver cubist doll / silver cubist doll" stand out in reference, only faintly veiled, to the artistic and poetic movement within which this poem is a participant as well as, perhaps, a critique. The only active verbs in the poem are in negation: "blue sky / can't see anything / can't see anything" followed by the lines "pale [*awai*, transitory] peach-colored flag / despair." The poem continues with empty-sounding effusions: "It is a happy lifestyle and me / it is happy ideas and me / it is transparent pleasures and me." And it ends: "evening formalwear / evening formalwear / evening formalwear / evening formalwear / boring." Unlike Yamamura Bochō's explicit evocation of the world of crime and darkness, Kitasono's images are relentlessly light and full of space and air. It is as though the "transparent pleasures" and "happy ideas" are being unmasked here, as though a purist aesthetics of poetry is being revealed and, by implication, cast in an ironic light.

In the introduction to *Shiro no arubamu*, Haruyama Yukio describes the need to go beyond the known realm of literature (*bungaku*): "As for literature, the part of it that has been written down is no more than simply literature. Only now for the first time, the unwritten part is [can be] called poetry [*poésie*]." In this essay, constructed of a fragmented series of thoughts, he continues: "By writing poems [*shi*] without meaning, one experiments with the purity of poetry [*poésie*]. To see meaning in poetry is not to see anything beyond literature in poetry."[23] Such statements, presented as the introduction to Kitasono's work, bring the implicit protest in *Kigōsetsu* to bear on the institution of literature. Haruyama's introduction is replete with whimsical remarks that mock the traditions of literary realism: "It is meaningless to look at a flower realistically. How do flowers look at us? When animals bark in front of flowers, they only reveal their disgraceful capacity for stupidity."[24]

Later, in a 1952 essay, Kitasono criticized his own early experimental poetry, including *Kigōsetsu*, for not sufficiently representing his individual poetic style (as he later conceived it): he found the early work too much influenced by the ideology and doctrines of the Surrealist movement.[25] Like Nishiwaki Junzaburō's work in the 1950s, Kitasono Katsue's at this time was no longer involved with the Surrealist movement; although both artists were considered central figures in prewar Surrealist groups, both (in different ways) are critical of their youthful writings, which they view as (mere) experiments. One recalls the phenomenon articulated by Bürger—changed meaning, or change in reception, of the works of avant-garde artists over time—although here it is a case of a change in the representation and construction of their work by the artists themselves, the reconfiguration and rejection of their own earlier methods and projects. Takiguchi Shūzō, however, maintained a vigorous allegiance to Surrealist principles long after other Surrealist writers had dissociated themselves from the movement, and for this reason he is often considered one of those responsible for the longevity and popularity of Surrealism in Japan, and for its enduring place in literature, theater, dance, and the visual arts.

John Solt notes the problem of Surrealism as fashion, given its marketability in contemporary Japan (it has several times attained the status of a boom, a periodic commercial trend). In terms close to Bürger's notion of "consumption," he writes:

We notice, somewhat alarmed, that the [Surrealist] movement has had more enduring impact in Japan than anywhere else, even its birthplace. Founder André Breton was aware that surrealism in a capitalist society would probably end up as just another trick in the arsenal of advertisers, rather than the self-liberation of the psyche that he and the other writers and artists originally had idealized. Present-day Japanese consumerism is living proof of Breton's realistic fears.[26]

Many artistic techniques once associated with Surrealism can no longer lay claim to the power to surprise, provoke, liberate in the same way as before. The technology of digital special effects and virtual realities, for example, includes the montage of disjunct and unrelated elements as one of its most basic mechanical functions. This use of images or techniques that were attributed a special power by the Surrealists, or of methods reminiscent of Surrealist techniques (especially in visual rhetoric), must be considered in the particular context of commercial advertising and contemporary culture: is Surrealism being cited, implicated, and (implicitly or explicitly) alluded to? The appropriation of "high art" elements within the mass media—both as a reinforcer of the myths and norms of the distinction between "high" and "low" and, at times, as a renegotiator of these terms—has received much attention in media and cultural studies. The presence of Surrealist art within the context of the *hyakkaten* (department store) art galleries, such as the Seibu galleries, places even the recollection and institutional recognition of Surrealist activities squarely within the realm of the commercial mass media. Still, revealingly, these exhibitions in contemporary Japan focus even now primarily on the European Surrealists and only relatively recently have come to give any sustained attention to the Japanese Surrealist artists and writers. This nexus of problems for the history of Surrealist ideas remains to be explored in more depth, for the implications of the value judgments enacted by such institutional and commercial choices, and for the reinscription of Surrealist ideas yet again within the logic of citation (with the reevaluation and changed meaning that such reiteration brings).

In the face of such a process of appropriation, however, Takiguchi's persistent close readings of Surrealism's earliest texts, his later reworkings of his writings and translations, and his well-known distrust and ultimate avoidance of mass media (on all but the most necessary occasions) appear all the more remarkable. Takiguchi's affiliation with Surrealism was among the most overtly political but was also deeply textual: it began in the rereading of French theoretical and poetic works and their careful translation into Japanese.

Takiguchi's series of poetic experiments reveals the functioning of this delicate balance between the political and the poetic aspects of Surrealism within the dialogue between French and Japanese artists. One selection from these works was entitled "Nanatsu no shi," or "Seven Poems"; each bore the name of a European artist (Salvador Dali, Francis Picabia, and so on). Published in the collection *L'Echange surréaliste* (The Surrealist exchange [original title in French], 1936), the selection was included with writings that Eluard and Breton sent to editor Toba Shigeru, some of which were thus printed in Japanese translation before their publication in France. *L'Echange surréaliste* also contained drawings received directly from the artists (unlike earlier Japanese Surrealist journals, which reproduced cuts from German and French magazines without permission).

As part of one of the earliest collaborative exchanges of its kind between French and Japanese Surrealists, the poem "Max Ernst," from Takiguchi's "Seven Poems," reflects subtly on the sense of distance evoked by such collaboration. The poem can also be read in terms of Takiguchi's ambivalence toward existing ideas about the possibilities of poetic language.

1. Cover of *L'Echange surréaliste* (The Surrealist exchange), November 1936. Courtesy of Uchibori Hiroshi, Shakujii-shorin, by permission of Hashimoto Akio. Photo: Y. Higashi.

The "Seven Poems" were later collected in the anthology *The Poetic Experiments of Takiguchi Shūzō, 1927–1937* (1967; *Takiguchi Shūzō no shiteki jikken, 1927–1937*); the title reflects a hesitation about the works' status as "poetry" per se,[27] and thus seems to reflect Takiguchi's continued idealism about the requirements that a work must fulfill to be considered in the category *shi* (poem).[28]

Max Ernst

A night traveler
Chomps bit by bit
On the incomprehensible handcuffs of night
As if they were scraps of meat

Into the voiceless depths of night
Care of the Gobi desert
A letter of simulation arrives

The eternal birds
Starved
Mistake the canned words
For scraps of meat

One night
Like a flower
A human gift
Burned

If one considers that evening curfews were a part of the political situation at the time of this poem's publication,[29] the term "night traveler" takes on implications of an illegal act: the image of breaking off handcuffs can be read as a protest or at least an allusion to such constraints, while at the same time it may mark the desire for freedom from censorship and poetic regulation. Takiguchi noted that his translation of Breton's "Speech to the Congress of Writers" (also included in *L'Echange surréaliste*) was censored in several places.[30] Breton's speech translated here ends with the assertion "It is not by stereotyped declarations against fascism and war that we will manage to liberate either the mind or man from the ancient chains that bind him and the new chains that threaten him."[31] When one reads in a poem in the same volume that the "incomprehensible handcuffs of night" (or handcuffs of puzzling night) are chomped on (*kuichirasu*, also chewed and spit out), this animal-like, vulgar gesture takes on a broader significance; the gesture implies a hunger for something unnamed and a relish beyond mere vulgarity (*nikuhen no yō ni*, as if they were scraps of meat).

Before proceeding further in a reading of this poem, one must confront a series of difficulties. The text, although it carries the title "Max Ernst," contains no further explicit reference to the artist. Is this an homage? The text is divided into four stanzas of three or four lines each. Unlike the works of Yamamura Bochō and Kitasono Katsue examined above, which immediately defy the attempt at hermeneutic interpretation by their elimination of verbs and grammatical particles, Takiguchi's work is composed of stanzas that can be read grammatically as sentences (although punctuation is absent). Each stanza appears as a separate entity, describing vivid and clear images (with some grammatical ambiguity); but the stanzas do not form any clearly "legible" narrative or immediately apparent series. Like Kitasono's work, the poem flirts with the reader's desire to interpret; the images lead toward a particular reading, only to turn upon it and suggest a contrary one, or to suggest that perhaps the effort to "interpret" the words as "meaning" per se is not at all what is called for.

I would suggest that the images of this poem strike a delicate balance between the poles of "meaning" and the protest against meaning, the connection of words (signifiers) to their meanings and the rupture of, and emancipation from, this connection. The image of the third stanza is particularly striking in this regard: the term "canned words" (or can of words, *kotoba no kanzume*) implies a prefabricated language (perhaps of poetic or linguistic convention, of old poetry). The "eternal birds" recall images of birds that appear frequently in Takiguchi's poetic world to evoke a figure of the poet or a figure of pure poetry. (The term *eien*, "eternal," recalls, too, Nishiwaki's insistence on the eternal as an aspect of his poetic theories.) One cannot determine whether these eternal birds are starved for lack of meat or for lack of poetry. They eat "canned words,"mistaking them "for scraps of meat." The image of meat appears twice in the poem: the handcuffs are chomped on "as if they were scraps of meat"; canned words are eaten. One is left with the question of the relation between "meat" and "words." Although in the first stanza the handcuffs are already marked as *fukakai* (puzzling, incomprehensible), what could be suggested by the image of the seventh line, *gitai no tegami*, translated "letter of simulation"? Like Kitasono's title *Kigōsetsu*, the *gitai* puzzles because it seems to stem from a different (theoretical, linguistic) realm of diction than the rest of the poem. This "letter of simulation" (or even "of mimesis") recalls the linguistic term *gitaigo* (onomatopoeia). It may indicate the imitative, sonorous capacity of words in poetic composition. *Gitaigo* are also those words in the Japanese language whose relation to the signified object is at the lowest possible degree of arbitrariness: might one infer that these words are closest to being "flesh"?

A letter has arrived from a great distance. One senses an ardent desire (for poetry) within a gaping absence: the night has no voice (*koe no nai ya-han*), the eternal birds are starved, the night traveler is tied in handcuffs. Has the hunger (for poetry) been fulfilled? Do canned words satisfy the appetite? Is the gift that has arrived from afar a gift of poetry? Or, rather, can one read these images as a scene of silence, darkness, and restraint, in which letters are only "simulated" and gifts burned? The poem's ending is romantic, un-abashed: "hitoyo / ningen no okurimono wa / hana no yō ni moeteita" (one night / like a flower / a human gift burned). What burns here may be po-etry itself, in an image of destruction—or, as in the expression *hana de moetatsu* (ablaze with blossoms), it may be the blazing vividness of a tree as it bursts into bloom: *moeru* is a conventional metaphor for blooming.

The dynamic of the poem is contained in the fact of the implicit promise of these images: in order to read the poem at all we must in some sense accept the promise proffered by the language of these stanzas, the "letter" it seems to send us. While in 1936 it would no longer be surprising to write a poem that made no gesture to fulfill the expectations of 5-7-5 form or traditional metaphoric diction, this poem goes much farther. Its construction of images in clear grammatical phrases seems to offer a promise of "interpretability" (poetic "meat") and at the same time betrays that assumption, and betrays it for reasons related to Haruyama Yukio's words: "To see meaning in poetry is not to see anything beyond literature in poetry." While attempting to free the image from the necessities of "good sense," to create, perhaps, the effects of the juxtaposition of elements "distant and true,"[32] these irregularly divided lines (belonging to a group of texts proclaiming themselves "Seven Poems") call attention to their sta-tus as "poetry." The proper names in the seven titles—Max Ernst, Salvador Dali, René Magritte—written in katakana (the syllabic writing system used, in its modern standard form, to write non-Chinese loanwords, ono-matopoeia, and emphasized words), stand as marks, perhaps even emblems of the "Surrealist exchange." The way of poetry is long, Takiguchi implies. It is a way marked by messages received from a distance, by exchange (like the letter or gift that appears in these stanzas). These distant gifts, like the names of the artists that entitle each poem, may have represented a promise, the hope of a method by which the poets could transcend the "re-alities" of 1936 Japan—although the realization of this promise became complicated within the conditions of the literary scene as well as the polit-ical situation of the time.[33]

Like *L'Echange surréaliste*, other exchanges and forms of direct contact with the European Surrealists were attempted by Japanese Surrealist poets. In 1935 Yamanaka Sansei (or Chirū), who adopted the "French" name Yamanaka Tiroux, had sent the Surrealist poetry anthology *Hiasobi* (with the French title *Jouer au feu*) to André Breton, to whom it was dedicated. (Although Breton could not have understood its words, the pink cover and dark rice paper, folded in the French style, are said to have provoked a strong reaction—"I am brought to the edge of illness with desire for the beauty of this paper." (Eluard and Tristan Tzara also perceived *Hiasobi* as an "object in rice paper.")[34] Takiguchi and Ebara Jun had translated works of Japanese Surrealism into French and wrote introductions to Japanese Surrealism for publication in France.[35] Nonetheless, the overwhelming volume of importation of texts, and of translation, was in the incorporation of translated French texts into Japanese avant-garde journals and poetry collections.

For Takiguchi the political aspect of the Surrealist project remained inseparable from his artistic production and poetic creation. In the case of Nishiwaki, however, one notes statements like the following in *Surrealist Poetics*:

> The bonds of habitual convention are to be broken not for their own sake but for the purpose of poetic expression. In other words, this act of destruction, with its consequential process of making reality exciting, must be committed in order to fulfill the aim of poetry. Yet if one breaks with custom and tradition *in actuality*, this act in itself is not poetry—such an act would belong rather to the field of ethics, of philosophy.[36]

One way of reading this assertion would be to consider its placement of poetry in a position of superiority (or exteriority) to that of ethics and philosophy; Breton's "First Manifesto of Surrealism" contains a statement that seems, on first glance, similar—that the "psychic automatism" of Surrealism should be "exempt from any aesthetic or moral concern." Yet Nishiwaki's statement can also be interpreted as a disclaimer, clearing the poetic realm—as a field of aesthetic creativity—from responsibility for transforming the world of the "actual," the necessity of "in actuality" making any breaks with custom and tradition. Futurist poet Kanbara Tai (1898–1997) attacked Nishiwaki and other Surrealists for this "reckless" attitude.

Recent analysis of Nishiwaki's work by Hosea Hirata can be read as an attempt to mobilize the terms of the Derridean "trace" in order to complicate these accusations, and to demonstrate the connection of Nishiwaki's poetics to a more subtle vision of "reality." By Hirata's persistent return to the problem of the real, and his central concern with the terms of reality (along with declaring some of Nishiwaki's avant-garde contemporaries "at least as guilty" as Nishiwaki), he shows this issue of reality to be the locus of a profound uneasiness, the center of a pivotal uncertainty in Nishiwaki's work, which refuses, finally, to be resolved. It is difficult to get around the directness of Nishiwaki's position in the above passage. (In examining Nishiwaki's attitude toward political revolt as it relates to his engagement in Surrealism, critics have noted that his position as a highly respected professor of English at Keio University was never threatened by his Surrealist activities.) A symptomatic moment here is a humorous anecdote related by prominent Nishiwaki biographer Kagiya Yukinobu. Kagiya narrates the scene of an encounter between Nishiwaki and Kanbara Tai, forty years after Kanbara's famous attack on Nishiwaki's poetics in the opening issue of *Shi: Genjitsu* in 1930:

> "Mr. Kanbara, I'll never forget that. Your attack was too severe!"
> "No, *sensei*. That's not right. I was praising you there. If you read it carefully you'll see I was praising you there."
> "Really? . . . I see, Mr. Kanbara was really praising me."[37]

The susceptibility of this story to rewriting suggests the difficulty that plagues any polemics centered on the issue of reality. Perception and interpretation are, it seems, not to be trusted in this story (even in a case as clearly documented and historically inscribed as the debate between Kanbara and Nishiwaki). Kanbara might argue that any critique, in giving attention to the object of criticism, may be considered as oblique praise (as in the dictum, all publicity is good publicity). But without such an explanation, this anecdote could threaten to unmask the hazy edges of what is considered reality in Nishiwaki's poetic theories; it could reveal the subjective force motivating, in practice, one's theoretical and analytic direction, and the difficulty of grasping and being certain of where in language one might begin to locate something called the "real" or the "actual."[38]

Although the anecdote of Nishiwaki and Kanbara represents an extreme (as a story that takes place after the fact), the story of Surrealism contains gaps and inconsistencies as dramatic as those one might expect in an autobiographical work.[39] The record of the historical development of Surrealism in Japan is due as much to the work of the members of the movement as to any external or "objective" critical eye. It is a history that, like many stories, crumbles in on its own invention and chooses its course in the process and at the very moment of its production. One may consider the example of a moment central to Japanese Surrealism—the manifesto entitled "A Note: December 1927," written by Kitasono Katsue, Ueda Toshio, and Ueda Tamotsu. "A Note" is often considered the first manifesto of Surrealism in Japan. In Kitasono's essay "Recollections of *Rose, Magic, Theory*" he places it at a crucial point in his summary of the history of the Surrealist movement in Japan:

> The Surrealist movement of those days [1927–1929] was divided into two groups, that of *Rose, Magic, Theory* [*Shōbi, majutsu, gakusetsu*] and that of *Ah, Fragrant Stoker* [*Fukuikutaru kafu yo*]; in any case the movement [both groups] had originated from the students surrounding Professor Nishiwaki Junzaburō of Keio University. The "Fragrant Stoker" group was faithful to the doctrines of Breton, but our "Rose, Magic, Theory" group was more interested in developing a world of Surrealism that would be original to Japan. This intention was summarized in "A Note," which was printed as a separate pamphlet and inserted in the first issue of *Rose, Magic, Theory* in 1928. . . .
>
> This manifesto was drafted by Ueda Toshio. We translated it into English and sent it to the Surrealists in Paris.[40]

Kitasono goes on to relate the subsequent joining of the two groups (Fragrant Stoker and Rose, Magic, Theory) to produce the Surrealist magazine *Ishō no taiyō* (The sun in costume, or The costume's sun). This journal, subtitled *Collection surréaliste*, makes clear its Surrealist intentions.[41] Kitasono's note that "We translated [the text] into English and sent it to the Surrealists in Paris," echoes the editorial in the third issue of *Rose, Magic, Theory* (January 1928). Following the proclamation "We are the young Zarathustras / We are the young Zarathustras," one finds: "The translation of 'A Note,' included between the pages of this journal, has been sent to the 'Communistes-Suréalistes' [so named in French by the editors of *Ishō no taiyō*] Louis Aragon, Paul Eluard, André Breton, and to 'Surréalist non Communist' Antonin Artaud." The young poets, presenting a manifesto in their magazine, record their sending it to the Paris Surrealists. They include the text of the note:

A NOTE DECEMBER 1927

We applaud SURREALSME's development of the abilities of consciousness and artistic desire—a baptism has come to us   We have accepted this technique

A NOTE   DECEMBER 1927

吾々は SURREALSME に於ての芸術欲望の発達あるひは知覚能力
の発達を謳歌した吾々に洗礼が来た　知覚の制限を受けずに知覚を通
して材料を持ち来る技術を受けた　吾々は摂理に依る POETIC OP-
ERATION を人間から分離せられた状態に於て組み立てる　此の状
態は吾々に技術に似た無関心の感覚を覚えさせる　吾々の対象性の限
界を規するのに POETIC SCIENTIST の状態に類似を感ずる　吾々
は憂鬱でもなく快活でもない　人間であることを必要としない人間の
感覚は適度に厳格で冷静である　吾々は吾々の POETIC OPERA-
TION を組み立てる際に吾々に適合した昂奮を感じる　吾々は SUR-
REALISME を継続する　吾々は飽和の徳を讃美する

Kitasono Katue
Ueda Toshio
Ueda Tamotu

2. "A Note: December 1927," *Shōbi, majutsu, gakusetsu* (Rose, magic, theory), January 1928. Reprinted (Tokyo: Nishizawa shoten), 1977. By permission of Hashimoto Akio.

which provides us materials through the modes of conscious perception, without having to accept the limits of consciousness   In a condition of separation from humanity we have assembled a POETIC OPERATION that relies on providence   This condition gives us a feeling of disinterestedness similar to that which would stem from the technical [literally "technique"]   We feel an affinity for the POETIC SCIENTIST as we measure the limits of our objective status [literally "our objectness"]   We experience neither melancholy nor joy   The sensations of those who do not consider their humanity as a necessity are properly austere and composed   Yet at the moment when we construct our POETIC OPERATION we feel an appropriate degree of excitement   We will continue in our SURREALISME   We extol the virtues of saturation.[42]

The text of "A Note" vacillates between words borrowed from science, implying a technical objectivity ("operation," "scientist," "technique" "saturation"), and the subjective fervor of a passionate, direct appeal. The scientific terms, describing the process of Surrealist creation as an operation of disinterested technicality, recall the wording of the Japanese Futurist movement, which attempted to apply technological and mechanical terms ("velocity," etc.) and scientific methods to the productions of language. Yet other words reflect the fervor and direct appeal of a religious tract: the repeated subject "we" (*wareware*), the references to singing praises or applause (*ōka*) and extolling or providential dispensation for the operation (*setsuri*), and the word "saturation" framed as a virtue or power (*toku*). One notes as well the initial image of a baptism in Surrealism. The speakers, both active and acted upon by an exterior force, are within the realm of the human (sensations, desire) and yet observe humanity from a distant, technical point of view. Thus the text vacillates between the two poles: the limitations of human subjectivity and the aspiration to the objective, the boundaries of human consciousness and the refusal to accept these limits, the sense of excitement and the call for a more appropriate calm and composure.

Like "A Note," the manifestos of Breton also employ the phrase "Surrealist operation"; for example, "the Surrealist operation has no chance of succeeding unless it is conducted under aseptic moral conditions, although there are still very few who are willing to discuss such conditions."[43] Similarly, on numerous occasions the necessity of dissolving the opposition between two poles (e.g., objective and subjective) is the subject of Breton's polemics. For example, in a later work, *Les Vases communicantes* (1932), Breton describes the necessity of surmounting the opposition between action and dream while maintaining the simultaneous presence of both terms of the opposition: "The internal development [of reality] and the objective consciousness of reality since this relation, by virtue of the sentiment of the individual on the one hand and universal sentiment on the other, contains, for the time being, a certain magic."[44] While the language of "A Note" incorporates some of the ideas and oppositions elaborated in European Surrealist writings—*chikaku-kinō* (the capacities of consciousness) invokes Breton's "perception-consciousness"[45]—the general sense of "A Note" seems to focus on an homage and celebration of Surrealist technique and on a transposed understanding of this technique's value into the new metaphors of the writers. The image of the "poetic operation" recalls the operating table in Surrealist imagery—for example, in Lautréamont's famous "meeting on an operating table of an umbrella and a sewing machine."[46] In other words, one might argue that here the Japanese Surrealists have performed their own operation on the Surrealist movement as they "perceive" it (or have been "baptized" in it).

Surrealist practice in Japan can be seen to reframe the narrative of Japanese modernization as an imposition of values from a hegemonic West.[47] The operation performed here is closer to the nature of a chance, or the functioning of a Surrealist image: a resonant and "true" juxtaposition. Here the "West" becomes a space that transcends its "real" position and begins to function as an ideal space, a place that provides material for the Japanese writers' poetic encounters, as well as a screen upon which their fantasies may be projected. As a distant reality, embodied in concrete representations and words (*renaissance, poésie, critique*), the signs of Surrealism provide an opening for the imagination (a space of the "beyond," like the *chō-* that names the Japanese movement). Between Japanese and European avant-garde movements, one may trace a vacillation between idealized moments of "pure" communication (or its imagining) and the realms of geographical, linguistic, and cultural disruption. Surrealism announces itself as a movement that refuses to remain within bounds, that crosses the edges of the theoretical or historical framework in which one might attempt to articulate it. From the precedent set by Yamamura Bochō in "Geigo," to the distant realities theorized by Nishiwaki or figured in Takiguchi's "Max Ernst," to the manifesto operation performed in "A Note" by Kitasono and the Ueda brothers, the texts examined in this chapter can be read as paradigmatic moments in the transfer of poetic ideas, moments that illustrate the functioning of contrast, division, and rupture that are an inherent part of the reformulation of the Surrealist's terms.

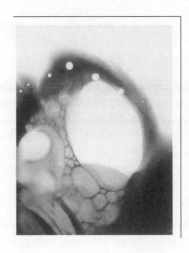

ON MEMORY AND DOUBT

Because its signification has wandered already . . .
—Harold Bloom, *A Map of Misreading*

While many have written of the profound effect of French and other European literatures on the writings of Japanese poets and novelists of the early twentieth century, rarely has the problem of the nature and functioning of influence, in its various forms, received direct or sustained examination in this context.[1] Studies focusing on the interactions between national literatures tend to emphasize a single direction of influence and thus lose sight of the process of cultural exchange as a complex and intricate series of relations.[2] With the emergence of postcolonial theory, the exercise of cultural and political power has taken a central place within the studies of literary and linguistic interaction; still, the process and functioning of "influence" has yet to be explored fully as a theoretical and analytical problem.[3]

When opened up to its possibilities as a question, the problem of influence permeates the relations between texts, between writers, between texts and their readers. More specifically, in the hypothesis or imagining of this project I am concerned with reconfiguring the discussion of influence, to open it to new models based on the study of memory as well as citation. Recent models and theories of memory are inspiring for the study of cross-cultural interaction because they manage to account for the movement, revision, or recollection of an entity across a significant gap without requiring the reification, oversimplification, or fetishization of the place from which it came (as idealized origin), nor of the place or topos of reception. Nonetheless, something is retained or recalled.

THE PROBLEM OF INFLUENCE

Walter Benjamin's studies of Baudelaire, written in several stages through the late 1920s until Benjamin's death in 1940, have brought into the province of poetic studies certain questions of memory, trauma, and consciousness that (as Benjamin notes) were first theorized by Freud in his studies of shell shock.[4] It is useful to return to Freud's surprising notion of memory and consciousness in order to consider its relation to the process of poetic composition. In fact Freud's vision of memory and dreams is already articulated in terms that suggest a textual model, and metaphors of writing and translation abound: for example, "the dream-content seems like a transcript of the dream-thoughts into another mode of expression, whose characters and syntactic laws it is our business to discover by comparing the original and the translation."[5] Freud writes of the process by which sensory or other experiences leave their traces in memory, that it is not necessary to be "conscious" of a stimulus for it to form a memory, and in fact, the most powerful impressions (such as traumatic experiences) are those that never enter the realm of consciousness: "All excitatory processes that occur in the *other* systems leave permanent traces behind in them which form the foundation of memory. Such memory-traces, then, have nothing to do with the fact of becoming conscious; indeed they are often most powerful and most enduring when the process which left them behind was one which never entered consciousness."[6] And more radically, "Becoming conscious and leaving behind a memory trace are incompatible with each other within one and the same system."[7]

Thus, Freud radically rewrites the understanding of the way memory traces are produced and recalled: there is no longer a direct or clear link between conscious experience and memory.[8] Freud's explorations of the unconscious and the nature of experience were taken up by Surrealist writers in their search for new forms of poetic composition. And for Benjamin, in his reading of Baudelaire, Freud's formulation leads him to make a distinction between two kinds of "experience," one that leaves a deep impression but may not necessarily have been registered in consciousness (*Erfahrung*) and one that passes through consciousness but does not necessarily leave a trace (*Erlebnis*).

How, then, can theories of memory enrich an understanding of cultural interactions? Rather than focusing solely on elements and techniques deliberately adopted by individuals within one culture from another, rather than taking for granted assumptions about the functioning of influence as cause and effect, one may take inspiration from recent models of memory (which in themselves focus on the psychic functioning of the individual subject) and bring them to bear on a reading of the larger cultural realm. By opening the consideration of cultural interaction and memory to an awareness of their own belated effects, linking them closely with a figure of shock and consciousness, we may discover the constitutive disruptions, disjunctions, and displacements that occur in the negotiation of cultural change. This model also illuminates the ways that literary and cultural appropriations provoke resistances, accusations of falseness, and imitation, just as theoretical research on memory that brings the status of the original into question provokes accusations of false or belatedly reconstituted memory.

This is emphatically not to defend the superimposition on a text of interpretations not to be found within it, or to say that a text need not show signs of an interaction in order to have been functioning within its logic. Rather, it is to question the possibility of reading such cultural exchanges "immediately." Instead, we open such a reading to the metaphors and models of memory (with its complexity, slips, deferrals, and disjunctions) and experiment with interpreting these texts within such a subtle, if at times potentially treacherous, framework.

One cannot but recall in this context Harold Bloom's extensive writings on poetic influence as synonymous with a particular form of misreading or poetic misprision. Bloom's vision of influence reads poetry as a function of the relation between texts, and as an effect of the text's own belated place vis-à-vis its forebears. (Belatedness, here, as part of the necessary process of transmission in every instance, is not to be taken in its pejorative sense: every poem, every cultural instance, would inherently be "belated" with reference to that which preceded it and destined to be "misread" by that which follows.) Bloom insists first of all on the distinction between the concept of influence and what has been known as "source studies": "The profundities of poetic influence cannot be reduced to source study, to the history of ideas, to the patterning of images." And, more emphatically, "Poetic influence, in the sense I give to it, has almost *nothing to do* with the verbal resemblances between one poet and another" (my emphasis). He then suggests it is not necessary that a poet have read a given poem in order to be influenced by it—the misprision that he posits at the center of writing may even be facilitated by not reading an acknowledged or clear precursor: "An ephebe's best misinterpretations may well be of poems he has never read."[9] Although the implication is that the later poet knows the poem, for example, by its looming reputation or through the legendary fame of its creator, one might hesitate for a moment without immediately trying to tie down the exact, literal form of the poet's grasping or interaction with these forebears, since this is precisely what the statement puts into question.

This radical understanding of poetic misprision or influence, itself often reinterpreted as a more simplistic Oedipal reading of the relation with a powerful poetic father, is particularly useful in placing emphasis on the poem's interaction with its own belated position as well as with its own future as an object of readings and misreadings: the intrapoetic situation Bloom describes can be applied to the situation of a poem in relation to its forebears, but also to a poem in relation to the future of its own reading, or in his words, "the poem's opening awareness that it *must be mis-read* because its signification has wandered already," so that eventually "influence comes to mean a kind of belated completion."[10] This reading of belatedness (or, in Benjamin's terms, "survival"), and of a signification that already wanders from the moment of its opening, radically undermines the hierarchy and temporal priority of what influences and what is influenced; such a reading also reconstitutes the notion of the "original" in consideration of a future and unavoidable misreading. It thus shakes (or even makes impossible) any originary stability of the influencing poem, even at the moment of its first appearance, since the poem itself is both the misreading and the completion of its own forebears.[11] While continuing to demand that the reader practice close textual analysis, this notion of influence undermines any positivist project of tracing influence that would be limited to clearly recognizable passages, bits of language, or stylistic techniques appropriated from one poet by another: it is not possible, according to Bloom, for the most important elements of influence to be contained in any simple notion of citation or source. On the contrary, he claims (taking this notion to the extreme) "not having read"(or in Freud's terms, not having been registered in the realm of consciousness) only places the poet in a more favorable position for this kind of creative misprision.[12]

If one were to consider, for a moment, the valences of the terms and their etymologies, one is struck by the differing connotations of the terms for "influence" in English and French—in contrast to the Japanese term, *eikyō*,—in their framing of the causal dynamics of the process they describe. In the English and French word "influence," one finds an emphasis on the notion of power:

Influence: 1. A power indirectly or intangibly affecting a person or a course of events. 2. Power to sway or affect based on prestige, wealth, ability, or position. 3. A person or thing exercising such power. 4. An effect or change produced by such power. 5. (*Astrology*) An occult ethereal fluid flowing from the stars to affect the fate of men. (From medieval Latin *influentia*, "a flowing in")[13]

Although the source may be intangible, there are clear implications of hierarchical structure not only in the "power to sway or affect based on prestige, wealth, ability, or position," but also in the astrological definition, in which the "occult ethereal fluid flowing from the stars" comes down from above "to affect the fate of men." That which is influenced is, by implication, projected as inferior in power or position, and the person who exercises the influence (by linguistically conventionalized synecdoche) is conflated with the effect of that influence, as though the person exercising influence had "flowed into" what was influenced and was represented in person by the change effected.

The etymology of the Japanese term *eikyō* (影響) which has been traced as early as the Chinese classic *Shu jing* (Book of documents; one of the five Chinese classics attributed to Confucius), comes from the perception of a "shadow following form" or an "echo responding to sound." In the *Shu jing*, the locus classicus is found in the chapter "Da Yu mo": "Yu said, 'To accord with those who follow [the proper path] is auspicious; to follow those who disobey is inauspicious. This is the shadow and the echo.'" Yu was the founder of the (probably mythological) Xia dynasty, which was, according to traditional Chinese records, the first dynasty in Chinese history.[14] The meanings of *eikyō* in modern Japanese include "influence, effect, consequences, repercussions, change, response." Although it maintains the binary oppositions between cause and effect (form and shadow, sound and echo), the nuance of the image is naturalized through the relation to trace, to shock, to a reverberation of a sound in emptiness.[15] The Japanese term is written with two characters that have multiple meanings when read separately: *ei,* meaning "shadow, silhouette, phantom, reflection, figure, trace"; and *kyō,* signifying "sound, resound, reverberate, echo, ring, explosion, effect, shock."[16] Thus in its etymology the term seems to combine notions of "trace" and "shock" in a figure that, strikingly, incorporates these primary features of the theories of memory.

The process of "cultural borrowing" here may be considered in relation to a number of possible models. All of these models bring radically into question the relation between the influencing and the influenced, and make that relation and the forms of that transmission into a matter for reevaluation rather than unspoken assumption. From the very etymologies of the terms for influence themselves we see that even the words for naming "influence" have undergone numerous passages and linguistic and semantic transformations. Beginning with the post-Freudian (and Benjaminian) notions of traumatic return and recollection, and incorporating the notion of a radical form of poetic transmission or misprision as a model of influence, we can propose an idea of the necessary, even constitutive, belatedness of cultural formation and interaction as deeply linked to the processes of memory. The interactions between cultures can be read as a practice of reading and misreading, citation and reiteration—with a difference, and "after the fact."

Here, too, come into play the relation between biographical readings of texts and the questions of the death of the author (as Barthes and Foucault wrote of them): "influencing" as a textual phenomenon or residue (textual survival) and "influencing" as a live and biographical or historical phenomenon, as a function of the memory of the real living being who wrote the works, who did or did not own or encounter or read certain texts. Each of these forms of biographical and historical as well as textual and theoretical influencing casts the others in a new light, or could, perhaps, inspire a reinterpretation and questioning of the others. Like Surrealism's history, which inscribes itself in the very process of its making, one might conceive of influence as a kind of performance, a citation (direct or indirect) that is both a demonstration of an alliance with something and the enactment or activation of that very alliance or reappropriation, in this case of a distant movement from another language and culture.

Recent theorists have written variously on cultural borrowing as it relates to problems of translation, to the very notion of translation and the construction of linguistic meaning itself, to the practice of writings and articulations that place themselves on the boundaries between languages. Lydia Liu has written revealingly of developments in modern Chinese language and literature in relation to questions of representation, translation, and cross-cultural movement. Just as Meiji-period translations into Japanese from European languages often adapted kanji compounds from literary Chinese texts to render European words, these uses of the terms might then be reinterpreted in a new vein in the works of modern Chinese writers. One might consider the Surrealist writers as engaged in a related practice of linguistic and cultural incorporation, in which it is a matter of reconfiguring and questioning artistic and poetic language and thought, along with the relation between language and experience, language and consciousness. Such processes ultimately affected the shape of languages, literature, and thought in both Japan and China.

In order to discover how this question of memory and influence works, it is useful to consider the resistances that the appropriation of Surrealism and other such cultural reiterations provoked. On the one hand, contemporary writers perceived Surrealist language as breaking away too far from the world of reality; on the other hand, they feared that the translations and transplantations Japanese Surrealism performed might not be true enough to the "original" movements. By analyzing the rhetoric of surface and depth, superficiality and authenticity, as it appeared in these attacks and in the critics' ideas of what the true purpose of poetry should be, we arrive at the question of the visual surfaces of the written word and the place of vision in the cultural crossings of Surrealism. Within a cultural milieu of increasing militarism and technological advances, the stakes of the poetic enterprise and of intercultural practices were clearly high, but at the same time the relation between poetry and the social or political world seemed increasingly uncertain. Many debates focused on the creation of a collectivity as opposed to the personal and idiosyncratic artistic consciousness or on an ideal of communication as opposed to certain poetic ideas: interiority, an encounter with the void, or a quest beyond the boundaries of language. Surrealist poets involved in a search for a new kind of engage-

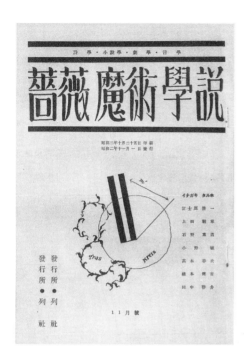

3. Covers of *Shōbi, majutsu, gakusetsu* (Rose, magic, theory). *Left*: November 1927. *Right*: January 1928. Reprinted (Tokyo: Nishizawa shoten) 1977.

ment with everyday life and the structures of meaning called the present state of reality and its perception "dull," thus shocking those whose notions of reality referred, in a more explicitly political way, to the rather too exciting everyday reality of Japan in the early 1930s.

Kitasono Katsue's writing becomes an example of one of these highly ambiguous and idiosyncratic writing styles. His wartime writings are a subject of debate (after a relatively long silence on the subject) in terms of nativism and complicity. Through a discussion of the resistances to Surrealism and the debates concerning reality, we come to the issue of how actuality/reality is defined and constructed, and the forms—collective or personal, coded or code-destroying, present and communal or involving a "void" or absence—in which one can engage it through language.

THE RESISTANCE TO SURREALISM: VISUAL POETRY AND IMPOSTURE

When critics accuse writers of Japanese modern poetry, particularly in the prewar period, of not having absorbed properly or fully the influence of European modernism, their descriptions contrast sharply with the profound "shock of consciousness" formulated in the figures of memory discussed above. While perfectly visible, claim the accusers, European modernism exists merely on the surface of the Japanese texts, too obviously a matter of putting on airs—a pose, not deeply enough absorbed to be considered authentic. The critics make these writings out to be, in a sense, forgeries, and their claims to influence are portrayed as illegitimate.

An early example of such an indictment would be the forceful claims of Hagiwara Sakutarō about various Japanese modernist groups, beginning with the naturalists, whom he saw as flaunting their relation to European literary trends. Hagiwara himself read and admired Baudelaire and especially Poe (and his work could be seen as a precedent for the kind of adoption of European poetic views that the Surrealists also practiced). He returned often to the writings of Baudelaire as he developed his innovative and influential poetics. Yet, in a series of aphoristic essays entitled "Shi ni tsuite no shō-essei" (Brief essays on poetry) published in 1931 in the magazine *Shi: Genjitsu*,[17] Hagiwara writes:

The members of the naturalist literary establishment [*bundan*] pretend to write novels scientifically. Certain recent poets also claim to write poetry according to the rules of mechanics. Such a forceful emphasis [accent] makes a strong impression on people, just as a well-designed poster leaves a strong impression in the mind. If one were to speak truthfully, however, their work is no more than Poster Literature in the end, a rhetoric exaggerated through cleverness. A novel written scientifically, or a poem made through mechanical means, has no place as a truly imaginative work. It is no more than a novel written with an attitude of objectivity, or a poem that mechanically reproduces some appearance according to one's tastes. As for those who claim to write Cubist poems, they have done nothing more than to take letters and, in foolish credulity, print them in the form of a pyramid.[18]

The pretense to scientificity, and the pretense to Cubism, in which poets and writers lay claim to various European movements' titles (not only Cubism but also Expressionism, naturalism, Surrealism, and Constructivism), are no more than affectation in Hagiwara's view. What makes the writers' attempts failures, or false, is first of all his impression of the exteriority of their application of these principles. "Novel[s] written with an attitude of objectivity" have failed to internalize, Hagiwara implies, the objective strategy they claim into any deeper structure: they strike a pose of objectivity. The question of what would constitute depth (or "spirit") rather than superficiality is not addressed explicitly here, but it is implied in his emphatic condemnation of surfaces and poses: *taido* (attitude) here, and in the case of poetry, "poems that mechanize an *appearance* according to one's tastes" (*shumi no gaibō o kikaiteki ni shita*).[19] The poems do not, as the poets claim, practice a writing of or with the mechanism through the rules of mechanics; as a result, Hagiwara claims, they are merely the reproduction through mechanism of an external appearance or exterior, like a poster, that catches one's fancy or tastes. The choice of the surface is flashy but does not reflect anything deeper than a passing interest, flirtation—and, interestingly, at the same time—a mass production, a mechanical reproduction. The poets' attention clings too much to the surface of words. Hagiwara, who well understood Baudelaire's notions of the solitary in the crowd and poetic intoxication, and whose readings and praise of Poe express an affinity for European poetics that was an important stepping stone for the younger poets he here condemns, portrays these younger poets as mere clever dandies (or foolish naïves). The works they produce become, in his neologism, "simply poster literature" (*tan ni posutaa no bungaku*).

What is "poster literature"? Hagiwara describes it as "rhetoric exaggerated through cleverness": his derogatory term "rhetoric" (*shūji*) implies only the formal aspect of words, or the surface of words alone separated from sense—an exaggerated materiality of language. The dishonesty of exaggerated rhetoric forms a contrast with Hagiwara's confessional suggestion of his own honesty: "If one were to speak truthfully" (*hontō no koto o ieba*). The use of language as surface, as external visual symbol separated from interiority, reveals that the new poets (as well as the naturalists) are using language dishonestly or manipulatively, in order to make a strong impression, as in an advertising campaign. Hagiwara highlights the mechanical reproducibility (as copy itself, and infinitely reproducible) of this poster literature and its absence of originality, of aura, in some deeper sense. In part, what is suspect here has something to do with mass production as well as with imitation, or with a certain notion of industrial modernity that goes along with superficiality and marketing. And yet, as he states in his condemnation of the Cubists, it may not be a willful deception, but simply a too naïve belief in the possibility of using language as a visual tool: "to take letters and, in foolish credulity, print them in the form of a pyramid." Not to pay attention to the interiority of language leads one to produce writing that is ultimately worthless as literature: the only use of these poems is as visual design, as pyramids of letters. He implies a condemnation of visuality as surface, as the merest exterior, as nothing that has any place among "true creative works" (*jissai no sōsaku*).[20]

We follow carefully Hagiwara's condemnation of these Japanese modernists, in their adoption of elements from European literary avant-garde movements, because it is symptomatic of that performed by many readers and critics who frame their understanding in terms of metaphors of depth and superficiality, interiority and costume—both in examining elements of European literature in Japanese writings and in considering the poets' use of language for its "surface" value as opposed to its underlying "meaning."[21] The simple credulity, the foolish naïveté (*bakashōjiki*), implies a blind importation of ideas without discrimination or understanding, the adoption of the surface of poetic structure. And strikingly, the very poetic ideas here criticized relate precisely to the breaking apart of traditional or ordinary notions of meaning and sense. It is just such binary oppositions as meaningful and meaningless, sense and nonsense, depth and surface, that, among others, Surrealist and modernist poets challenge in their work. Hagiwara's reading and resistance, then, are not an isolated case but can be taken as a paradigmatic strategy for the condemnation or dismissal of Surrealism up to the present day by various readers and critics. This includes critics, like Hagiwara, whose own work is closely related to similar poetic ideas in its exploring of the horizons between readability and figural ambiguity, the borders between European and Japanese notions of the poetic. To demonstrate this point, let us consider one of the most sympathetic and fully cognizant readers of the prewar Japanese Surrealists, a critic and poet whose understanding of both European and Japanese Surrealism places him in a privileged position as a reader of influence.

Tsuruoka Yoshihisa (1936–) writes extensively on Japanese Surrealism. One of his most significant critical works is the collection *Nihon chō-genjitsushugi shiron* (Japanese Surrealist poetics) published in 1966. There, in assessing the contribution of Kitasono Katsue to Japanese Surrealism, he speaks of the warp (*yugami*)—not unrelated to the idea of misprision—in the understanding of Surrealist poetics (and of other European movements) upon their importation into Japanese literature. This series of misunderstandings has as much to do with the assessment by literary historians of the poets' contributions as with the poets' own knowledge of European thought. This image of warping (distortion, bend, skew) becomes a key term for his analysis. Following a discussion of the lyrical and sensual aesthetics of premodern poetry in Japan (from Sei Shōnagon's late tenth-century compilation *Makura no sōshi* [Pillow book] through Matsuo Bashō's seventeenth-century poems), Tsuruoka offers this criticism—and recall, it was written in the postwar period, with the benefits and biases of hindsight:

Thinking once again about the Surrealist poetry of Japan [*waga kuni*, our nation], we realize that it had an intimate [*missetsu*] connection with such traditional aesthetics. The Japanese poets, unable to acknowledge openly the difference in their basic spiritual/mental [*seishinteki*] conditions from those of the European Surrealists, dazzlingly imitated the example of the Western works and theories, but, before one had a chance to notice it, they secretly substituted for it within themselves the sensuous lyricism of traditional aesthetics. The fact that this switch went unnoticed is another important reason for the warping of Japanese Surrealism.[22]

For Tsuruoka, much of the shaping of Surrealism in Japan takes place through a false substitution—outside the consciousness even of the Japanese Surrealist poets themselves, who are unable to acknowledge the differing fundamental conditions that make the direct adoption of ideas from

European Surrealism an impossibility. The ideas that they import are thus replaced by a secret, or fraudulent, substitute (*surikaeteita*), and the displacement goes unnoticed by the poets themselves and by the readers/critics of the movement, who take their Surrealism for authentic. Striking here is his description of the way the poets relate to the Western works and theories: they "learn by observing, apprenticeship, following an example" (*minarau*, implying a strongly visual model of learning), and the results may be dazzling, radiant, beautiful even, but, Tsuruoka implies, precisely not deep, dark, or interior, not more than a shining visual surface.

In this sense his descriptions are similar to the understanding of surface—the imitation elaborated by Hagiwara in 1931 (the creation of works that leave a "strong impression on the mind"). What is dazzling, what is learned in a visual mode, is, in the terms of *seishin* ("mind," "spirit," implying interiority and depth) no more than a fraud, a substitute. Tsuruoka accuses the poets of not changing anything within, and not expressing anything more new than the most traditional sentiments of Japanese premodern poetry. But what is most troubling to him is not this repetition of tradition; rather, he is most bothered by the false surface, the dazzling exterior, and by the fact that the poets pretend to accomplish something that, in his estimation, they do not even begin to attain.

Tsuruoka's unhesitating judgment brings to bear a certain moral force ("unable to acknowledge openly," "secret substitution," "before one had a chance to notice"). Further, through the term *missetsu* (secret intimacy) the rhetoric of his accusation gains a sexual connotation—the Surrealists have, in secret, been too intimate (surprisingly) with the tradition. In particular, for Tsuruoka, the case of Kitasono is representative of this deception: in other Surrealists, particularly Takiguchi Shūzō, he perceives a depth that would allow him to acknowledge an authentic importation of ideas from Western literature. He elaborates on his ideas of a "true" or original Surrealism, in describing what Kitasono failed to attain.

It is instructive to examine Tsuruoka's view of what would constitute a Surrealism properly understood:

Originally, Surrealism (and there is no need even to borrow the words of Gaëtan Picon)[23] is a movement that passed through and was drawn from Dadaism as a rebellion against modern reason [rationalism]; it is a passionate intermixing that leads toward life, and must be constituted and continually supported by an impeaching [*kyūdanteki*] attitude toward the world and existence itself. Kitasono's

spirit [*seishin*] in these poems expresses its lonely sadness within an absolutely traditional spiritual climate [*fūdo*]; for him, there is nowhere a reality that one must
confront with one's bloodstained (desperate) flesh.[24]

What Surrealism means, for Tsuruoka, does not even require the citation of
the French poet Gaëtan Picon (*kotoba o kariru made mo naku*): it goes without saying, or in other words, has been internalized by him; it has become
obvious, a matter of course. But the structure of this assertion, which is the
most open definition of Surrealist thought he gives within this part of his
argument, is both a citation and not a citation: it borrows the authority of
having absorbed Picon's words, but (in eliminating any quotation marks)
makes them Tsuruoka's own. The traditional term *fūdo*, roughly translatable
as "climate" or "atmosphere," is often incorporated into arguments about
the uniqueness of Japanese culture, as springing from elements of the cli-
mactic or regional specificity: drawing upon the term *fūdo* as a characteristic of Kitasono's spirit, he places Kitasono on the side of a nationalist/tradi-
tional view of Japanese culture and implies a complicity on Kitasono's part,
made explicit later, with such nationalism. The terms of a true Surrealism,
for Tsuruoka—*hangyaku* (treachery, treason, insurrection, mutiny) or *kyūdanteki taido* (denouncing, censuring, impeaching attitude)—are full of political rebellion against nationalist projects, a violent revolt that must be willing to risk physical engagement. In this critique (written during the rise of
the 1960s student movements) the willingness to confront reality at the risk
of one's flesh becomes the precondition for authentic Surrealism.

Tsuruoka's view of Surrealist engagement recalls, among others, the
statement by Michel Leiris in the foreword to his autobiographical *L'Age
d'homme*: in "De la littérature considerée comme une tauromachie," Leiris
elaborates a view of literature that requires writing to contain what he figures as the "bull's horn," or at least "the shadow of a bull's horn" (*l'ombre
du corne du taureau*):

Is it not true that what occurs in the domain of writing is devoid of value if it remains 'aesthetic,' anodyne, deprived of sanction, if there is nothing in the fact of
writing a work that would be the equivalent . . . of the piercing horn of the bull
for the torero, which alone—because of the material menace that it harbors—
confers a human reality on his art, and prevents it from being merely the vain
graces of a bailerina?[25]

That Leiris tests the relation between writing and reality, and proposes
putting a certain kind of threat in writing to give it a "human reality," can

be seen as analogous to Tsuruoka's understanding of a "true" Surrealism with its "reality that one must confront with one's bloodstained flesh": it is in a similar kind of autobiographical truth that Tsuruoka locates the signs of a deep connection with Surrealist ideas.

Tsuruoka claims that what one adopts or cites must relate to what was already, autobiographically, present—it must echo a trace that has already been written within one. Thus, in the case of Kitasono, the only thing already present within him onto which he could write, or for which he could substitute his Surrealist understanding, was the lyrical and sentimental past of Japanese poetry. By contrast, in the case of Takiguchi Shūzō, there is an autobiographical condition on which his reading of Surrealist poetry can be superimposed (or perhaps overwritten, like a palimpsest), and for this reason his is seen as an authentic absorption. Tsuruoka quotes Takiguchi's essay "Chōgenjitsushugi to watashi no shiteki jikken" (Surrealism and my poetic experiments) in which he relates the events of his youth that led him from a reading of Blake's "Songs of Innocence" to suddenly dropping out of Keio University and departing for Hokkaidō: "When I left for Hokkaidō, I sold my entire library of literature—I intended to liquidate everything. Actually one might say that [it felt as though] Surrealist thought pierced that emptiness."[26] Tsuruoka rightly notes this description of the strangely violent way in which Surrealist thought enters Takiguchi's world and begins to play a critical role in his thinking.

The image of piercing (*tsuku*, stab, transfix, gore, attack)[27] implies a depth or a shock of impact having to do with the flesh, with a form of imminent danger. ("Surrealist thought pierced that emptiness.") We recall Leiris's terms for this process of conferring "reality" along with (still, however, metaphorically) the threat of physical danger: the point of the horn, the piercing of the skin. Takiguchi's description links the place of emptiness (*kūkyo*, vacancy, hollowness, fruitlessness) with an absence of content; the same word, *kūkyo* (without content), that might be used to describe a superficial or pointless piece of writing, here is subject to the piercing of a thought that is therefore, by definition, given a plenitude rife with danger. Beginning with a certain realm of liquidation, getting rid of all of his library of literature, Takiguchi does not seem to place Surrealist thought in an equivalent relation, as a replacement or substitute for "literature": it is not literature, but that which pierces through the vacancy left by the liquidation of literature.

On Memory and Doubt 51

Although Takiguchi's initiation into Surrealism remains distinct from
that of the European Surrealists, it gains for Tsuruoka a certain validity for
being an experience that Takiguchi engages in a highly personal way, without which he could not have accepted Surrealist thought. "Unlike Kitasono
and the others, [Takiguchi,] as a prerequisite for his acceptance of Surrealism, had to pass through a state of spiritual turmoil, as a highly personal
experience [goku kojinteki na taiken to shite]."[28] Thus, for Tsuruoka as for
Leiris, there is a profound relation between the personal experience of danger or disequilibrium and the possibility of being pierced, touched, or violently affected (written on) by a text. It is in part because of this personal
preparation, the period of violent uncertainty and turmoil, that readers are
able to believe in the depth, the reality of (as well as the threat posed by)
Takiguchi's acceptance of Surrealism.

This way of seeing Takiguchi's "personal experience" of Surrealism
has been adopted by several critics who have attempted to understand the
importation of Surrealist thought in Japan. In his essay "Takiguchi Shūzō
and André Breton," for example, critic Iwaya Kunio traces a number of
analogies between the lives of Takiguchi and Breton: their rebellion against
parents who wanted them to become medical doctors, their upbringing in
northern sea landscapes (Brittany and Toyama), their common aversion to
the stabilization of "literature," and their common search for the absolute.
In Iwaya's words, which go farther in implying a kind of objective chance
at work in these similarities, the two were "destined for each other."[29] He
takes the biographical or autobiographical links as evidence of the authenticity of both writers' engagement with Surrealism:

Although in those days, other Japanese poets were also influenced by Surrealism,
they understood it merely as a formal or stylistic novelty, a different way to write
poetry. Takiguchi was the only one who was committed to Surrealism as a spiritual adventure—a matter of life or death. Surprisingly, the very mental process
which tempted him to a "self-abandonment almost equaling violence," can also be
recognized in the *life of Breton himself.* Because of his experiences during the war,
the latter also decided to give up a medical career. . . . Was he not tormented by a
craving for self-abandonment?[30]

Tracing the possibility of recognizing the connections between Takiguchi
and "the life of Breton himself," Iwaya, too, recognizes depth in Takiguchi's approach through another figure of "life and death" (through the
possibility of being touched in a violently personal way), in opposition to

the other poets for whom Surrealism was merely a "formal or stylistic novelty, a different way to write poetry," a mere superficial technique. Even if the two writers are not the same, Iwaya sees their differences as further proof of the deeply personal nature of their approaches, and hence the authenticity of both Takiguchi's and Breton's ways of viewing and practicing Surrealism.

In contrast, Tsuruoka views Kitasono's way of adapting Surrealism as merely superficial, in part because it does not pierce the surface or express the potential of language to enact any "real" or threatening action. It is seen as weak, lacking; Tsuruoka's analysis recalls the earlier depiction by Hagiwara of literature that only mechanically reproduces "some appearance according to one's tastes" or takes on, superficially, "an attitude of objectivity." Tsuruoka writes of Kitasono:

In other words, his spirit [*seishin*], penetrated by traditional lyricism, did nothing more than put on and take off the language and the various -isms, merely as an ornament to his external appearance, a *nouvelle vague* that varied with the seasons [*sono tokidoki no nuuberu baagu*].[31]

He describes European poetics as a pure fashion show: to "put on and take off the . . . -isms." (Reducing Surrealism to one -ism among many, he uses the katakana -*izumu* to emphasize its foreign aspect, rather than the common equivalent, -*shugi*, which would perhaps depict the movement as a more coherent or specific set of principles or doctrines.) These -isms can be changed at will; *izumu to gengo* (-isms and language) are, Tsuruoka claims, mere surface for Kitasono, ornaments (*kazari*) to embellish his external appearance, in a specifically visual sense (*gaiken*, outward show, exterior view). Tsuruoka uses the French *nouvelle vague* in its most ironic sense, bringing the French term into his description as if to demonstrate precisely the effect of such an importation within his Japanese sentence, emphasizing its pretension and ephemeral superficiality. What Tsuruoka perceives in Kitasono's spirit (in the place that, finally, would reveal depth and underlying intention, the aspects of poetic interiority with which Hagiwara, too, identified the ultimately meaningful place in poetic language) is that it is "penetrated with traditional lyricism" ("dentōteki jojōshugi ni tsuranukareta seishin," his spirit is pierced, penetrated, struck through, perforated). The term "pierced" (*tsuranukareta*, although not the same as Takiguchi used earlier, *tsuku*) can describe the way a light strikes through the darkness, a theme through a work of literature, or, even, a bullet through flesh. What is deeply hidden within Kitasono, what one can perceive underneath, this critic claims, is the "traditional lyricism" that can be identified with the history of premodern Japanese poetry. And the reason he finds such an allegiance insidious is not merely because of the exterior superficiality of the costumed -isms, but also because of the political valence that such allegiance serves to conceal. The crux of the matter is Japanese national identity and the relation to tradition:

> And further, [Kitasono] himself in *Shiro no arubamu* [White album] denies the basic attitude of taking pure aesthetics as the object of experimental poetry, and in the poems after the Great East Asian War[32] he becomes obsessed with the view of poetry that finds its purpose in a study of the value of East Asian culture and civilization. This floating, weak spirit of his selects one of the most emotionally shallow poems from the Man'yōshū: "From today, great lord, I depart without looking back, to become your humble shield and to resist the foreign enemy." He calls it "pure and complete" [*junsui de jūjitsu shita*] . . . and, a strange kind of patriot, he praises the poem, saying that if he could he would like to have written it. This patriot goes on to become an active champion of war, praising it in his essays and poems, beginning with "Essays in Contemporary Poetics" (in *Gendaishi*, Spring 1942). Be it in Surrealism or patriotism, the reason for his metamorphosis is that he ultimately lacked an independent subjective stance of engagement with respect to a central core of reality.[33]

Tsuruoka attacks, openly and vehemently, Kitasono's "weak" (*nanjaku*) and "wafting" (*fuyū*, floating, suspended) spirit, in which he praises a poem from the Man'yōshū (20.4373) that Tsuruoka sees as reflecting only the most shallow and patriotic emotions. What makes Kitasono's Surrealism superficial (from the perspective of this postwar critic) is the fact that he can change with the times to defend a national imperialist project and would turn the purpose of Japanese poetry to such unconscionable ends. Kitasono's later obsession with East Asian civilization is rooted, Tsuruoka claims, in the lack of a firm subject position (*shutai*) in his engagement with reality: again, Tsuruoka seeks evidence of depth, of real underlying connection to the "core" of Surrealist thought.

Let us turn, for a moment, to Kitasono's own words of praise for this poem from the Man'yōshū, so that we can consider the implications of such a seemingly insidious and nativist praise. If one examines the brief essay "Aikokushi" (Patriotic poetry), in which Kitasono cites and praises this poem from the Man'yōshū, one finds that he laments the sentimentality of most of the new patriotic poems that surround him, which compare unfavorably, in his opinion, with this often-cited premodern poem. The earlier poem, he says, was often recited on the radio and in newspapers; it is not, then, a favorite chosen from among all the poems of the anthology, but rather a poem chosen from among the available patriotic poetry he heard around him. Kitasono's point in this brief essay is that modern patriotic poetry fails as poetry; he claims to be incapable of producing a worthwhile patriotic poem. So, although his explicit point is that he would like to write a poem as good as this one, the essay functions also to provide an excuse for his not producing a sufficient volume of patriotic poems, or for not responding to requests for patriotic poetry:

I have had patriotic poems requested of me, but when I think of this poem from the Man'yōshū, I cannot bring myself to take up the pen. Up to this point I have not written any such halfhearted [irresponsible] poems that I could not include in my poetry collections. . . . I have not written a single such poem just for the occasion; although I am ashamed to be unable to write a satisfying patriotic poem with such a content, at the same time somehow I can't feel right about publishing any until I can write a patriotic poem with which I can be satisfied. Recently this circumstance has been truly vexing [*jirettai*].[34]

Although one cannot excuse clear complicity by pointing out areas of ambivalence, it is possible to view these statements of Kitasono's (in their historical context) as taking the Man'yōshū poem as a kind of shield in itself, if only a humble one. Without losing sight of the larger context of this argument, which expresses a stated desire to write a poem of such sentiments, one can at the same time see the "vexing" position of the speaker, surrounded by bad nationalist poetry on the radio and in newspapers, and threatened with the suspicion of disloyalty because, prolific though he is, he is not composing, or not composing a sufficient number of, such poems. Although his text does not evade the term *aikokushi* (patriotic poem), it often refers to the kind of sentiment that such a poem would express with vague pronominals that become difficult to interpret: *sono ba kagiri* (limited to such a circumstance), *sōshita naiyō no shi* (poems with such a content). The pressure to write and the concomitant inability to write such poems are evident here, even if couched in terms of an artistic dilemma and the difficulty of writing well.

The anxiety Kitasono claims in relation to this Man'yōshū poem (an "anxiety of influence" in the most stereotypical Bloomian sense, the inability to live up to the expectation set by the earlier poem) could benefit by a reading in which, in this case, Kitasono *would* be found to be insincere, or substituting one sentiment for another. In this case, oddly, Tsuruoka does not give Kitasono's language the credit for insincerity that he is ready to give to the language of his earlier Surrealist works, although deriving his reading of the latter in part from the existence of the former. The fact that Kitasono is capable of arriving at such a point of nationalist sentiment, or of producing convincing language to this effect, becomes the proof for Tsuruoka of his lack of connection with any "core" of reality. Put another way, Tsuruoka has succumbed to the temptation of taking the words "pure and complete," as themselves the only terms that can be found pure, and sincere, within an otherwise slippery and elusive language.

Tsuruoka's critique may be understood not merely as a single reader's idiosyncratic view of Surrealism in Japan; it is, besides, a revealing example of an understanding that, as we shall see, permeated the readings and critiques of Surrealist works in Japan even at the time. The veiled anger running through Tsuruoka's accusing words echoes the raw anger of Kanbara Tai in his famous essay in *Shi: Genjitsu*, "The Fall of Surrealism" (*Chōgenjitsushugi no botsuraku*). Tsuruoka's critique of the Surrealist's lack of contact with reality echoes the accusations that precipitated the split among the contributors to the magazine *Shi to shiron* in 1930 and the founding of *Shi: Genjitsu*, a division centered on the debate between *poésie engagée* (socially and politically engaged poetry) and *poésie pure* (pure poetry).[35]

Kanbara cites and censures in the strongest terms Nishiwaki Junzaburō's view of reality and of the purpose of Surrealism:

This is a truly irresponsible theory! It is not merely that we cannot allow such intemperate language on the part of the Surrealists: but for us contemporary people whose concern for reality is increasing with each passing day—a reality that surrounds us with nearly overwhelming power—Nishiwaki Junzaburō's words expose his extreme lack of awareness of reality, and, moreover, deceptively adorn and whitewash the escape of those who lack the courage, power, justice or honesty to confront reality directly.

Kanbara goes on to argue that a tendency to evade or ignore reality is typical of the Japanese Surrealists:

This tendency is held in common—with greater or lesser degrees of difference—by the Japanese Surrealists.

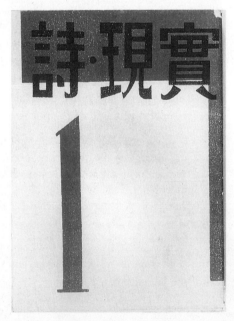

4. *Left*: Cover of *Shi to shiron* (Poetry and poetics), June 1921. *Right*: cover of *Shi: Genjitsu* (Poetry: reality), June 1930. Courtesy of Kanagawa Museum of Modern Literature.

This way of thinking about "the dullness of reality," these pompous parting words [*mottaibutta sutezerifu*] of those who flee reality, necessarily slight reality, despise it, and immediately arrive at the *mistranslation* that gives Surrealism the same meaning as "nonrealism" or "antirealism."

Their mistranslation deserves admiration for its simplicity, and for being so illogical as to constitute a veritable leap of thought.[36]

Kanbara here, first, argues that despising, loathing, and evasion of reality are characteristic of Japanese Surrealists in general. He reads their thinking about "the dullness of reality" (a citation from the first line of Nishiwaki's *Chōgenjitsushugi shiron* [Surrealist poetics]) as a pompous putting on of airs and takes the Surrealists' attitude to be a deceptive ornamentation of words that can be assumed and removed at will. Like Tsuruoka, Kanbara sees this superficial posturing not only as a lack of true connection with reality, but also as a direct means of evading contact with reality. He frames this evasion in the terms of a mistranslation: the Japanese Surrealists, in ignoring or despising reality, have arrived at a mistranslation (*goyaku*) of the "meaning" of Surrealism; they have arrived at "nonrealism" (*hi-genjitsushugi*) or "antirealism" (*han-genjitsushugi*). Constructing an oppositional model (realism versus anti- or non-realism), Kanbara then attacks this vision that he sees represented by the Japanese Surrealists (who pretend to be so important as to be above reality), with the ironic praise that "it is so simple and illogical as to represent a veritable leap of thought." The mistranslation here takes the terms of Surrealism and makes a simple and clear leap (*hiyaku*, a logical leap, a flying jump, a rapid progress): the motion is almost wonderful, he comments bitingly, for the clarity with which it leaves behind what it translates (a true Surrealism, he implies) and arrives at something completely different.

Kanbara attacks the Surrealists for leaving reality behind and at the same time accuses them of oversimplifying the terms of Surrealism (of instituting a too-clear division or opposition between the real and the surreal—as nonreal, antireal). He cites a passage from Ueda Toshio's essay "My Surrealism" ("Watashi no chōgenjitsushugi," published in *Shi to shiron* in June 1929)[37] that he sees as representing Japanese Surrealists' view of reality; yet if we examine Ueda's passage more closely, we see that the views on reality explicated here are not nearly so absolute or clear-cut as Kanbara would have us think, and they contradict this representation of a unified Surrealist point of view.

The title in itself ("My Surrealism") suggests a personal vision of Surrealist practice: by giving his essay this title, Ueda claims Surrealism as his own and highlights a subjective vision of Surrealist thought. Kanbara's accusation does not allow for (extreme) individuality among the Japanese Surrealists; they have followed Nishiwaki's "irresponsible" view too closely ("This tendency is held in common—with greater or lesser degrees of difference—by the Japanese Surrealists"; and Nishiwaki's words "deceptively adorn and whitewash the escape of those who lack the courage, power, justice, or honesty to confront reality directly"). Both Kanbara's and Ueda's essays employ frequent imperatives, overt, strong condemnations and assertions, and a telegraphic and explosive style. One might raise the question, then, of who speaks, in so strongly subjective and personal a mode, in these Surrealist essays? Who can lay claim to the title of "Surrealist" as his own? Who has the right to define and trace the understanding of the meanings of Surrealism (the proper translation or mistranslation)? The accusation of mistranslation invokes the legitimacy of some prior understanding on whose "authenticity" both speakers' positions depend.

What is it in Ueda's "My Surrealism" that evokes so violent a rebuke? When Nishiwaki claimed that breaking convention is not to be done for its own sake, but only in the service of poetic expression, for Kanbara this represented an avoidance of the larger questions of social and political "reality." In Ueda's case, one discovers another kind of polemic, one that slips precisely at the site of the personal pronouns, in the space that opens between the "my" of the Surrealist speaker (*watashi no*) and the "you" of the listener (*shokun*, you, the addressees of an essay).[38] Ueda Toshio writes (in the passage cited by Kanbara):

[You must] understand the Surrealist's abhorrence of the world of reality. A great literary movement conceals [contains] a new truth that contradicts conventional values. Therefore, you must understand the truth of Surrealism. Oh, most excellent journalists of the world of reality, understand the new truth of Surrealism! And understand the new dream of nihilism [nihility]. To say it properly, one ought to be ignorant of the rules of art.

The world of reality is a world of death, and a world of sleep. You people who dream in this world of sleep! You do not exist. Living things, you deserve to be abhorred. The mortal muse of imagination gives dreams to you who are asleep in the world of sleep. You who were given these dreams then give [the dreams] expression. This is possible in the world of sleep, and it is the work only of those who are asleep. Thus, you do not exist. And further, you are living beings who deserve to be abhorred. You are asleep. You are dreaming. You are in a world of empty daydreams. You are in the world of death. You are in the world of sensation. You are those who have been captured [*toraerareta*] by death, and you are prisoners of the world of death. Tell, departed spirits. Dream, oh ghosts. Be blessed, apparitions of the dead.

Ueda begins with a sentence that seems to be a clear object for Kanbara's attack: he speaks of the "Surrealist's abhorrence of the world of reality." A doubling occurs with the address, "Oh, most excellent journalists of the world of reality!" While it would seem, from the general context of the essay, that this would constitute an attack on the addressees (you, who are mere journalists of the world of reality), it eventually becomes less clear whether the addressees (you) or the Surrealists themselves are living within this problematic "world of reality." In other words, while his essay appears to be a polemical tirade against those who do not understand Surrealism, with its repeated sentence endings "You must understand" (or, "let us understand," *rikai seyo*), it is not always clear who is to do the understanding, and who composes the group of addressees: are the Surrealists themselves included in this situation, with the difference that they possess a "new truth" or way of understanding it?

The ambiguity in part lies in the persistently repeated subject term *shokun* ("you," plural), who seem to be attacked here for being asleep, for living in a world of death, for not existing; they are "living beings who deserve to be abhorred." On the most explicit level, this is simply a tirade against non-Surrealists, against the regular members of the society, for thinking that they are living and awake when they are dead and what they perceive as reality is a "world of sleep." This is the aspect of Ueda's statement that Kanbara so vehemently attacks. If one sees the world of reality as not really existing, as being dead, asleep, a land of daydreams, it would provide an excuse for escaping this world to seek another place that, in this scheme, would be considered more alive, more awake—existence in some other sense, in terms of the "new truth of Surrealism."

And yet, in the essay one finds a moment when the "you" seems no longer to refer clearly or exclusively to those outside of the speaker: "The mortal muse of imagination gives dreams to you who are asleep in the world of sleep. You who are given these dreams then give [the dreams] expression." The "muse of imagination" allows one to die and gives dreams;

then one "expresses" (*hyōgen o nasu*) or gives expression (to something that remains unspecified): this would seem to describe the creative impulse. Gradually the polemic directed at "you" (*shokun*) comes to include the speaker himself, and to elide with the vision of Surrealist poetic creation that would incorporate the dream, death, and reality into the process of creation, rather than keeping distinct boundaries between these realms. Thus the "dream of nihilism" seems to contain a more positive possibility. The "you" who are in a world of daydreams, a world of the senses, could be those who have not yet "woken up" to Surrealist thought. It seems that this world of daydreams, of death, could be profoundly connected to a Surrealist view of reality, in which reality is precisely linked to a vision of death, dream, and sleep and is not clearly separated from these worlds as conventional values would have it.

Thus the final invocation, "Tell, departed spirits. Dream, oh ghosts," seems to be also a call to the creative impulse, in which all beings are seen as ghosts (*bōrei*) capable of telling, of dreaming, of being prisoners trapped in the "world of death." Perhaps for Kanbara this use of the idea of death appears irresponsible, when "real" death presses in all around; yet, for Ueda, it represents a profound identification with a view of reality *as* death, as dream, and not at all a despising or condemnation of reality because of its association with death, with nonexistence, with sleep. In this sense, Ueda's is a more ambivalent description than that of Nishiwaki, with his view of the breaking of convention. Convention is broken here in the "new truth" that is concealed within Surrealism (and in ignoring the rules of art); but Ueda does not effect as clear a split between the "real" and the "non-real" (surreal) as Kanbara would have claimed.

Kanbara's focus is on science and its uses in the poetic process: he would like language to be clear and clean, and, one infers, would like writing to apply and correspond to reality through a kind of empirical method. For him, Ueda's understanding of reality is merely an escape, an attack on those who are engaged with the "world of reality." (In Ueda's view, however, it is "journalists" like Kanbara who are trapped.) In fact, his view contains both an attack and a gradual, implied inclusion of the speaker in the larger dilemma implied by this attack. We shall return, in the section "'Examines narratives': Poetry and Actuality" (Chapter 4), to the question of the dream and the relation of the dream to the project of writing and to the will. But for the moment, one can see that the pivotal dilemma for those who claimed Surrealist thought as their own, even at the time of these earliest formulations and debates in Japan, was the way a writer might engage with something like the world of reality, rather than falling into a use of language as a putting on of airs.

We can see a clear link between the reasons for Hagiwara's damning of "poster literature" and Tsuruoka's questioning of the superficial pasting of a new aesthetics onto an unaltered root of traditional aesthetics, the criticism with which he attacks Kitasono's writings. Important turning points for the contemporary debate on the status of reality include Kanbara Tai's "The Fall of Surrealism" and Miyoshi Jūrō's "Surrealism, etc." (to be discussed in the next section, "The Extinction of the Personal"). The latter, again, accuses the Surrealists precisely of criminal "mistranslation" as they leave reality behind. In relation to those critiques, we find that deep ambivalences are revealed in Ueda's invocation of ghosts and death and in his confrontation of the problem of reality and dreams. In the next section we continue to examine the ways in which Surrealists questioned what reality might have to do with dreams. To do so, we examine how within this poetics the direct access to something called reality, finally, is seen as a difficult if not impossible demand, just as translation, at its limits, contains within it the force of a rigorous and perhaps unattainable requirement for immediacy.

What is the role of the emptying out of the self, including the voiding of purpose or personal identity, that the Surrealists saw as a prerequisite for receiving inspiration or creating something new? What is the status of "everyday reality" for avant-garde writers in Europe (including certain ideas that were incorporated from Russian Constructivism), and how can a reading of that status illuminate these debates on translation and everyday reality in Japan? (What happens when the word "reality" is both an ordinary, nonpoetic term for the world around us and a metaphorized and highly charged center for a literary and artistic quest, and what happens when it vacillates between these two levels?) Perhaps there is a particular purpose in the Surrealist's "leap," so often accused of representing a mistranslation; perhaps there is a use or a reason for their overturning the logical hierarchy between the "real" and the "unreal." What, then, is the role of the emptying of identity, the specific qualities of the kind of "night" that poetry invokes? And what might this have to do with, and how might it serve to alter, a "world of reality"?

The Extinction of the Personal

A reading of Ueda Toshio's essay "My Surrealism" raises the question of the self, and the place of the self in Surrealism. As Iwaya claims, there is a violent search for "self-abandonment" closely linked with the Surrealist work of Takiguchi and Breton. One might approach this issue through the questions posed by Ueda's essay: How is it that a writer might be "captured by death"? What does it mean to be "prisoners of the world of death"? One recalls in connection with these questions a later essay by Maurice Blanchot, "Inspiration," and in particular the segment entitled "Death, Trap." Echoing and moving beyond the terms of Mallarmé and Novalis (who were among the poets translated by Ueda and other members of *Shi to shiron* at this time), Blanchot writes of night, death, and sleep as they relate to the written "work" and to language. He elaborates two versions of night, one of which is the "ordinary" one (like that which might be envisioned by Kanbara in his rationality, the clear opposite of day) and the other closer to the world of reality as death or sleep referred to by Ueda.

Kanbara's reality is analogous to what Blanchot would term "the day"; it is a reasonable and present power, with which one argues and labors in the realm of conscious action. Ueda, however, writes that the "work" of "you who are asleep" is to "give expression [to dreams]"; he applies a logic that eludes Kanbara's view of reality. Kanbara is right to note that this view is "so illogical as to be deserving of wonder" and that what is illogical in it takes the form of a "leap" (and we recognize in the leap a critical and fundamental term of Blanchot's thought). Thus, we may propose that Ueda's death and sleep are closer to what Blanchot calls the "*other* night," that which is no longer susceptible to control or purpose, a night that is not merely the opposite of day or life but contains and conceals its own specific fascination and strange nonlogic: this night, for Blanchot, "has no power, does not call; it attracts only by negligence." The ignorance and the despising of reality that Kanbara attributes to the Surrealists is a form of such neglect: Kanbara accuses the Surrealists of neglecting reality. But in Blanchot's terms the opposition between negligence and attention is overturned. What appears to be useful work in the "real," in the day, is seen as an elusion of "inspiration" and a burrowing attempt to shelter from the "void" that surrounds them nonetheless.

Kanbara attempts to throw off the weight and ambiguity of the terms of death, of sleep, making them appear negative, irresponsible, insincere; yet he does also locate within them a leap that we can read, not as a defect but as a necessary and critical point linked to the process of writing and to the form and practice of translation—in Blanchot's terms, "the leap is inspiration's form or movement."

Blanchot also describes this "other night," as "the sparkle of something baseless and without depth."[39] In other words (taking the liberty of following Blanchot's logic), the perception of the depth of this other night comes with viewing it logically, through the day: from within itself, this other night appears precisely baseless and without depth. But again, the depthlessness (emptiness), as in Takiguchi's emptying out (*kūkyo*) in preparation for receiving inspiration, is not here to be taken in the conventional negative sense; rather, it is precisely the opening to possibility, to inspiration. Blanchot writes, "Apparitions, phantoms, and dreams are an allusion to this empty night."[40] And Ueda calls on these apparitions, phantoms, and dreams: the distinction between what is "baseless" and what has depth is no longer a clear determinant of what is "real."

The hierarchy of real and unreal is overwhelmed here, and it is no longer possible to speak so definitively, as Kanbara does with his emphatically positivistic statements ("I agree with the following statement 100 percent," he affirms several times in his essay). It is interesting, then, that Kanbara calls this way of thinking of reality *sutezerifu*, a throw-away line, a parting shot, last words. We may agree that this way of thinking represents in fact a moment of departure from something, from a certain kind of logic and scientific understanding that Kanbara values, and it does enter the dangerous realm of eluding one's grasp, carrying out translation so that it becomes a leap rather than a link or a logical connection.

Ueda exhorts these inhabitants of the world of dreams to speak and to dream: they are not in the world of death in the conventional sense precisely by virtue of the fact that they can be addressed by Ueda, and that they remain capable of expression, of receiving dreams from the "muse of imagination." In a sense, the slip occurs because the world of "sleep" and the world of "death" in Ueda's description are not significantly differentiated: it is another night but not one that would be outside of the reach of a call, or outside the possibility of being invoked by Ueda's words ("Oh, ghosts") and commanded by him in the imperative mode: "understand" (*rikai seyo*), "tell" (*katare*), "dream" (*yume miyo*). Even in the space of the leap from one world to the next, a link is created by the address itself, and by the command. This is the aspect of Ueda's reality that Kanbara either refuses to see, or upon seeing, finds to be all too abstract for the contemporary situation in which he would like to find a purpose, a possibility of intentional and effective action in relation to the "reality that surrounds us now with an overwhelming power."

Kanbara's essay "The Fall of Surrealism" finally becomes a central (as well as symptomatic) treatise for analyzing the forms of the resistance to Surrealism—and for mapping certain textual moments and sites in which Surrealism was perceived as doing something dangerous and irresponsible. In my view, this irresponsibility was related to the attempts by Surrealist writing to induce a disorienting and radical slippage in the language's foundations and referential capacities. This slippage itself has to do with appropriation and translation. It also is related to the way the poets (and their poetry) link—or, in the opinions of critics, fail to connect—to the world.

Later in the essay Kanbara reiterates an attack of Surrealism by the poet Miyoshi Jūrō (1902–1958). Miyoshi was a poet and playwright who began his literary career as an anarchist and later became involved in the proletarian literary movement and Marxism, until the mid-1930s when he underwent ideological conversion (*tenkō*) and renounced his Marxism.[41] In the essay "Chōgenjitsushugi nado" (Surrealism, etc.), which focuses explicitly on the problem of translation, Miyoshi writes:

How is Surrealism being translated against itself [literally antitranslated] in Japan? How is it being mistranslated? And furthermore, how will those reactionary poets, those highbrow poets [aloof from the world], skillfully redesign the camouflage clothing of this mistranslated Surrealism, this Surrealism translated against itself, remaking it in the Japanese style, then hiding themselves stylishly behind it? . . . What kind of meaning does this have for society? . . . I will merely say here how disgusting and how intolerable it is to see you Japanese Surrealists wear this stylish camouflage of Surrealism that hides the truth.[42]

Miyoshi, like Kanbara, is concerned with the societal meaning or significance (*shakaiteki igi*) of how Surrealism has been understood in Japan. The fact that Surrealist poets remain "aloof from the world" (*kōtō shijin*; *kōtō* can also mean "Parnassian") and are "reactionary" represents a serious problem for him. In Miyoshi's terms, the Japanese Surrealists have designed a Surrealism that covers up the real situation (here he uses the same term for "design" that Hagiwara did in the earlier passage, *ishō*, and the related term for skill, *kōmyō ni*). Once again, what is problematic for Miyoshi, Kanbara, and Hagiwara about the Surrealists in Japan is described in terms of a stylish costume worn (*kikonasu*) to cover up one's true intentions, one's real situation. The mistranslation of Surrealism, or the "antitranslation" (*han-yaku*, the translation against itself), Miyoshi characterizes with the idiomatic term *kakure-mino*, rendered here as "camouflage outfit"—literally, *kakure-mino* is a straw raincoat in which to hide one's body. (As early as the *Makura no sōshi*, this term comes to mean the concealment of the truth, of the facts of one's real situation.) To describe the Japanese reworking and transformation of Surrealism as a straw raincoat, by employing a figure from the *Makura no sōshi*, prefigures Tsuruoka's view that the stylish costume of Surrealism conceals no more than the oldest traditions of Japanese poetry. Although the condemnation here comes from a different perspective, Miyoshi, too, implies that these traditions have nothing to do with contemporary reality and society. He finds such a Surrealism "intolerable" and "disgusting," both for masking the truth and for remaining aloof from the present reality in a "clever" concern for style.

We shall consider again the Surrealists' notions of tradition, the related problem of originality, and the terms in which they defend their project. In his essay, Miyoshi accuses them of precisely a lack of originality: they have cleverly redesigned elements of the tradition in which to hide themselves, but they have neither invented anything new nor contributed to the resolution of contemporary problems in society. They have made Surrealism ambiguous and personal, when what is needed, according to Kanbara, is science, progress, speed, sincerity—the search for positive values. Kanbara's denunciation of the Japanese Surrealist's view of reality hinges on the notion of the "dullness of reality" or of everyday life (*tsu-maranasa*) elaborated by Nishiwaki. Such a notion of dullness may also be compared to the related Russian concept of *byt* (everyday life) used by Russian (Constructivist) poets such as Vladimir Mayakovsky (1894–1930) and adopted and translated from his work by French Surrealists in the phrase "la vie courante."[43] The term denotes the dull humdrum of everyday existence, or the conventional plane of the everyday world against which the poet struggles. Roman Jakobson defines *byt* in his article on Mayakovsky, "On a Generation that Squandered Its Poets":

Opposed to this creative urge toward the transformed future is a tendency toward stabilization of an immutable present, covered over by a stagnating slime, which stifles life in its tight hard mold. The name of this element is *byt*. It is curious that this word and its derivatives should have such a prominent place in the Russian language, while Western European languages have no word that corresponds to it. Perhaps, in the Western European collective consciousness there is no concept of such a force as might oppose and break down the established norms of life.[44]

Byt is linked to the problem of how Surrealism will transform society: the year of Mayakovsky's suicide, the Surrealists changed the title of *La révolution surréaliste* to *Le Surréalisme au service de la révolution*, and Breton dedicated the central article in the first issue to Mayakovsky: "Ljubovnaja lodka razbilas' o byt" [Love boat has crashed into *byt*]. The path of this concept of *byt* and its relation to the dilemma of revolution and poetry, or the place of poetry in society, can be traced beyond Breton to the crux of the polemical debate on *tsumaranasa*, which led to the split between the journals *Shi to shiron* (Poetry and poetics) and *Shi: Genjitsu* (Poetry: Reality). *Byt* can be a metaphorized view of an omnipresent ordinariness (pettiness, stifling convention) as well as a nonpoetic term for "simple, everyday existence"; this ambiguity is echoed in the Japanese Surrealists' argument and in their vacillating understanding of the terms of their debate: *tsumaranasa*, everyday life, and reality.

The division between the personal and the collective (in Mayakovsky's motto, "personal motives about the common *byt*")[45] becomes another central problem in the critique of Surrealism: the Japanese Surrealists are seen as guilty not only of wearing Surrealist thought as a costume, but also of expressing views that are "merely" personal and cannot be shared with others or are not susceptible to adoption by the collective. Kanbara writes, speaking for his own group: "In the present era of perfectly mechanized industrial capitalism, we find most attractive that which is systematic, scientific, clear (*meiryō*), exact, and speedy. We can feel no attraction today, in 1930, to that which is not precise and clear." Kanbara seeks a positive model of purpose and progress, which would embody the qualities he specifies: system or structure (*soshiki*), scientificity, clarity, and precision (*seikakusa*, also "authenticity," "veracity"). His understanding of the present era, as an era of "perfectly mechanized industrial capitalism," matches his mechanized, scientific desires for poetic experience. Known as a Futurist,[46] he applied the model of industrialism to the production of poetry. Thus he finds the views of Kitasono, for example, to be intolerable: "This Surrealism of theirs has turned itself into a faded nonsense that is completely individual-istic and cannot evoke the sympathy of anyone but themselves."[47] He em-phasizes the absolutely personal and individualist (*zenzen kojinshugiteki*) quality of the Surrealists' thought as proof of its being no more than *tawa-goto*, or drivel, nonsense, foolish talk (like the title of Yamamura Bochō's poem "Geigo"). The language of Surrealism must be shared and under-stood (with precision, clarity, exactness) in order to be considered valid.

At various points in Kitasono's essays and theoretical writings, he elaborates his view of the "collective" and the "personal" in poetry. In the ten-part essay "The Limits of Surrealist Poetry" ("Chōgenjitsushugishi to sono genkai") published in 1930, the same year as Kanbara's critique, Kita-sono writes: "Surrealism is an antipersonal (antibourgeois) artistic system." In his parenthetical definition, then, the personal would become analogous with the bourgeois; later on in the same essay (section 8) he names "taste" or "fancy" (*shumi*) as the "last opium of individualistic art." An art that de-pends on the principles of taste is "bourgeois" and individualistic: one should "spit," Kitasono writes, "mercilessly and with extreme cruelty, as if one were spitting on the Bible, on this agitation for [good] taste."[48] Kita-sono's language, in this essay as in much of his critical writing, is full of enigmatic images and ambiguously embedded clauses, linked by multiva-lent phrases that break up the grammatical flow (such as *to shite, ni oite*, and *ni tsuite*), making it difficult at times to determine where exactly the argument is headed. His readers tend to appropriate the clearest moments of approval or condemnation and let them stand in for his whole argu-ment, glossing over the numerous difficulties and complexities in the in-tervening theoretical language.

In "The Limits of Surrealist Poetry" and other essays from the 1930s collected in *Haiburau no funsui* (The fountain of the highbrow), Kitasono outlines a certain doubt about the principles elaborated by the early Surre-alists (such as Breton and Aragon) and suggests a "second phase" of Surre-alism that would resolve some of the problems of this first phase. Kitasono elaborates here a vision that he saw as a "second Surrealism," but that crit-ics see as Kitasono's development of his personal poetics, which continues in his postwar works.[49] To call these essays individualist, however, would be to miss the force of their anti-individualist stance, and their positioning of themselves as a latter phase but still a part of Surrealism.

What Kanbara found most individualistic in Kitasono's writings was not simply the idiosyncratic views he espoused, but rather most specifically the language in which he explicated these views. His language was so elliptical as to evoke the accusation of evading reality—not settling into any clear, single, or exact "meaning." In essays such as "The Limits of Surrealist Poetry," the sentences are slow and curve back on themselves in circles: they are anything but the fast instrument of clarity that Kanbara would have admired. Nonetheless, his language is precisely crafted and creates its ripples with intentional exactitude. Kitasono writes (in a moment that Kanbara calls "faded nonsense"), in the essay "Chōgenjitsushugi no tachiba" (The Surrealist position):

Surrealism, as a literary movement, defines "vacuum tube" [*shinkūkan*] as "the vacuum tube that is [has] nothing at all." Thus the materials and the world of skill that constitute this vacuum tube vary [*sōi*, differ, disagree, are at variance] in accordance with the vacuum tube and are subject to its command.

As for being "nothing at all," this "nothing at all" is a result of [exists by dint of] nothing at all. The work that leads to this "vacuum" is the essence of art.[50]

Kitasono here is explicating the "void," describing the place of emptiness, and runs into the rhetorical difficulty of speaking of "nothing." Furthermore, he is attempting to explicate the terms in which the void or the "vacuum," "nothingness," are spoken about. To speak of nothingness, of the "vacuum tube," as something that stands in command over the world of skill and materials (*sono shihai o ukeru*) would provoke Kanbara to a vehement condemnation: How can nothingness rule over the world and objects? How can a vacuum tube be the essence of art? And yet this is what Kitasono here asserts, and further, he articulates a kind of doubled nothingness: the "vacuum tube that is [has] nothing at all." It is not only "empty" but also, even as the "container" of emptiness, it disappears once again—becomes the equivalent of "nothing at all." The repetition of *nanimono mo nai* (itself a kind of doubled negative) fills Kitasono's language with nothingness, with an almost palpable absence of the thing. The world of skill (*ginō*: ability, capacity, talent) prescribes and articulates the concept of this vacuum tube but is ultimately governed by the very vacuum it prescribes. Interestingly, the word "vacuum" (*shinkū*) in addition to its scientific meaning has a Buddhist usage in Japanese as the term for the nirvana of Hinayana Buddhism and the Mahayana "finality" (the void that is the truth). Art's essential work, at the core of art (*shinzui*: kernel, pith, soul, lifeblood), is to work toward this very "nothing at all."

Kitasono's concept of the vacuum, or the void, recalls Maurice Blanchot's articulate and moving descriptions of the relation of the void to the work of art. Blanchot's language, too, has a tendency to turn upon itself, to use double negatives, and he posits a "void that comes from a void" as he takes on the task of describing and articulating nothing, or nothingness. Blanchot writes in the essay "La Littérature et le droit à la mort" (Literature and the right to death), "Let us suppose that literature begins at the moment when literature becomes a question." Literature "professes to be important while at the same time considering itself an object of doubt."[51] This idea of literature's originary doubt is connected to Kitasono's claim that the place of the "literary" (*bungakuteki*) in Surrealism appears in the moment of naming the vacuum tube (the aim of art) as nothing at all.

Blanchot writes in the same essay of the simultaneous force and emptiness of this void in relation to Surrealism: literature is "null, and as long as this nullity is isolated in a state of purity it may constitute an extraordinary force, a marvelous force. To make literature become the exposure of this emptiness inside, to make it open up completely to its nothingness, to realize its own unreality—this is one of the tasks undertaken by Surrealism." To make literature open up to its emptiness, to realize its nullity: this pure vision of the literary work echoes Kitasono's statement that "the work that leads to this 'vacuum' is the essence of art." And it is a work that is the result of "nothing," the nullity resulting from nothing: in Blanchot's words, it is "starting from nothing and with nothing in mind—like a nothingness working in nothingness, to borrow an expression of Hegel's."[52] This larger sense of encompassing nothingness opens the understanding of literature beyond a logic of "purposefulness," in which a writer sits down with a given prior intention in mind and produces or reproduces this as a result on the page.

It is notable that both Blanchot and Kitasono express their views of writing (as nothingness) while citing and borrowing terms from *other* writers about this nothingness. In Blanchot's case, it is Hegel's expression, "like a nothingness working in nothingness"; for Kitasono, it is the Surrealist's words "a vacuum tube that is nothing at all" (*nanimono mo nai shinkūkan*). In turning over these (implied) preexisting prescriptions about the artistic process, they arrive at their own understanding of nothingness (the void, the vacuum) as the core of the work of writing: in citing other writers' words, a communication is already implied. There is a moment, however,

when the cited work disappears and is overwritten: Kitasono's repeated citing of the words *shinkū, shinkūkan* and *nanimono mo nai* loosens them
from the sense of a context from which they are taken, and in turning
upon themselves, the sentences may bring us to the empty, "pure" space
they propose. The sentences empty themselves out, even as they propose
to describe all of "art" and the core of art's work. Similarly, when reading
Blanchot, one finds a moment when nothing becomes everything or everything nothing, as the sentence turns upon itself in oxymoron: "If literature
coincides with nothing for just an instant, it is immediately everything,
and this everything begins to exist: what a miracle!"[53]

To say that these visions of the void are "non-sense" (*tawagoto*), as
Kanbara has, does not wound: writing, here, would not stand on the opposition between sense and nonsense, between logic and illogic. To say that
it is "pale, faded" (*iroasetaru*) gives it back a part of emptiness. For the view
of art espoused here, the negative words of Kanbara that "no one outside
of himself could share" this Surrealism ("*jibun igai no nanibito to mo kyō-
kan o motanai*") are overwhelmed by the multiple and dizzying negatives
of the repeated *nanimono mo nai* that he critiques. The loops of Kitasono's
language, in other words, undo the force of a clear, simple negative with a
particular object, and the Surrealists' views of language place no credence
in Kanbara's "100 percent agreement," or the logical, scientific progress
that he proposes as a substitute for the "ambiguities" he sees as the Japanese Surrealists' failing. This is not to say that Kanbara is "wrong" in his
accusations:[54] the view of language espoused by the Surrealists may not be
an effective tool for action with respect to the kind of 1930s "reality" of
which Kanbara speaks. Yet their debate is not merely the pushing and
pulling between the "artistic doctrines" of Futurism and Surrealism in Japan: rather, it contains all the force of the question of artistic purpose and
the functioning of language, and of the relation between the individual
artist and the collective movement, the question of the void and the possibility of communication with a reader.

The operation that Surrealist language and method perform and
claim within the context of these debates may, even in this quest for the
void, have an impact on the realities it describes. It reveals a central locus as
well as an Achilles heel in the transmission of ideas and forms from one
culture to another, one language to another. The Surrealist intervention in
the Japanese language, under the sign of the "vacuum" (as scientific absence

and Buddhist void, artistic aim and ultimate emptiness), has been read as a dangerous moment for the stability of social understanding and the construction of individual or personal identity. The language and poetry of Kitasono Katsue, for example, have been read in terms of this "warping" that Surrealism represents and, at its limits, effects. We have explored how some of the central resistances that Surrealism provoked, the terms of this resistance and its trajectory, have a certain continuity from contemporary writers such as Hagiwara Sakutarō and Kanbara Tai through post-war critics and readers such as Tsuruoka Yoshihisa. The terms of this resistance, and the attempt to anchor language to reference or make ethical demands that poetry take responsibility for its link to "reality" during an age of crisis, resonate with the critical questions being raised in our own day.

The relation between ideological agendas and paradigms and the capacity for interpretative violence, for language to work against itself or against the intended purposes of its author or speaker, have become the subjects of pressing analysis in the wake of deconstruction. The processes of cultural interaction thus become a place, a framing moment, for the exploration of these issues. Through an analysis of the metaphor and process of "warping" of and within the language of Kitasono Katsue, we go on to explore the further impact of these resistances of language and meaning, and consider the perceived effects of Surrealist thought on social discourse and on the construction and deconstruction (or, at its limits, destruction) of the "personal" realm.

Surrealism's Warp: Kitasono Katsue

Kitasono Katsue's understanding of his proposed second phase of Surrealism is predicated on an abolition of the "personal" or "individual" (*kojin*). As he describes in "The Limits of Surrealist Poetry":

The poetry of second phase of art that will flourish [arise] after the extinction of the personal, will have the following special characteristics: a systematic process of resuscitation of the individual; a phenomenological figure [*zukei*] beginning in the hands of the crowd; and, as a montage, a fixed period and quantity of discontinuity.[55]

The second phase of (Surrealist) art, as described by Kitasono in this essay, requires as its precondition the extinction (*shōmetsu*, nullification, disappearance) of the individual, although it will lead eventually to a rebirth or resuscitation of the individual. It will involve a "phenomenological figure" (*genshōgakuteki zukei*) or diagram, a plan, that begins in the control or command (*shōaku*) of the crowd. The third quality involves a montage (Kitasono uses the French term in katakana, *montaaju*) and a discontinuity, but it is not a discontinuity that is indeterminate: it contains a fixed term or quantity of discontinuity, and thus contains both the fixed and the uncertain, or a fixed space linking elements that are otherwise not linked, in the manner of a montage.

One finds, then, that in his formulation of what the second phase of poetic art will bring, Kitasono incorporates contradictory terms into each of the three characteristics. The discontinuous brings with it the "fixed quantity and period" (a certainty within a disjunction, to form a montage); the rebirth of the personal is described as "systematic" or "structural"—so that the institution, or the structure, intervenes within the reappearance of the individual. The "figure" that is to begin in the grasp of the crowd is "phenomenological": it appears to have both the "design" or intention of a figure, an "intellectual intuition" (like the noumenon) and at the same time to be "phenomenological" (if one were to take this term in its philosophical sense of an object of sensual perception, as opposed to an object of intellectual intuition).

Such a description by Kitasono of his ideal second artistic phase of poetry begins with the rhetoric of a clear and readily understood program: the "special characteristics" of the "second phase of art that will flourish after the extinction of the personal." It seems that one wants merely the disappearance of the individual, whatever that would entail, in order for this phase to begin. And yet, in the elaboration of the particular terms of these characteristics, the contradictory world of Kitasono's philosophical language arises, bringing his proposal into the realm of the "beyond" not merely in its sense but also in its way of formulating that sense. It becomes, in its own words, a kind of "fixed term" (three named characteristics, a brief sentence, ending with the copula, *de aru*) of discontinuity; these characteristics are a kind of montage, three discontinuous or unconnected elements whose link we may or may not supply.

At the same time, Kitasono's proposal traces the poles of the "individual" (his individual formulation of Surrealism) and the institution or system (*soshiki*) in that it is the design of a program for a poetic movement; it is both a design and that which will be seen to arise, as if by its own accord, by the dictation of the "crowd" (the poets who would be its proponents). Thus we may read his proposal as an attempt to enact, grammatically, its own understanding of the second phase, and in this sense it is paradigmatic of Kitasono's ways of formulating his poetic theories and interpretations. At the moment of the most clear, polemical, and "transparent" argument, Kitasono's language will suddenly become figural, contradictory, and allusive, only to recuperate a sense of secure "clarity" in his firm grammatical closure ("X *wa* Y *de aru*"). This characteristic (repeated at many points in his theoretical writings) may contribute to the disorienting effect of these writings on certain readers, the sense of a "warp" in his understanding that places it in a relationship of disjunction with the collective movement.

Tsuruoka writes:

One cannot deny that one of the reasons for the warping of Surrealism in our country overlaps with this warping within Kitasono Katsue. One can look forward in the future to the correct recollection and assessment of the Japanese Surrealist movement in poetry, as well as the more careful assessment of the poems of this unique poet [Kitasono], that are superior in other respects. At the same time, one must hold on to the correct understanding of them, not believing myths such as that written by Andō Ichirō in his essay "The works of *Shi to shiron*" (*Shigaku*, vol. 5, no. 5) which calls Kitasono a "pioneering Japanese Surrealist."[56]

What is this "warping"? How is it that only by separating Kitasono's contribution as an individual from an understanding of the more general movement of Japanese Surrealism can one arrive, according to Tsuruoka, at a "correct" understanding of the movement?

In another passage in the same essay discussed above—in which Kitasono is concerned precisely with "The Limits of Surrealist Poetry"—the disorientation of his language takes an extreme form. Here, Kitasono writes of the "misunderstanding" or "misunderstandability" (*gokaisei*) of the image (*imaaju*, the French term discussed earlier in relation to Reverdy's poetics). At moments, his description appears as a kind of polemical tirade against "today's popular trends," and yet its figural intricacies render such a singular reading impossible:

Anything would be fine, but for the time being the misunderstanding of "image" moves toward the edge of the ice at the back of a transparent octopus. Because we have nothing but a perfectly black page when it comes to the boundary between reason and feeling, and the ultimate boundary between the world of matter and the world of the spirit, we produce a result no different from that of the seventeenth century. Without an absolutely certain despair toward the limitless infinite quantity of endless ribbon leading toward this blackness, the musician, as a pedestrian [*hokōsha*] on the spherical surface of feeling, was polishing the back of his head with the tongue of the somewhat despicable fanatic [*kyōshinsha*]. The remaining portion of the individualistic art we were telling of. It is one group of impressive line-ups from the school of vomit and bowel discharges [*toshabutsu-ha*] that constitute today's popular trends as salesmen [*baikyakusha*] of what is merely taste by obscure hands. Namely, it is the "necessary and sufficient" ax leading us toward understanding. Or the farming implements. The road of animals, in the shape of a chrysalis, used detonating discoveries (rules of limits) as a pose of sight. We spit phlegm mercilessly and with extreme cruelty, as if spitting on the Bible, on the agitation for [good] taste (the last opium of individualistic art).[57]

The image with which he opens the passage, "moves toward the edge of the ice at the back of [the movement toward] a transparent octopus," places the reader immediately in a realm of overwhelming disorientation and transparency, which, however, is a realm of movement toward some kind of limit. It is a liminal and provisional space of the image: opening with the words "anything would be fine" (nan de mo kekkō de aru ga toriaezu), he makes arbitrary the words that follow. Any aspect of the "image" (not just mistranslatability) or any figure to describe that aspect (the "transparent octopus" is a provisional choice) would have done as well, he implies, for his purpose.

While he indicates the arbitrariness, artificiality, the "set-up" or framed quality of the images and argument that follow, certain poles of Kitasono's polemic are clear and open: most virulently attacked among his objects are "today's popular trends," described as *toshabutsu-ha* (roughly translatable as the "school" of "vomit and bowel discharges"). His language here is reminiscent of the Dada manifestos and earlier polemical writings (such as those of Takahashi Shinkichi or the writers of the magazine *Aka to kuro*) that attack the literary establishment, using terms that break the conventions of decency or politeness and incorporating vulgar language and expletives. Yet if this is the moment in which he is "clearest," and in which the "other" school that can be opposed to his own group (*bokura*, we) is most explicitly named, his own group by the end of the passage is seen spitting mercilessly (*yōsha naku tan wo haku*), and thus perhaps they lose the clarity of their distinction from their enemies (figured in terms of bodily discharges and vulgarity).

Another moment of clear binary opposition that helps to structure this passage is in the "boundary between reason and feeling," a recognizable and conventional distinction that describes a familiar terrain, as does the "boundary between the world of matter and the world of the spirit" (*busshitsukai to seishinkai*). These terms in Japanese are modern neologisms, coined to translate philosophical concepts that appear in the writings of Kant and Hegel, among others.[58] *Risei* would correspond to the concept of reason, or the German *Vernunft* as opposed to *kansei* (sensibility) or the German *Sinnlichkeit. Busshitsukai* and *seishinkai* are "matter" and "spirit," or the material world and the spiritual world (as, for example, in Hegel's dialectical materialism). So these terms are coded as a part of a European philosophical quest, and the idea that "we have nothing but a perfectly black page when it comes to" these distinctions, or when it comes to the boundaries between these concepts, can be read in several senses: we (*bokura*) have no idea about these distinctions, the "page" (in katakana, *peiji*) is illegible, dark, full but unreadable. Whose seventeenth century ("a result no different from that of the seventeenth century") does he describe? Is he adopting part of the project of European philosophies as a critique of progress that has been made (by the Japanese Surrealists)? There is an odd disjunction here: the sudden moment of clarity in Kitasono's rhetoric surfaces only in order to point to an absence of clarity, a "black page"; the intervention of a modern vocabulary appears only in order to indicate a continuity that encompasses the seventeenth century, without any change.

Another complex metaphor intervenes, a figural description of a "musician, as a pedestrian on the spherical surface of feeling," and the reader is left to decipher the place of this musician in relation to the quest for understanding of the boundary between feeling and reason, and of the black page that they describe. This musician, then, only meanders on the surface of feeling (and does not penetrate within): another liminal image, another walking on the edge, like the "edge of the ice" in the earlier metaphor. The musician does not feel the despair (that the rhetoric implies he should) at the endless blackness, the obscurity, the distant and "infinite quantity of endless ribbon." One is struck by its repetitions of the infinite, the endless, in the face of which the only certainty is despair. "The musician, as a pedestrian on the spherical surface of feeling, was polishing the back of his head with the tongue of the somewhat despicable fanatic." How is such an image to be read? It is associated in the next sentence with "individualist art": one may thus assume that it is a condemnation, a negative expression, related to "today's popular trends." The musician here does not enter the world of feeling; he performs what seems to be a pointless gesture with the tongue of the fanatic (*kyōshinsha*), a mere polishing of surfaces. "We" (humans who need to grasp or understand, or cleanly divide up the world), in ways that are "necessary and sufficient" for our understanding, use the ax or "farming implements," "use detonating discoveries (rules of limits)," as a *pose* of sight, at an edge of a violent or extreme limit.

The "discoveries (rules of limits)" contain the potential for detonation, but we contain them in a narrow, encapsulated road, or exploit them for a "pose" of sight or understanding. What would be blasted apart has something to do with "rules of limits," although the limits he has named here are the boundaries between reason and feeling, the material and the spiritual world, which remain, in his words, "a perfectly black page." If one were to follow along with his image, it implies that a special emphasis must be placed on limits and rules, and yet, Kitasono performs a certain kind of "breaking apart" of rules in the very act of critical writing. In speaking of the "image," he reveals that which can be misunderstood (*gokaisei*) not only in abstract "images" but also through an incorporation of metaphoric and allegorical language that we can consider within the rubric of his idea of images. It can thus be read as a "performance" of the use of images, and, as a discussion of misunderstanding in relation to images, it contains a profound anger: "deserves to be despised" (*bubetsu subeki*), "we spit phlegm" (*tan wo haku*), "schools of vomit and bowel discharges," "salesmen of what is merely taste."

In a sense, then, this text predicts its own future of being misunderstood, and of being read (as Tsuruoka reads it above) as part of a project of profound misunderstanding of Surrealism, and of mistranslation. Kitasono leaves us with a text that, in its elliptical style and many embedded phrases, still requires a translation and remains susceptible to mistranslation (even before it is rendered into English). It exists, then, as a kind of object in itself. Resistant to paraphrase or to reencapsulation, Kitasono's theoretical writings (at such moments as this) launch an attack against reading in the conventional sense of "understanding" or distillation. The images remain there, in their material presence, while at the same time they imply (through the use of polemical attacks, through layered modifying clauses) a (suspect) desire for transparency, clarity, readability. "Anything would be fine": the image's only necessity is in its very articulation (its presence on the page at this moment is its only requirement and encompasses its full reason for being). To read Kitasono otherwise, at such moments as this, is to fall into the misunderstanding of insisting on good taste, on maintaining limits and boundaries where all there is is a blank page.

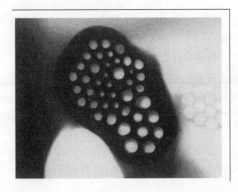

4

POETRY AND VISUALITY, POETRY
AND ACTUALITY

> Any piece of writing, outside of its treasures, ought, in deference to those from
> whom it borrows, after all, language, to present, with words, a meaning however
> indifferent: one profits from thus turning away the idlers, charmed that nothing
> concerns them in it, at first sight.
> —Stéphane Mallarmé, "The Mystery in Letters"

The disruption of meaning in Surrealist poetry and criticism leads us
to raise the question of the place of the visual in these literary works, the
role of sight in the articulation of a movement whose visual production (in
the plastic arts) has overwhelmingly dominated in its reception. Particularly in the case of Japanese Surrealism, the visual and plastic arts remain
the aspect of the movement that is best known and well received in Europe
and America, in part because of the preconception (or misconception)
that, because the art is visual, it can be apprehended "directly," without the
mediation of translation. And yet, as Věra Linhartová has pointed out, the
role of critical writing in the modern painter's work is not merely to explain
a finished product after the fact but also to project the horizon of the
work's future, to outline the artist's understanding of process in a way that

is integral to the appreciation of the work and to the continuing creative process. In other words, the hierarchy between the critical writings of the artist and the visual work is unsettled.

GRAPHIC POETICS

> Speak, transparence, whoever you are!
> —Takiguchi Shūzō, "Tezukuri kotowaza"
>   (Handmade proverbs)

For Japanese Surrealism, as we have seen, the visual arts and the literary were closely allied. Takiguchi Shūzō wrote art criticism and poetry and made works of visual art (such as *décalcomanie* paintings, a Surrealist technique of pressing a piece of paper onto a painted surface and peeling it off, to collaborate with chance). Kitasono was a designer, graphic artist, critic, and poet and had a background in the visual arts. Nishiwaki Junzaburō painted oil paintings and watercolors; Koga Harue, the painter, wrote poems to accompany his painting. The magazines that presented Surrealism to Japan contained reproductions of the latest developments in European art, architecture, machinery, and fashion. It is an artificial separation to consider the poetic and critical works of Surrealism outside of their link with the visual, as it would be difficult to conceive the visual works of Surrealism in isolation from their verbal explications and theoretical projects. Although this book is most concerned with the literary aspects of the Surrealist movement, we must consider the numerous ways in which the verbal realm suggests or explores visual terrain, or the ways in which one can perceive an entry of the visual into the terrain of the literary.

Regarding the relation of the visual realm and poetry, one may recall the enthusiasm of Ernest Fenollosa (1853–1908) and Ezra Pound (1885–1972) for Chinese poetry and Pound's (rather whimsical) understanding of the functioning of Chinese characters as visual signs or pictures that, at least in his view, maintain their concrete functioning as "pictures of objects in nature" within the poems in which they appear.[1] Thus, for example, the sentence from the Confucian Analects that would read, "The Master says: to learn and to practice from time to time—is this not a joy?" Pound translated as, "Study with the seasons winging past, is not this pleasant?" He analyzes the components of the character for "practice" (習, *xi*, made up of the character for "white" below that for "feather") to arrive at his metaphor

July 17, 1936

Dear Mr. Ezra Pound,

       We greet you with our deepest thanks
for your sending us your beautiful book. How glad we
were when we saw your splendid work. Mr. Katue Kitasono
has shown your friendly letter to all of us.

       We, the Japanese younger generation,
heartly wish to success in our work, staying always at
the twenty-one years old, as you hoped us in your letter.
Thank you again for your present.

                Yours truly,

Minoru Nakahara

Katue Kitasono

Shugo Iwamoto

Doko. Yoshida.   *Akiko Ema*

Shuichi. Nagayasu.   *Haruki Sou*

Takeshi Fuji.

Chio Nakamura.

Itiro Isida

M. Tasoshima

5. *Left*: letter from members of the journal *VOU* to Ezra Pound, 1936.
Right: letter from Ezra Pound to Kitasono Katsue (Katue), 1937 (excerpt).
Courtesy of the Yale Collection of American Literature, Beinecke Rare Book
and Manuscript Library.

Dear Katue KITASONO

All right Kitasono is your family name.
We occidentals are very ignorant. You must TELL us , patiently
even these details.

The poems are splendid , and the first
clear lighting for me of what is going on in Japan.

The NEW Japan. Sur=realism without the half baked
ignorance of the French young.

I shall try the poems on GLOBE. It is not
a literary magazine. They have printed me on Edward Viii th
abdication , and announce that they will print my note on
Roman Empire. Then they say my note on Geneva is too serious
for their readers. That may be because I mentioned George
Tinkham , who kep NH the U.S.A. OUT of that sink of
hypocracy the League of Nations.

" Uncle George " is crossing the Pacific next summe
and I hope you will be able to meet him. He IS the America
I was born in , and that may have disappeared entirely by
now.

My daughter was shocked at his lack of sartorial eleganc
(age eleven) but she decided that " l uomo piu educato "
had spent too MUCH time on his face massage etc

" l uomo piu educato " is a S.American more
or less millionaire fop.
diffuseness...

of "winging past."[2] In *Of Grammatology*, Jacques Derrida calls Chinese poetry the "irreducibly graphic poetics" that constitutes "with that of Mallarmé, the first break in the most entrenched Western tradition." He reads the ideogram from the functional perspective that Pound gave it, as a challenge to the transcendental authority of some founding categories (in Western tradition) of language and grammar, of "being."[3] Sinologists have challenged Pound's and Fenollosa's understanding of the functioning of the Chinese sign by pointing out that Chinese is as much a process of understanding conventionalized signification as any Western language and is apprehended in relation to sound as well as pictorial representation.

And yet, perhaps at the moment of the Surrealists' espousing aspects of European philosophy, at the moment of their sympathy with poets such as Mallarmé, who would question the constructs and conventions of poetic meaning, the Japanese poets may have taken on the challenge of making kanji (Chinese characters) signify in a way analogous to that "breaking of the most entrenched Western tradition" of which Derrida speaks. In other words, they adopted a project for poetry in the Japanese language that fulfilled an aim of the European poets they read and translated, and gave to the kanji character (or attributed to it) some of the qualities it was envisioned to have in Europe. Their attention to the visual qualities of the word and the use of written language as a means of pictorial construction (besides many precedents in the Japanese calligraphic tradition) has several sources and can be read in relation to the poetry and poetics of French Surrealism. The Japanese Surrealists recast in their own terms an ambivalence about the relation between writing and seeing that exists already in the work of the French Surrealists, Breton among them.

Rosalind Krauss describes the privileged place of the visual in European Surrealism, and the ways it is ultimately overcome by the supremacy of the medium of writing, in her essay "The Photographic Conditions of Surrealism." In Breton's *Le Surréalisme et la peinture* (Surrealism and painting; Takiguchi published a Japanese translation in 1930) one finds a eulogy of vision in the famous opening lines: "The eye exists in its savage state. The marvels of the earth . . . have as their sole witness the wild eye that traces all its colors back to the rainbow."[4] The supremacy of vision is established here as well as in the "First Manifesto of Surrealism," only to be (in Krauss's words) "immediately challenged by a medium given greater privilege: writing. Psychic automatism is itself a written form, a 'scribbling on paper,' a textual production. And when it is transferred to the domain of visual practice . . . automatism is no less understood as a kind of writing."[5] Krauss traces an ambivalence in Surrealist theory that begins by privileging the visual, for its direct and transparent relation with reality, and yet ultimately focuses on this reality itself as a form of representation, as a form of writing. Thus photography takes its place as a central form in which this paradigm can be enacted, containing both the "traces of reality" and the "spacings and doublings" of the photographic process that are to reproduce those inherent in that reality: "It is precisely this experience of *reality as representation* that constitutes the notion of the Marvelous or Convulsive Beauty—the key concepts of surrealism."[6]

As Krauss demonstrates, the Surrealist aim toward immediacy or directness (an impossible, yet urgent demand) rests on a continual overturning of the hierarchy of "the real" and representation, presence and sign. At times, Breton's thought appears to align itself with a Platonic view in which representation remains ever secondary, fallen, as a reflection or echo of a veiled presence. At other moments, writing seems to possess the capacity to transcribe directly from the marvelous, to bypass the machinations of logic and conventions. It offers the possibility of a significant encounter beyond the intentionality and subjective limitations of the writer. The Japanese Surrealists in their distinct poetic practices also vacillate between prioritizing the role of visuality and that of representation, or engaging a notion of visuality as representation that challenges the structure of this opposition.

We may return first of all to the essays of Hagiwara Sakutarō, in order to trace the development of the controversy in modern Japanese poetry over the priority of the musical in relation to the visual. For in modern poetry, in Hagiwara's view, the visual has taken an unfortunate precedence over the musical, the expressive "song," that was the traditional function of poetry as early as the kana preface to the *Kokin wakashū* poetry anthology (905). Nearly every study of Japanese poetics returns to these words of Ki no Tsurayuki, the compiler of the collection, as the first known critical work on poetry in the Japanese language:

Japanese poetry [*uta*] grows from the seed of the human heart into leaves of ten thousand words. Many things happen to people in this world, and they express their feelings through the things they see and hear. When we hear the bush warbler that sings among the flowers, the voice of the frog in the water, we know that all living things must have their song.[7]

This statement that "all living things must have their song" (*ikitoshi ikeru mono, izure ka uta o yomazarikeru*) expresses the idea of poetic composition through an image of singing: *uta o yomu* contains the meanings "chanting" or "reciting aloud" (its primary sense, focusing on the aural aspect), or more broadly, "poetic composition." Yet the comparison with natural elements repeats the emphasis on the aural: "the mountain thrush sings" (*naku*) or "the voice of a frog." Thus, although poetry may seem to embody equally the things that people "see and hear" (*miru mono kiku mono*), this is merely the outward form of the expression that is more fundamentally an act of singing, originating in and growing organically out of the thoughts and feelings of the heart. We note that the linking phrase *to shite* appears here (as it does so many times in Kitasono's critical language above), marking the entry to the figural realm, where the heart becomes a seed leading to the blossoming forth of leaves of words. It marks a doubling, and a gap for the reader to fill, or infer the link between heart and seed—aided by the paralleling of the conventional expression *koto no ha* (words, leaves of words, language)[8] here used in its literal and idiomatic senses.

The question of poetry as an aural medium, with its traditional understanding as described in the *Kokinshū*, continues to be raised in the writings of Hagiwara Sakutarō: Hagiwara, incorporating a consideration of Poe and Baudelaire, and examining this question as a dilemma in modern poetics, still retains the primacy of the aural as the underpinning of the poetic process. He uses this prevalence of sound and music in his defense of free verse, in spite of its having lost the 5-7-5-7-7 rhythmic pattern of *waka*, traditional Japanese vernacular poetry in the classical forms. For example, one of his aphoristic essays, entitled "Shi wa masa ni horobitsutsu aru" (Poetry is surely becoming extinct, 1931), traces his perception of modern poetry through the opposition of the auditory and the visual. His text deserves examination in full:

The poetry of ancient times was passed down from mouth to mouth, from ear to ear. Modern poetry, on the other hand, is read from the printed page. Moreover, with modern poetry, there are even those who claim that the auditory aspect has become unnecessary, and only the appearance to the eye as one reads is important.

But let us consider this for a moment. How many of the ancient poems, from the time before the advent of writing, actually remain recorded today? Aren't almost all of the poems we know from ancient times those that were written down after the advent of civilization [and writing]? And if the problem [of an overemphasis on the visual] were going to occur, should it not have happened much earlier than the present age—at the time of the invention of writing, or at the latest with the invention of printing techniques? Yet even in China, the country of the invention of ideographic characters (originating from the direction of visual sensation), this problem has not once occurred. The poetry of China has from ancient times taken beauty of rhythm to be its highest condition.

Again, it has been claimed that people do not read books aloud, but in silence; therefore the musical aspect of poetry has become unnecessary. Yet those who read silently still move their vocal chords inside their throats—like deaf-mute students practicing speech under their breath. And when one reads poetry that has a beautiful rhythm, one naturally finds oneself tempted to move from silent reading to reading aloud. With silent reading as with reading aloud, one feels strongly accented words strongly, and those with a weak accent are felt weakly. Therefore, this second claim cannot be a sufficient explanation.

A third explanation says: the modern era is an age of business, and people's minds have become fatigued through overwork. People who desire the intense stimulus of poetry cannot tolerate the dullness of the pursuit of passages of text in order to read them. Rather than "reading" they would prefer to "see"; they desire the instantaneous efficiency of "looking" at printed materials. If this were the case, however, poetry would have been completely obliterated, buried [*maibotsu suru*] under works of visual art—or under moving pictures [*katsudō shashin*]. In that case poets would do better to toss aside their words, and to switch to a more efficient visual medium of art. Or, as Yvan Goll has said, it would be better to make poetry into a brand-name [trademark] poster on the street.

All these reasons are mistaken. The true reason that today's poetry has lost its music is that ever since the advent of the old naturalist poetic establishment—which thoroughly denied poetry—poets themselves were swallowed up in the tide of realism, lost their own "poésie" and poetic feeling, and were assimilated into the opposing principles of prose. The poets themselves have become prosodic. Therefore, it is natural that modern poetry started as prose, and from the beginning did not demand musicality. In other words, the art of poetry in the true sense of the word, which would contain real poetic spirit [*shiteki seishin*], is in the process of becoming extinct today. I have only two concluding proposals to make here. Either we must dispense with all traditional attachment and nostalgia, and bravely fling poetry into the dustbin of history, or, if not, we must make an altogether new departure, and rebuild the architecture of poetry from the start at its correct position, [on the foundation of] its true essence. Now that today's literary establishment is approaching its last hour, a new return [*shinkaiki*] to classicism would constitute a most drastic revolution, and would be counted among those major surgical operations that led to miraculous revival.[9]

Hagiwara here discusses from various perspectives the proposal that "modern poetry has lost its music," and therefore, in his opinion, is in the

process of dying out. Although his own proposals rely on a paradoxical return to the past figured as a "revolution" or major operation to revive the poetic establishment, the argument he makes by countering the three proposed
reasons for the prevalence of the visual in modern poetry shows that he still
perceives contemporary poetry as having the possibility of incorporating
both the auditory and the visual, both the written and the rhythmic. At least
in the case of China, visual ideographs and auditory beauty (originating in
the earliest classical poems) can coexist. The music of poetry has survived in
spite of "silent reading": people still "move their vocal chords inside their
throats" and, if the beauty is overwhelming, are seduced or tempted to read
aloud. The visual and print media have their place, but the highest goals of
poetry relate to a return to the origins of poetry: although a complete return
is impossible, Hagiwara imagines that through rhythm and the stronger or
weaker accents of words, one can attain at least a partial return to the aural
mode of poetry, to something on the order of the "poetry of ancient times"
that involved the mouth and the ear, rather than merely the eye.

  This idea of a "return" is emphasized in his repeated use of terms associated with death: in a sense, he is advocating a return to an unattainable
past, and his language is full of the specter of the death of poetry. Poetry is
surely "becoming extinct," he claims, and the current literary establishment is reaching its "last hour"; if people desired only the visual, then poetry would have been "obliterated, buried" (*maibotsu suru*) under the various visual arts. Among the visual media that threaten poetry in the current
"age of business" is film, or "moving pictures" (*katsudō shashin*)—he employs the term from the earliest days of film, before the word *eiga* (movie,
film) had come into common use. His description here strikes one as
strangely correct; his fears, to a certain extent, are realized in the developments of the commercial film industry in the following decades. The idea
of the fatigued mind that has had so much of business that it can only seek
"intense stimulus" through easy, efficient media resonates with the current
age as much as with Hagiwara's own. But, as Hagiwara argues, poetry has
survived, if only barely, in spite of modern efficiency and the tired minds of
businessmen; if poetry has lost its music, this is because it has come too
close to the principles of prose. (Here he refers to the prose of "realist" fiction, which he sees as a "tide" that sweeps unsuspecting poets away and,
figuratively, drowns them; that tide at least makes them lose their place as
poets and stifles their "poésie" and poetic feeling.)

The final image of his description incorporates conflicting figures. On the one hand, Hagiwara advocates a return to "classicism," presumably in the sense of valorizing the auditory aspect of language. On the other hand, in his own poetry and in his poetics he defended the use of free verse and helped to advance the development of modern Japanese language as a poetic medium; his work in this area did much to make possible the kinds of innovations that ensued in the poetic avant-garde groups. There is a strange mix of nostalgia and revolution in his work as in his theories, well summarized in this final line: "Now that today's literary establishment is approaching its last hour, a new return to classicism [*kotenshugi e no shinkaiki*] would constitute a most dramatic revolution, and would be counted among those major surgical operations that led to miraculous revival."

His image of a "surgical operation" to be performed on the art of poetry recalls the words of Kitasono, Ueda Toshio, and Ueda Tamotsu in "A Note" of 1927, in which they proclaimed: "We have assembled a *poetic operation*," and "at the moment when we construct our *poetic operation* we feel an appropriate degree of excitement." The changes poetry needs are framed in terms of scientific/technological innovations, in that they seem able to perform miracles of *kishikaisei* (revival, return to life from death). Kitasono, too, employs a scientific vocabulary to explain the Surrealist's project, although his "poetic operation" is proposed in the English term, while Hagiwara's *daishujutsu* (major surgical operation) would involve a return to elements of poetry that he sees as present in premodern Japan. Hagiwara proposes a new "architecture," a (modern) construction, and his proposal once again implies a technological process, but it also opens an image of poetry as "located" at a specific site: the site (perhaps) of Japan's ancient rhythms, although the goal, for Hagiwara, is expressed equally in the French term "poésie." While Hagiwara cites Yvan Goll (himself a dislocated figure in language, both German and French at once), he does not oppose Japan to non-Japanese ideas of poetry, or claim (directly) an authenticity based on national allegiance: his language contains moments that seem to stem from the incorporation of Western philosophy into Japanese modern language, even as he longs for the old language and its classical rhythm.

This dilemma is played out in Hagiwara's career: his early books of poetry (*Tsuki ni hoeru* [Howling at the moon], 1917, and *Ao neko* [Blue cat], 1923) are written primarily in colloquial modern Japanese, while his last book of poetry (*Hyōtō* [Frozen island], 1934, written between 1916 and

1933) is composed in classical Japanese (with an abundance of Chinese characters), a language that Hagiwara himself considered to be a kind of return, a retreat from his endeavors to work with colloquial modern Japanese. The essay cited above was written between these phases (although it is not possible to identify a clear temporal break between these styles, since he wrote both kinds of poems during various periods of his career).[10]

Rhythm is a central concept for Hagiwara's poetics, and one that is intimately interwoven with the problems of translation: for Hagiwara, free verse contained a "rhythm without rhythm," and poetry "translated" the "inner rhythm of the heart" into the rhythms of language. Thus, for Hagiwara, the process of poetic creation involves a translation; but he considered this translation from the heart's rhythm to the poetic rhythm to be present in Western poetry, and he thought Japanese poets should incorporate it into their poetry. He recognized that this kind of translation was not unique to Western poetry, but was present also in classical Japanese poetry:[11] he desired to translate into Japan something that already existed there. Still, it is certainly not the visual elements of poetry that are of crucial importance for Hagiwara, but the various aspects of the questions of sound.

By contrast, for the Surrealist poets the question of the visual was integral to poetic composition and to the poetic spirit. In Kitasono Katsue's only published interview, he makes explicit the importance that he believes the visual elements of poetry have had throughout his career. Speaking with the designer Sugiura Kōhei and poet Matsuoka Seigō, he says, "Design is the foundation of what is important to my sensibility. That is why I am always careful with it."[12] He describes his love of working with typography and for small press magazines. Besides his own drawings, photography, film, and design work in the postwar period, in his last decade he created the genre of the "plastic poem" or "concrete poem," sculptural objects created to be photographed—recalling Hans Bellmer's and Man Ray's constructions that also existed only temporarily for the photographic record that was made of them. This form of poetry was to transcend the limitations of language: it did not use language, except in the form of newspapers, usually French or English, crumpled into shapes or cut-out visual forms (like a walking frog figure, upright, who seems to suggest a figure of the poet, or a round ball of crumpled paper in the corner suggesting a moon). They suggest dispensing with words (crumpling, cutting) in order to reconfigure paper and type in the service of visual forms.

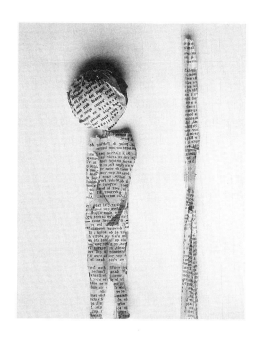

6. Kitasono Katsue, plastic poems, "A Study of Man by Man." Courtesy of Chiba City Museum of Art.

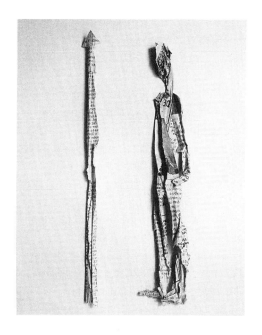

Sugiura comments on Kitasono's poetry in the interview: "Color used as an expression in your poetic vocabulary can be considered the archetype of color. Most of your colors are simple. Also, it seems color is being sent through metamorphosis in lines such as 'within black, yellow.'" This understanding of the place of pure color, primary color, shape, and simplicity in his poetry incorporates the terms of modern abstract art, the simplification of shape and line. Sugiura raises the issue of sound and the voice in relation to Kitasono's poetry (and his vigorous refusal to read his poetry out loud), and he rightly describes the quality of sound in Kitasono's work in terms of silence, visuality:

> If I am in an airplane looking down, I don't call out because the distance is too great for me to be heard. Rather, it is more common to *absorb the sounds of nature below with my eyes*. If this is seen as one kind of poetry, then there is an inside and outside to the relationship between voice and poetry. I cannot state it very lucidly, but I think what you mean, Katsue, by "uninhibited design" is not simply "to abandon" but to gaze from a certain distance, assimilating the self one observes as an object.[13]

Sugiura's comparison of the place of sound in Kitasono's poetry to the absorption of the "sounds of nature below with his eyes" leads him to subsume sound in a visual realm, in a distant object, and he takes the figure one step further in describing this process as "assimilating the self one observes as an object." If sound, here, were to be read in poetry as associated with the self, the lyric voice, then the self in Kitasono's poetry is absent in its traditional form and is replaced by a self that is absorbed (silently, without a speaking voice) through an exterior object. Sugiura's description falters at this point, as if stumbling over the difficulty of the leap between these concepts, self/other and voice/visuality. Kitasono's work (seen as "uninhibited design") would then be "uninhibited" in the sense of not being constrained by the limits of individuality or a given notion of "self."

In order to clarify this visual emphasis in Kitasono's Surrealist poetic works, one may examine the poem entitled "Shi no gūzō," or "The Icon of Poetry," from the May 1932 edition of *Madame Blanche*, published along with other journals by Bon shoten as a vehicle for the poetic coterie Club D'Arcueil (named after the town where Erik Satie lived). The group included among its many members Kondō Azuma, Iwamoto Shūzō, Nishiwaki Junzaburō, Sagawa Chika, Ema Shōko, and Yamanaka Chirū (Sansei).[14]

The Icon of Poetry

For the eternal brain that rejects the quivering rose
There was an inevitable solitude
Inside the net of early summer light [I] put the grape-colored
      upper air and desolation

For the clear-[voiced] friend   Or for the day of a clean parting
Like a lofty monarch already [I] bless the crystal rose
That poet's made-up pupil is dying

The title "The Icon of Poetry" evokes a sense of poetry freezing into an image of itself, a stillness. Although the various meanings of *gūzō* have different connotations—from idol to image, statue to icon—all are human creations, constructions visually frozen in space; they are observed with the eye, symbolize but do not speak. Similar in form to many other poems of *Madame Blanche*, this poem stands in the center of the page, surrounded by a wide blank margin, a kind of poetic icon in itself. The title immediately suggests that the poem will also constitute a comment on poetry, on poetic composition, or on that which remains after the process of composition has been completed: not the poem but the image, icon, statue, of a poem. This icon seems to be associated in the first line with the "eternal" (timeless, immortal) brain, in opposition to the quivering, ephemeral, living rose. The weight of the Chinese characters for "brain" (*nōzui*) and "rejects" (*kyozetsu suru*, refuses, repudiates) in the first line contrasts with the light gentleness of the hiragana *furueru* (quivering) of the rose. The "for" (*no tame ni*) that is repeated three times "for the eternal brain," "for the clear-[voiced] friend . . . for the day of a clean parting") is both a dedication and a mark of causality (on account of, for the sake of): if it is a question of poetry here, these elements followed by *no tame ni* might be the causes, the points of origin, or the eventual beneficiaries of the poetic composition. This ambiguity highlights the dynamic relation between poetry and icon. Is the purpose of poetry to be found in the process of composition (the live process) or in the (static) result created in the end? Which is the "cause," and where the "result"?

    In the third line, the verb "to place" or "to put" (*oita*) highlights the conscious act of creation, the trapping of "desolation" (*sekiryō*) and "grape-colored upper air," ephemeral entities placed (by an unnamed subject, translated above as "I" but precisely not specified in the poem) within a "net" of "summer light." Here, more than the "meaning" of the image, what stands out is the sequence of colors and shades: from the rose in the first line to the early summer light, grape color, and light clarity (of the friend and the sun) leading to the crystal rose and then the dark dying pupil. If the image of placing the "grape-colored upper air and desolation" into the "net of early summer light" seems to describe the catching of the most ephemeral element, the freezing of that which cannot be caught, then what is caught and frozen seems to be the color, the motion, the visual elements described through their qualities of light and dark, movement and color. Who does this placing? The "inevitable [inescapable] solitude" in the second line that is "there" and animate (*soko ni . . . ita*) can also be read as an inevitable "solitary," a solitary person, who appears when the brain rejects the quivering rose. It may be possible to link this solitary figure, or its metonymy of solitude, with the desolation (*sekiryō*) of the third line or alternatively with the poet of the final line. The term "clear-[voiced]" (*rōrōtaru*) that modifies "friend" is usually used to describe the clarity of a voice (or the silvery clear shining of the moon): thus, the friend may suggest a source of clear sound in relation to the silent icon, the voice or friend from whom one parts clearly, leaving the implied speaker alone, desolate.

Yet the traces of this human story of a parting that leads to loneliness and (eventually) to the poetic composition that (in this reading) monumentalizes the relationship, the parting and the poet's solitude are immediately undercut and made complex by the uncertainty of causes and effects in the poem: this text suggests an homage (in the usual sequence) that results from a relationship ended or, possibly, the benediction or prayer for the clarity of such an end. It is, however, neither of these. The "crystal rose" suggests yet another figure for the frozen icon, the crystallized statue that is the motionless poem.

As the poem closes into the darkness of an eye, a dying "pupil" (*kesshō suru hitomi wa shindeiru*), a blackness, we see that the "depth" that would be expected in a lyric is denied here: the pupil is covered with makeup, it is neither dark nor the "mirror of the soul," but rather, a return to the surface, to the question of color. Even if the pupil is to be read as black, it is not a blackness of depth but of paint, a doll's black-painted surface pupil that does not seem to see. With the appearance of the poet's pupil one would expect the poem to resolve into a lyrical point of view, to conclude so that the balance of the images in the poem might "crystallize" into a more unified or clear perspective, or that the images would be given a point of view from which rereading could decipher meaning or even the bare suggestion of a narrative in the earlier lines. Instead, however, the subject position of the poet is made explicitly "false": if the "poet's . . . pupil" is to be read as a figure for the poet's alleged point of view, it is as much an artifice, a color to be incorporated into the canvas of the poem, as any other moment or image in the poem. It has surrendered its place of privilege to the tapestry of chromatic images that surrounds it.

In one possible reading of the poem's trajectory, then, we see the fluidity and quivering of the first line, the life of the rose, resolve into a death in the final line, as the overarching point of view (linked, perhaps, to the "lofty monarch" of the fifth line) causes the rose to become crystal even as it is blessed or prayed for. The construction of an homage to the rose, to the living thing, both blesses it and crystallizes it, closes it from pale, gentle colors (of the early summer air) to the absence of color in a crystal (clear, white) or an empty, depthless (made-up) pupil. The clarity of the "parting" or farewell in the fourth line is not the sensual clarity of light or sound, like *rōrōtaru* (used to describe the "clear" friend), but rather, a verbal construct of clarity, *meikai* (lucid, articulate, explicit, unequivocal). The sun (or day) of this unequivocal or lucid verbal clarity is either the purpose and goal of the benediction or (*no tame ni*) the underlying causal principle of the process of benediction and poetic composition: clarity, light, attained through words.

Even as one reads, one feels the poem's desire to eradicate the possibility of these constructed readings, the fight that is taking place on the grounds of the poem between the ephemeral, fluctuating, and quivering words that function as visual signs, as icons just as they hold a place in the possibility of interpretation. The images "rose," "solitude," "poet," and "crystal" are themselves visual "icons" in the poetic vocabulary of Kitasono, compositional elements that resist being placed in a net, distilled by the mind, or crystallized into a pure and lucid point of view. These repeated visions of clarity and lucidity suggest a pull to allow the poem to stand, without interference or analysis, as a visual icon, a statue to poetry—a poetry that might exist apart from any solitary subject or poet, and break free from the lofty monarchical poet's eye and attain the autonomy to cause the illusion of his (or her) being. The poem takes over the poet and becomes the cause, causes him/her (thus gaining the power, as in the last line, even to kill the author's eye), rather than (in the usual sequence) being the result and the product of the poet's existence, vision, and construction. Thus, even if the "inevitable" figure of the solitary or poet is "there" (*soko ni . . . ita*), he/she does not "do" anything, does not necessarily have control over any act: he/she merely "is," necessary or inevitable perhaps, but as much a product of the poem as its imagined point of origin. The origin is a surface, the pupil (eye) is "made-up."

In reading Kitasono's poem, then, one sees the dynamic pull between the elements of meaning and the visual image or the poetic surface that nearly usurps the primacy of a more traditional lyric mode. Even so, the text remains in continuous relation with the possibility of such a lyric mode, through the grammatical structure of the poem's sentences (no punctuation, connections between the lines left open), and through the suggestion of familiar poetic/thematic terms: loneliness, isolation, poet, death, friend, and farewell. The primacy of the visual within the poetic here seems to lead toward the death of the lyric, and the sonorous "poetic spirit" (*shiseishin*) as a basis and origin for poetic composition in such texts may have begun to disappear. As Hagiwara's notion of "rhythm" can no longer justify composition in colloquial Japanese, the visual icon of poetry takes its ambiguous place.

The lack of photographs and drawings in most issues of *Madame Blanche* is notable; other avant-garde and Surrealist magazines freely wove photos and dramatic nontypographical designs among the texts, or at least placed them prominently on the cover. Here, in a magazine of nearly pure typography, the visual status of the poem as image takes an unusual precedence. Before Kitasono's experiments with Constructivist poetry and long before his attempts with plastic poetry, this tension in relation to words and the possibilities of poetic creation, dynamic and static possibilities for poetic language, is revealed in his work. The "net" that catches the desolation and high air in the third line is the only "foreign" word (in katakana) in the poem, although Kitasono often included roman letters and katakana words in his works. At that crucial juncture, the moment when the fluid and ephemeral are caught in the net—trapped, made articulate and clear —the clarity of the foreign word (*netto*) intervenes. What is the relation of foreign poetry to this moment of trapping the ephemeral, to the clean, clear, distinct, to the crystallization of elements of color, air, and emotion? (*Netteté* also means clarity in French—*net*; clean, clear, distinct.) It is not a question that is answered by the poem, but rather remains as an odd moment of crux, a central opening of the poem to the ways in which *shi*, as icon (statue, image) functions in relation to translation, grasping of the foreign, and bringing such language (of colloquial poetry) and conceptions of clarity into Japanese. To open up the question of this "net" (*net, netteté*) of clarity and foreignness, one must consider the place of European and French poetry within the poetic compositions of this time, and the ways in which an absence of foreign words, or the presence of only a single foreign word, says as much as a proliferation of such terms within a given poem. How does this flash of foreignness here function within the problematic of the "death of the lyric" in this poem, and in relation to its visual emphasis? What does the foreign net, the foreign clarity, bring in?

For Kitasono, the questions of surface and depth (without stopping at mere opposition) are intricately interwoven into his poems. It is possible to stop (as some readers do) at a sheer refusal of his poetry as mere "surface," or "design." Yet his poems themselves open and engage this question in a more complex manner in relation to their own reading and textual surface, fluctuating ambivalently between meaning and surface image. In certain readers, his poems provoke resistance, refusal; others admire them simply, silently, wonderingly, without comment or reading. Many imitate his style and uses of language—imitation or reenactment becomes the only permissible comment that leaves the integrity of the poem untouched. The poems' own ambiguous engagement and refusal of meaning, the play and intricacy on their surfaces, provoke these multivalent and contradictory responses.

For a contrasting vision of the place of the lyric subject in a contemporary avant-garde text, one might consider the poem "Pélerin"[15] (Pilgrim) in the same issue of *Madame Blanche* by the poet and Club D'Arceuil member Asuka Tōru,[16] a poem that passes through the masculine "I" (*boku*) in a meditation on a wanderer's experience of loss:

Pilgrim

The many things I lose • lovers • dancing girls • possessions • glory • and then memories • all were desolate things • "busy, busy" and I forget my youth • friend! (what one has can be lost) might this general truth cast the shadow of happiness on me? Goodbye • I who desire nothing was I who do not want to lose anything • and day after day by the sea the painful sun continues

In the three long vertical lines of the original untranslated poem, "I" (*boku*) is repeated many times: "I lose," "my youth" (*boku no wakai nengetsu*), "happiness on me" and most emphatically in the words "I who desire nothing was I who do not want to lose anything" (*nani mo hosshinai boku wa nani mo ushinaitaku nai boku datta*). The line frames an equation based on the figure of *boku*: the "I" that does not want to lose anything becomes the "I" that no longer desires anything (knowing, perhaps, that the "goodbye" is inevitable, that "what one has can be lost"). He mourns the loss of his youth, his lovers, his glory, and even memories: nothing that can be possessed is immune to this process of loss. It seems, in this text, that only the repeated "I," the subject himself, is certain to remain. And yet even that "I," in the final sentence, seems to succumb to the passage of time, to the "day after day," to the rising of the sun on the seashore that, for the last line of the poem, wipes out the traces of the persistent *boku* and goes on without him: "day after day by the sea the painful sun continues." The poem hovers between anthropomorphizing the sun ("the painful sun," *itai taiyo*) and attributing to it the sentiments that the subject feels: is it I who find the sun painful, or, more literally, is it the sun that is itself in pain? Similarly, the quality *sabishii* (sad, lonely, desolate) becomes ambiguous: is it I who feel deserted when "many things" are lost, or is it the objects themselves that become lonesome and desolate?

"Lovers, dancers, possessions, honor": Asuka's diction is simpler and more traditional than the more abstract images of Kitasono. Here, lost youth, lost loves, are clearly designated and mourned, and the passage of time is explored in its relation to the self. Part of the contrast, if one were to compare the two poems in their balance of rhythmic and visual elements, comes from this poem's extended line length and its repetition of the sounds *no*, *o*, and *u*, particularly at the opening: *o* and *u* are often understood to connote mournful melancholy (*boku no ushinau ōku no mono*). Similarly, the direct attribution of the loss ("the many things I lose," "goodbye") gives the poem a narrative aspect, legible in terms of a personal reaction to the passage of time, as opposed to Kitasono's more abstract designations of solitude or desolation (caught "inside the net of early summer light"). The speaker hopes that the sharing of such loss by others ("this general truth") might begin to make up for his personal loss, to "cast the shadow of happiness on me." This moment of shadowed hope comes with a call to a friend, an address (*tomo yo*, oh, friend) and a statement of parting that also seems to express the recognition of a mutual regret, or at least the presence of an addressee for the parting (*sayōnara*).

Asuka's typographical use of the "•" between the objects, particularly in the first line, functions along with the repeated melancholy lament to give the poem the appearance of a collection of abandoned objects or abandoned phrases: "lovers • dancing girls • possessions • glory • and then memories • all were desolate things." Hardly an imposing "icon" or "statue" of a poem, this poem appears more as a remnant, a scrap-heap of language, in sequential (though still visual) links; one thing follows another like the repetition of "day after day" (*kuru hi mo kuru hi mo*). The pain continues, time passes—and the adult's "busy, busy" life (even this is doubled) merely masks the process of forgetting and loss that constitutes the "pilgrim's" life.

The phrase in parentheses, "what one has can be lost" (*aru mono wa ushinawareru*), which seems to represent the simple "general truth" that the speaker hopes will cast its shadow of happiness, creates an ambiguity between the objects and the self who loses them because of its different possible readings (*aru mono*, those who have, that which one has). The sentence may be read "some things will be lost" (loss is inevitable), "those who have will lose," "those who have will be lost," or "that which one has can be lost." The multiple possible readings of this "truth" are enabled by the use of the word *mono* in hiragana (mono, without its Chinese character, can denote a person or a thing). And when the "I" who desires nothing folds in and collapses into the "I" who does not want to lose anything ("I" = "I"), this moment seems to trigger the disappearance of the "I," the moment the "I" itself is lost. Thus, the repetition of the term for self causes the collapse of the "I" into one more isolated term among the objects, one more word in the rhythmic sequence of words, reduced to the status of object and, perhaps, lamented. The moment of hope and questioning (for the "shadow of happiness"), the moment of abstraction of the situation of the self, can then be considered as the only moment in which the "subject," as it were, emerges from this heap of desolate objects, but only in order to bid farewell (*sayōnara*): in a sense, the poem as a whole is encapsulated in this farewell, or as a farewell in itself, on the part of the wandering pilgrim in time.

As in Kitasono's poem above, only one word brings in the realm of the foreign: in this case, the title, "Pélerin," is in French in the original, suggesting a wandering not so much as a space of the exotic but—if one might read it allegorically—as a loss for the poetic associations of words. No longer do these lists of objects, these words, seem to maintain their classical associations of love and nostalgic longing, as in the numerous classical

poems about the ephemerality of things. In a sense, the foreign term becomes the key to the novelty of the loss (the departure from language's
"home," on what may be a holy voyage), which is a loss not only of the objects in question but also of the subtle connections between words, the
warm environment of classical rhythm and poetic diction that is disappearing as a new poetic mode is being invented. This poem speaks too directly of loss to suggest the subtlety of classical poetic association. The
poem itself becomes a pilgrim, a wanderer toward a new poetic terrain. The
relentless repetition of the subject *boku* can be seen only as an emptying
out of the subtle associations of the poem's terms. Similarly, "happiness"
and "loneliness" have become abstract and cold, written over by the "busy,
busy" way of contemporary life. The words "busy, busy" appear in quotation marks in the original poem: is it the very language of daily life, the
speaking ("busy, busy") that wipes out youth and the association with former times? Without the intervention of a foreign term or perspective could
one no longer perceive what is being lost, too busy within contemporary
culture to gain the distance required for the elaboration of poetic thought?

Within the apparent simplicity of this poem's diction there is an intricacy that contains a certain irony and a hopelessness toward the terms of
its own lament. Loss becomes identified with the banality of a term like
sabishii, not the more elaborate *sekiryō* or *fukahiteki na kodoku* of Kitasono.
All terms are made equivalent in their sadness, to the point of the only remaining hope, perhaps, being in their very equivalence, in the very (abstract) similarity of the speaker to anyone else: "Might this general truth
(in the very generality, banality of that truth) cast the shadow of happiness
on me?" Generality, banality, lonesomeness in the most conventional sense,
are all that is left, so in this the speaker places the last remnant of hope.

In relation to the place of the visual and typographical in poetry,
then, Kitasono's poem makes more abstract use of the visual in opposition
to the lyrical and sonorous elements in his text, while Asuka's text touches
on the metapoetic level through the lament of its rhythmic melancholy, or
through the force of its very repetition and the emptying out of the "I" that
the repetition brings about. Both poems invoke the foreign only through a
single but critical term: "net" and "pilgrim," as foreign words, stand out by
realigning the perspective of the poem in relation to the view they create.
Asuka's text does not mention color at all, while Kitasono's is full of color;
yet Asuka's use of a typographic caesura ("•")—like a "pupil"—perhaps

takes a place analogous to Kitasono's moments of darkness in relation to color, or silence in relation to sound. The overlapping of qualities of objects and the self—"desolate things," "painful sun"—recalls Sugiura's words in the interview with Kitasono when he speaks of poetry as a process of "assimilating the self one observes as an object." Through such terms the poem closes into its silence, leaving the subject for the natural world, and the "I" seems to collapse back into itself, leaving only the painful continuation of the sun on the seashore, day after day.

The "surgical operation" that Hagiwara proposed for poetry involved a return to the "true essence" of the poetic spirit and breath. Poetry's loss had to do with an overemphasis on the visual surfaces of writing. The works of Asuka and Kitasono have a more ambivalent and sometimes contradictory relation to the visuality of poetry, and reading their work and that of other Surrealists reveals that the seeds of this ambivalence are already present in Hagiwara's diagnosis and prescription as well. Perhaps it is true that the way Japanese Surrealists use Chinese characters takes its inspiration from a Western philosophical misprision about the Chinese characters and their functioning, not as sound, but only as visual graphic sign or icon. A certain disillusion of language, or with language, is reflected in these poems, and along with it a certain lament. Perhaps the lament, for a loss related to the disillusion with language, leads to a new kind of creation in the fallout of this disillusion. The poet, a wandering pilgrim, undertakes a new kind of negotiation with language that comes from a place of solitude but that paradoxically creates community, a community even in lament. Yet these works enact a more ambivalent relation to this loss than a sheer nostalgia would entail, as they are aware of the icon of poetry, or the icon of solitude, that remains.

TRANSLATION UNVEILING

The night is not like the day. It is so supple.
—Henri Michaux, "The Night of Disappearances"

Both Kitasono Katsue's and Asuka Tōru's poems open the larger question of the relation of French writings to Japanese writings: how, precisely, were the French writings being translated, and how can one understand the ways in which they were read, the effects they had? How did the gap between the grammatical and poetic possibilities of French and Japanese languages affect the writing of these poets, nearly all of whom also spent time translating poetry from the French in addition to writing their own poems? How did the breaking apart of traditional notions of poetic meaning, the French avant-garde poets' rending of syntax and uprooting of the foundations of linguistic interpretability, affect their own notions of poetic expression and the use of language, including colloquial language? We shall explore these issues by examining some works of the Japanese poets and their relation to aspects of French Surrealist texts, as well as by considering an instance of direct translation from French to Japanese, in order to see exactly how a particular French text was read and the tensions such a reading opens within Japanese modern language.

But first we will digress briefly for the sake of a rather striking comparison. At about the same time as the Japanese Surrealists' experiments, a large number of modern Chinese poets were deeply engaged in reading and citing French poets and alluding to French poetic techniques. Michelle Loi, writing of this interaction in her monograph *Poètes chinois d'écoles françaises*, emphasizes that at times there has been a tendency to misattribute influence or importance to French authors (or schools of poetry) in the reading of Chinese poets' work, and that this tendency can contribute as much to a misunderstanding of the significance of the work as it adds to our reading through the connection it reveals. Many Chinese poets were called "Occidentalist," "symbolist," or "modernist" in China after the May Fourth Movement (an anti-imperialist protest after World War I, it popularized the "New Culture" movement already underway, which assured the development of the literature of colloquial Chinese as opposed to classical language). Many poets sought models in Western literature as they distanced themselves from the structures of the classical language and the forms of classical literature; yet as many such attributions of influence were spurious or misleading as were accurate.

Loi cites the case of Ai Qing (1910–1996), imprisoned in the French concession in Shanghai by the French from 1932 to 1936 for his "patriotic activities," after he returned from France where he had studied painting. In prison, he began to translate poetry (such as that of Emile Verhaeren), but he gained a reputation as a disciple of Guillaume Apollinaire because of a few citations, a popular (mis)understanding of his work that remains to this day. He claims only to have "remembered a few phrases": his citations of Apollinaire were, in his words, a "reproach to the French who retained [me] in prison." Thus, according to Loi, here "the reed pipe [*mirli-ton*] of Apollinaire brings nothing of Apollinaire, but tells much of the sentiments of a Chinese poet in a French prison." She argues that "a biographical or historical event can quickly let fall an ill-fitting costume that masks the work for better or for worse—or rather for the worse than for the better." For most of the Chinese "Gallicist" poets, "when it is not simply a fashion, the original text becomes a pretext for 'revealing oneself [*se dévoiler*] by hiding oneself.'"[17] The use of the French text, in Loi's analysis, becomes a costume, a play of veils: using a French text is both a form of unveiling, unmasking, disclosing (and this may reveal some secret that has nothing to do with the French text itself) and a hiding of oneself—behind the textual "veil" that the French "original" text provides.

We note here the figures of costume and veil that pervade the description of the importation from one language into another, both for readings of Chinese and for Japanese poets. Further, Loi notes the case of the Chinese poet Luo Dagang (1909–?), whose mastery of the French language was "perfect" (he translated many Chinese poems into French and for many decades wrote poems in French). Luo Dagang wrote in 1945, when he published his first poems in French, "The highest praise that one could accord these poems would be to say that they are *not at all French*."[18] Here, it is not a matter of the multiple veils of a Chinese poem containing allusions to French, partial translations of French, or stylistic borrowings. Yet at the precise moment when these difficulties of translation would seem to have disappeared—when the poem itself has completely concealed the marks of its being "Chinese" and has been written "perfectly" in the French language—then the Chinese poet would want all the more for the poems to have disclosed completely their "foreignness" ("*not at all* French"), to speak clearly and absolutely of their status as strange, as other.

One recalls the writings of Nishiwaki Junzaburō in Latin, English, and French, or the writings of Takiguchi Shūzō in French and English, the treatise on painting published in French by the artist and essayist Okamoto Tarō (1911–1996). Do these writings (like those that combine elements from Japanese and translated French) participate in a similar play of veils, such that, whatever the language of the writing, the interaction with the foreign language functions as "a pretext for 'revealing oneself . . . by hiding oneself,'" removing a mask by placing a new one? It is striking that the "original text" is seen as a "pretext for" revealing while hiding—a

pretext, the site of a pretense, an excuse, thus one more layer of concealment. Although Loi seems to be referring clearly to a *French* "original" in
her description of the Chinese poets, a second look reveals that ("when it is
not *simply* a matter of mode, or a fashion") it is the Chinese text that one
must "read with great care before daring to make affirmations" about the
connection with French poetry. The Chinese text, too, has its place as
"original text," so even here, the ground is highly unstable at the location
of the original. "The original text becomes a pretext for 'revealing oneself . . . by hiding'": this phrase, when mobilized to warn against the facile
misreading or mislabeling of a poem in its connection to French poetry
(the *mirliton* of Apollinaire "brings nothing of Apollinaire"), brushes in its
own rhetoric against the difficulty of arresting the lifting of veils once it has
begun. According to Loi, the term "Occidentalist" (or "Gallicist"), in describing Chinese poetry in relation to French, can become a "dangerous label" that is "stuck on too quickly": it is a piece of modernity (the adhesive
label, an image from the realm of mass production) that masks the partic-
ularity of the poetic content. For Loi, a crucial part of this content is that
it is not merely "Gallicist," and possibly, ultimately, not French at all.
While in her view, what one must not ignore is finally the "Chinese" aspects of the poetic content that veils itself in Occidental "costume," once
one begins to raise veils one finds always another layer and a continual dis-
location of any such "ultimate" core of the "original."

   For the Japanese poets who interested themselves in French poetry
and poetics, one finds many analogous dilemmas, and the rhetoric of unveiling the layers of text and "pretext" contains similar dangers, including
the possibility of a too-quick labeling that leads to a dismissal of the work.
This has been the fate of much of Japanese Surrealist poetry: identified either with the Japanese classical tradition or with a derivative imitation of
French avant-garde work, the poems themselves are quick to "hide" among
the play of influences and elusive textual origins that make up their fabric.
How, then, might one consider the work of interaction and translation that
brought Surrealism to Japan, without haste or dangerous labeling, without
ignoring the difficult slippage of location between text and pretext—at the
same time without resorting to a simple nostalgia of "origins"? Perhaps a
reliance on the writings of Breton is in itself an attempt to invoke a most
recognized locus of Surrealism's "origins," acknowledged in both Western
and Japanese criticism, as well as in the early texts of the Japanese discov-

ery of Surrealism. Without taking Breton as a point of ending, one may nonetheless recognize in the translations of his work, by Takiguchi in particular, all the difficulty and multiple layering of text and pretext that inhere in the Surrealist writings that surround them, by the numerous writers whose work is connected in various ways with Surrealism.

TAKIGUCHI SHŪZŌ AND ANDRÉ BRETON

One might consider, for example, Takiguchi's 1928 essay "Shururearisumu no shiron ni tsuite" (On the poetics of Surrealism), published in the March issue of *Sōsaku gekkan*, when Takiguchi was only twenty-five years old. Its appearance, before the publication of Nishiwaki's *Chōgenjitsushugi shiron* (Surrealist poetics), and before the translation of Breton's *Le Surréalisme et la peinture*, marks among the earliest and most direct introductions of Surrealist principles through a reading of Breton's "First Manifesto of Surrealism" (1924), which Takiguchi acquired in 1927 along with *Les Pas perdus* and other related works.[19]

In the second paragraph of the essay, Takiguchi states:

Freud's research into the unconscious world, and in particular his interpretation of dreams, truly excited the Surrealists. The opposition between "reality" and "dream" is a very old one. In spite of a strong belief in the agency that works in the spirit of dreams, many saw dreams as no more than followers of reality or as temporary incarnations separate from reality. What André Breton attempted to see was the essence of the spirit [*esprit*] as manifested in dreams. Dreams are made up of things that would be impossible [in reality]. In dreams, judgment and selection are banned, and only the pure flight of the spirit is permitted free passage [*tsūka*]. Breton calls dreams, in opposition to reality, "surréalité." Memory is an obstacle and because of it reality is continually [endlessly] muddled.[20]

Takiguchi seems to be reading along with Breton's "First Manifesto of Surrealism." After mentioning (in the first paragraph) the development of Surrealism from Dada, he begins his description with a discussion of Freud and the impact on the Surrealists of Freud's inquiries (*tankyū*) into the unconscious world and the interpretation of dreams. (As Breton states in the "First Manifesto": "It was, apparently, by pure chance that a part of our mental world which we pretended not to be concerned with any longer— and, in my opinion by far the most important part—has been brought back to light. For this we must give thanks to the discoveries of Sigmund

7. Takiguchi Shūzō and André Breton in Breton's library, their first meeting, Paris, 1958. Photo by François René Roland. Courtesy of Satani Gallery, *André Breton and Shūzō Takiguchi: The 13th Exhibition Homage to Shūzō Takiguchi.*

Freud.")[21] Takiguchi's essay belies a common assumption that the primary difference between Japanese and French Surrealism was an unawareness of the work of Freud in Japan. Although the place of Freud's work for the Japanese Surrealists remains in question, it is clear that from the earliest phases of Surrealism in Japan there was at least some recognition of the importance of his work—such that Takiguchi begins a description of Surrealism not with the name of Breton but with that of Freud.

Immediately interpolating his own view that "the opposition between 'reality' and 'dream' is a very old one" ("'genjitsu' to 'yume' to no tairitsu ga mottomo furui mono de aru"), Takiguchi seems to allude to the poetic opposition between dream (*yume*) and reality (*utsutsu*) as thematized in Japanese tradition as early as the mid-tenth-century *Ise monogatari*.[22] Because the opposition, as well as the confusion, between dream and reality is so well-known as to be a classical trope and almost a cliché in Japan, Takiguchi needs to explain and justify the excitement that the exploration of dreams evoked in the Surrealists, and the profound effect of Freud's thoughts on dreams and the unconscious. Yet one senses a simultaneous resistance to this realm, or to its presentation as a novelty; there was already "a strong belief that existed in the agency that works in the spirit of dreams," a belief that was a critical one in the past (*jūdai de atta*). But in spite of their former importance, dreams are currently seen by many as subordinate to "reality." Disconnected from their former belief, people's current notions of the opposition between dream and reality place dreams at the *service* of reality (as *jūsha*, literally followers, attendants) or describe them as "separate entities" (*bekko*, separate, individual) that are merely temporary incarnations (*kagen* 仮現 a term that recalls the Buddhist notion of reality, *utsutsu* 現, as that which is presently alive, temporarily incarnate in this world: *kagen* are the temporary appearances of Buddhist deities in this world as human beings). Takiguchi, in his description, must negotiate the boundary between existing concepts of the dream in Japanese thought and the French terms, such as those he uses (*esprit*, that I have translated as "spirit," which in French also contains the sense of "mind" or "intelligence").

The human spirit or mind as it is expressed or manifested in dreams is thus viewed anew here, neither as subordinate nor as a temporary and inessential aspect of existence: rather, it is the "essence" or true substance (*honshitsu*) of the mind or spirit (*esprit*) that Breton recognized to be revealed in dreams. Takiguchi's language emphasizes the physical, corporeal presence of the dream's elements: dreams are constituted, composed, made up physically (as their tissue, their structure: *soshikitai*) of any impossible thing (*arayuru fukanō na mono*). Here, he brings in also the language of censorship—these impossibilities are prohibited in reality by the faculties of judgment or selection, but "pass" in dreams where these censors are absent. The reality he describes is also a reality of art ("judgment, selection," and description) like, for example, that of Stendhal's narrator whom Breton describes in his manifesto as selecting from the available stock of images and verbal possibilities ("the superimposition of catalogue images . . . he seizes the opportunity to slip me his post cards").[23] Thus it is the "impossible" that is of greatest interest, that which would not "pass" (*tsūka suru*) the censorship of judgment and discretion. (This term for the "impossible" may be Takiguchi's rendering of Breton's notion of the marvelous, in life and in art, "le merveilleux.")

In his direct translation of the following passage from Breton, Takiguchi describes the circumscribed realm of reality that allows people to consider only that which "belongs to our experience" (or, as Breton has it, "des faits relevant étroitement de notre expérience," that which falls narrowly within the province of our experience). Breton writes:

> The absolute rationalism that is still in vogue allows us to consider only facts relating directly to our experience. Logical ends, on the contrary, escape us. It is pointless to add that experience itself has found itself increasingly circumscribed. It paces back and forth in a cage from which it is more and more difficult to make it emerge. It too leans for support on what is most immediately expedient, and is protected by the sentinels of common sense.

Takiguchi translates and explains (I render his version literally):

> "Pure theory allows us to consider only facts belonging to our experience. Experience circles round and round inside a cage and it becomes increasingly difficult [*konnan*] to escape. Grounded in direct utility [expediency], it is protected by common sense." An act in a dream [the act of dreaming] and an act in reality are both absolutely physiological parts of life, and where reality ends, dream may also reach its conclusion [*ketsumatsu*]. Breton's "surréalité" does not have as its aim to be a supplement to reality.[24]

Takiguchi skips over certain segments of the passage he translates from the French, in particular those in which Breton emphasizes (possible) positive uses of logic, if turned to different and more relevant problems than the ones it currently addresses. Thus pure logic (or, as Breton has it, "absolute rationalism") as well as "common sense" (*jōshiki*) and "direct utility" (*chokusetsu no sayō*) are blamed for the imprisonment of "experience." Takiguchi's term *ori* represents as much a jail cell as an animal cage, and he assigns a relatively clear blame; experience is imprisoned and desires escape, but the process becomes increasingly difficult ("dasshutsu suru koto ga iyoiyo konnan to naru"). In contrast, Breton portrays experience as an animal that one would like to coax out of the cage but which refuses to budge: for example, we might assume the point of view of the poet, who would like to have access to the higher and more marvelous realms of experience but is unable to get "experience" to leave this cage composed of immediate utility, guarded by good sense, and restricted by rationalism. "Elle tourne dans une cage d'où il est de plus en plus difficile de *la faire sortir*" (It circles a cage from which it is increasingly difficult to *make it emerge*; emphasis mine).

Although the difference is small, the effect on the relation of the speaker to experience is profound: in the case of Breton, it makes the speaker complicit, in a sense, with the dominant use of logic; only now is it beginning to be possible to engage in other ways of thinking that would allow the dream and the wider realm of (antirational) experience to be explored. Takiguchi's thinking places a stronger emphasis on the seemingly external forces of selection, judgment, criticism, imprisonment, censorship: the desire for freedom is strong, but the hindrances seem to stem from the realm of "reality," and, by implication, from social mores, traditions, even Buddhist-related patterns of language and ideas, as much as from the internal (or internalized) logic of one's own thought. Takiguchi speaks of the end of reality coinciding with the end of dream, in what seems like a refutation of the concept of reincarnation. Both realms are temporary, both exist in this world; thus the actions that one performs in dreams and in reality are both "physiological." It is this which, for Takiguchi, distinguishes Freud's view of dreams that excited the Surrealists from what might otherwise, translated into Japanese, be in danger of appearing a mere repetition of an already familiar and accepted view. The "rationalist" mode that Breton claims reigns at present, and against which his polemic is directed, seems a matter of less concern to Takiguchi here than the attack on "common sense" and the explications of the usefulness and specificity of a new view of dream and "surréalité" (and the relation between them, given the new form of the term *chōgenjitsu* with the reading *shururearite* noted alongside it).

This is not to invoke the common essentialist argument that would cleanly oppose the valence of Breton's text to that of Takiguchi's, in terms of some kind of priority of (or preexisting disposition toward) the "irrational" or antilogical in Japanese culture. In fact, what is perhaps most striking about the two texts alongside one another is the extent to which they *are* able to be parallel, in spite of the differences in language: the ability of

Japanese modern prose to trace the nuances of the French syntax, in its extreme figurativeness and abstraction—and, presumably, still to remain within the bounds of Japanese grammar, syntax, vocabulary—marks a pivotal moment of rewriting or overwriting of meanings that, in the end, changes our view of both texts.

To a singular degree, in this passage, one can observe the reconstruction or reexplication of the notions of the "real," of "dream," of "experience," through and in relation to an implied tradition and at the same time through the reading and translation of a foreign text. The position of Takiguchi in this essay is divided: at times he is identified with Breton as speaker, taking in the concepts from the manifesto and reproducing them, with or without quotation marks; judging society along with Breton, he comments on the prior tendencies of rationalist thought and critiques these "enemies" along with Breton. At other moments he judges Breton's argument, relating it to European and American thinkers whose notions of the image, reality, or experience he is familiar with: most notably, he recognizes connections with Gertrude Stein and Nietzsche (while the links he traces to Rimbaud and Baudelaire are already constructed by Breton in the "First Manifesto"). As commentator, translator, gloss, Takiguchi is in a dual position of identification and distance from the text of Breton. Through nuances of diction and argument, one can observe Takiguchi's grappling with the preconceived notions inherent in Japanese literary tradition or in past uses of the words that form the core of his translation of Breton's ideas: it is a struggle, in a sense, to renew these terms and to wrench them from the force of their own past and nuance of usage. Thus, to explain Surrealist thought in Japanese, to read and to translate a single paragraph of a manifesto, entails a struggle analogous to that facing poets in their attempt to rewrite and rearticulate, or rather, to break down and then, perhaps, to reconfigure as possibility, the syntax and conventions of Japanese poetics.

"ETAMINES NARRATIVES": EXPERIMENTS IN ACTUALITY

Before continuing to explore Takiguchi's understanding of the concepts of "dream" and "reality" in relation to poetic composition, we will examine briefly Takiguchi's first attempts to put into practice the Surrealist suggestion of an exploration of the realm of dreams. How, in his poetry and later critical writings, were the notions of dream and reality enacted? How did the struggle between them play itself out in his later writings?

Two works of Takiguchi Shūzō contribute to this reconfiguration of poetic language along the "fault line" between Japanese and French: an early poem entitled "Etamines narratives" (Narrative fibers) from 1927, written at approximately the same time as his first discoveries of Surrealism, and, in relation to it, his famous theoretical essay elaborating his poetics entitled "Shi to jitsuzai" (Poetry and actuality, 1931). These works engage enduring questions and struggles that concerned the Japanese Surrealists, about the relation between language and actuality, about poetry and dreams, and about the possibility of beginning to write (or, the will to write and the difficulty of writing). Through them, one can discover hints about ways to read the relation between Japanese and French Surrealism—and the problems this reading poses for an understanding of the functioning of translation, transpositions, and the materiality of languages.

"Etamines narratives" was first published in the literary journal *Yama mayu* (Mountain silkworm) and in the Surrealist collection *Fukuikutaru kafu yo* (Ah, fragrant stoker). *Yama mayu*, a magazine of art and literature, in thirty-six issues between 1924 and 1929 introduced Japanese readers to translations of Baudelaire, Apollinaire, Rimbaud, Jean Cocteau, and Yvan Goll and to excerpts from the *Chants de Maldoror* of Lautréamont, as well as the first narratives and critical reflections by future members of the Japanese literary establishment, such as Kobayashi Hideo, Nakahara Chūya, and Hori Tatsuo. "Etamines narratives"[25] takes the form of a prose poem in six parts, each segment a single paragraph composed of grammatically unbroken sentences. It opens with these lines:

> When copper and a white rose compose a harmony, winged sleep lets out a scream.[26]

A disorienting opening, undermining ordinary sense, suggests itself to be the narrative of dream. A harmony composed (formed, made) by the coin and the rose causes sleep to begin to scream; this sleep has wings (*tsubasa no aru suimin*), but if it carries a message, what comes through is an incongruous combination of sounds, a harmony (*kyōwa-on*) and a scream (*sakebi*). Critic Iwanari Tatsuya terms this effect in the opening of "Etamines narratives" the "diffusion of meaning" (*imi no kakusan*), the retreat of "subject" or "theme," "giving the phrases and words autonomy from the constraints of a given poetic style."[27] I would agree that a "diffusion" is happening with meaning in this image, but it is deceptive: like the image of the line itself, it is a juxtaposition of a violence, a rupture of meaning (like the scream) and a gentle, figurative coherence of the grammatically smooth, unbroken image-sentence (like the harmony).

On the page, "Etamines narratives" is structured like a poem in prose, positioning itself at the boundaries between the language of Japanese modern prose and free verse poetry that would have been familiar to readers by this time. The title announces the encounter with a narrative of some kind, with its title alone in French: "Etamines narratives." "Etamines" can be translated as "fine cloth," or threads of that cloth, its fibers —thus evoking the conventional figure of the threads of a narrative (a figure that exists in Japanese as well, in the term *suji*, meaning both "thread" and "plot" of a story). It can mean also the whole cloth, or the stamen of a flower; one could speculate on what kind of a narrative could be figured as a stamen, or where in a narrative one would locate its stamen. These six short pieces generate the beginnings of a plurality of stories or fragments of stories. Each sentence seems to be the seed of a new narrative whose connection to the previous line we can attempt to reconstruct but which, while flowing in smooth grammatical and rhythmic sentences, defies coherence.

Later in the first segment of the poem, the sleep (*suimin*) returns in the form of a question:

Like any material that emits sound, did that sleep too belong to the will?[28]

"Like any material that emits sound"—again we have the cleaving of the sentence in the middle; what do all the substances that emit sound have to do with sleep? Earlier, we heard winged sleep emit a scream: the opening to sound, the opening to sleep—are these the results of an act of will? This question recurs in Takiguchi's work: "Ano suimin mo ishi ni zoku shiteita no kashira?" (Did that sleep belong to the will?) The work of the will, of intention, of control in sleep, and in the narrative threads of dreams, remains an issue for Takiguchi in his later attempts to grapple with the poetics of automatic writing: To what extent can the writing be automatic? Where can the dream take over the power of the will?

To bring this question for a moment into the context of a larger issue: Takiguchi and his colleagues were engaged in translating theories of automatic writing, and in translating texts of automatic writing themselves, into Japanese. How can translating, creating that well-wrought result through a painstaking process of continual rewriting, be compatible (or even begin to be reconciled) with the automatic, the spontaneous, as a means to break with/transcend literary convention? We know that Takiguchi was a perfectionist as a translator, and that he continued work on his translation of Breton's *Le Surréalisme et la peinture* long after his first translation of it was published in 1930. Until the end of his life he always planned to go back to it and work on it again. Perhaps one can understand the possibility of combining translation and automatic writing in terms of Maurice Blanchot's suggestion, when he argues against the confusion of the "immediate" with the "facile," in his description of automatic writing:

In reality, where the most facile means were being proposed, there hid behind this facility an extreme demand, and behind this certitude—this gift offered to everyone and disclosed in each . . . —was concealed the insecurity of the inaccessible, a probing of what never is in evidence, the exacting demands of a search which is no search at all and of a presence which is never granted.[29]

"The immediate is not close," he says; perhaps in the approach suggested by automatic writing, the demands and troubles that beset the translator may already be found. What seemed an incongruity, a rupture may be reconsidered as a point of contact, a common exacting and even unfulfillable demand.

To return to "Etamines narratives," one is immediately tempted to ask: who is sleeping here? This *suimin* named by the lines is a personified sleep, but the sleeping subject, if we were to call it that, is absent. The idea that what one hears in this work are dreams is only implied, never named. The only person who appears in the first segment of the poem is the figure of an architect: "the architect scheming a new architectural trick by means of overflowing useless things." The crafting, consciously composing figure of the artist is seen here as merely playing tricks, working with an abundance of useless things: if this image can be read in relation to the absent figure of the poet, to reflect on the poet's work with language, then it is not in conscious tricks, scheming creation like that of the architect that anything of interest is to be found, any worthwhile task for the will.

In the third stanza, we find the figure of "a boy who lays his head on a book of poetry that changes" (*Henka suru shishū ni atama wo noseru shōnen wo kokyū suru*).[30] Poetry makes its appearance in its own name, *shishū* (book of poetry). A boy lays his head on the book: is he sleeping? But here, again, an explicit narrative subject is absent, as is the grammatical subject of the sentence. The boy who lays his head on a book of poetry is the direct object of the verb to breathe: "[I/you/it—something that is left out] breathes a boy who lays his head on a book of poetry that changes." What breathes? In Japanese the absence of a subject in this sentence is not ungrammatical or even strange, but it leaves the poem without any body that does this breathing, leaves us, one might say, with a kind of anonymous inhalation, an inspiration, related here to poetry and to a boy, related to the connection between sleep and language.[31]

Takiguchi's images tempt the reader with the ends of threads of narrative and metaphors to follow, but these threads do not necessarily lead toward any determinate or determinable place, or even any exit: the threads proliferate. Without abdicating the task of reading, however, one takes up the challenge posed by the poem, to read and to follow the threads of the grammar and their initiated narratives, knowing all the while that they threaten to (or certainly will) break off at any moment.

Takiguchi, a faithful translator, was not always a literal translator. Perhaps this may be in part because the "proper" limits or boundaries of a translation were not respected in his case—the texts he worked on spilled over into his own critical writings, into his poetry, into his way of living.[32] In his critical essay "Shi to jitsuzai"(Poetry and actuality) Takiguchi articulates his theories of the relation between writing and the encounter with the actual (*jitsuzai*). The word *jitsuzai* can be defined as real existence, actual being, essence, actuality, entity, or (in philosophy) absolute being. For literature, it is used also to describe the effective illusion of reality created by language: the characters in a play seem as if they were "real" (*jitsuzai no yō ni*, taken from life, flesh and blood); their illusion causes one to suspend one's disbelief.

The text of "Shi to jitsuzai" published in *Shi to shiron* in 1931 confronts the problem of the will and its relation to writing (through the encounter with the "real"). The essay, which opens like the beginning of a story—a narrative of writing—begins as follows:

Noon, it is just noon, eyes enormous, and my pen, maintaining an odd equilibrium like the Tower of Pisa, begins to move. My fingers, obeying the law (*sic*) of my will, grasp this penholder.[33]

The speaker is wide open to an encounter, ready to begin: "eyes enormous," sitting in the bright light of noon as if to guarantee that whatever comes will not be missed. The first words of the first sentence, *sore wa shōgo* (it [that] was at noon) imply that something is about to happen, we don't yet know what. This "it" or "that," an emphatic *çela* with no antecedent, is neutral, like the unknown; perhaps it is what the pen waits for—only premonition.

The opening passage (as in Asuka Tōru's "Pélerin") insists on the personal pronoun, the masculine, informal *boku* (I), who possesses the pen, the fingers, the will (*boku no pen, boku no yubitachi, boku no ishi*) at the moment of waiting for writing; but still, it seems, the actual moving of the pen is left to happen by itself. The I, here, *does* nothing except that these attributes *belong* to him: vocal cords, fingers. Yet the fingers grasp the pen as a result of the "law" (*hōsoku*) of the writer's will. Here a curious intervention of the word *sic* appears in parentheses—among the few roman letters in the entire text—to qualify the idea or the term "laws," or "laws of the will." *Sic*: "thus; so." (My dictionary says, "used in written texts to indicate that a surprising or paradoxical word, phrase, or fact is not a mistake and is to be read as it stands"—or if there is a mistake, it is present already in the original, and should not be misattributed to the quoter.) The idea that the will has laws is, for this text, a surprise, a paradox, and perhaps even a mistake transcribed from some "original." The phrase casts the position of the speaker into doubt and foregrounds the relation between the speaker and the event being transcribed. Is this a translation? It is as though Takiguchi were commenting that he is being faithful to some original, a text or even the event of writing itself, that posits the laws of the will—strange as that may sound—and the personified fingers' (*yubi-tachi*) obedience to these laws.

Immediately, a further paradoxical comparison appears, with the image of the statue of Niobe (daughter of Tantalus, who turned to stone while bewailing the loss of her children). In this analogy, the eternally immobile statue and the flowing fountain of water beside it create "the same effect":

If my vocal cords—in a manner similar to that in which the eternal silhouette of the fountain [stream of water] beside Niobe's marble statue produces the same effect as she does—confess to an irresistible force, as if their vibrations obeyed a single precise law of the will (*sic*), how can my fingers, traversed down to their tips by these stirrings, proudly [valiantly] resist my vocal cords?[34]

The dynamic is between the vocal cords (which would speak, confessing to the presence of an irresistible force, an inevitability conditioned by a single law of the will) and the fingers, resisting this urge, these stirrings toward expression; the fingers hold back and hesitate, resisting (writing). A similar phrase comes up later in the text as well: *karōjite hatsugen suru*, the difficult entry into language, into utterance. The animated vocal cords confess, and the fingers are personified as well (*yubi-tachi*, with a plural suffix used primarily for people) in their capacity for pride and resistance.[35]

If we can read this description as a pursuit of the questions of the will that begin to be raised in "Etamines narratives," we note that the will to writing described here is diffuse, located in part in the voice, in part in the fingers, giving rise to vibrations, forces, and necessities. Between speech and writing, there is a proud resistance, replicated in some form in this figure of Niobe and the fountain—the flowing, ephemeral stream of water maintains an eternal silhouette, freezing into a form that produces the same effect as the statue itself. (We might recall in this context Baudelaire's famous lines about beauty in "Salon de 1846": "Toutes les beautés contiennent, comme tous les phénomènes possibles, quelque chose d'éternel et quelque chose de transitoire,—d'absolu et de particulier." "All beauty contains, like all possible phenomena, something eternal and something transitory—something absolute and something particular.")[36] Takiguchi, in his search in this essay for the relationship between poetry and actuality, between real existence and the absolute, touches on a related paradox, embodied in the relation between the impulse to write (as a stirring or vibrations in the vocal cords) and the actual act of moving the pen on the page.

The hesitation to write implies a sense that there is a danger involved, the threat of some contact/collision between the word and the "real"—as he later claims, "Reality [*genjitsu*]: if my lips are not burned on the word, is it not rather a miracle?" What is in question here, as becomes more evident later in this fragmented and idiosyncratic essay, is the hesitation or difficulty, even the impossibility, of approaching this *jitsuzai* (actuality) in an immediate form; and yet the essay expresses a dissatisfaction or disillusionment with the various possible mediations. Most people, the essay claims, mistake *seikatsu* (livelihood, living, daily life, the everyday, or *byt*) for *genjitsu* (reality/actuality), and this mistake, this substitution related to logical thinking is a convenient cultural convention that makes it easier for people to deal with reality, allowing them to define their position:

[People] probably felt strongly that it was convenient to have an ever-present logic ("pan-logicism"). And it is a fact that people have secured a certain position for themselves by speaking of daily living [*seikatsu*] in the place of reality [*genjitsu*], or by abstracting so-called "living" from reality. And certain people persist in repeating this way of speaking (substituting one for the other) over and over, endlessly.[37]

What is to blame here is, in a sense, theory or logical thinking: by abstracting (*chūshō suru*) living from its basis in reality, through the use of logic, or what Takiguchi terms a "pan-logical" approach, people have been able to gain a mastery or secure a fixed position (*hitotsu no ichi wo kakutoku shita*). The price of this, however, is a loss of the sense of a difference between reality and this thing that becomes its poor substitute, that Takiguchi here calls "living" or "daily life."

This leads, he implies, to an outcome of perpetual repetition of the same—not only the same way of living but, more particularly, certain kinds of habits of language that say the same thing over and over again, making the same substitution in speech endlessly, without ever touching what he would call "reality." (*Soshite aru ningentachi wa sore wo ikudo mo ikudo mo iikaeru no de aru.*) The repeated *ikudomo, ikudomo* (again and again, time after time) emphasizes the monotony of this abstract replication. Thus an entrance into language would be made possible by a certain logic, by the clinging to certain abstractions, but as he says later in the essay, "when I have been able to begin speaking through logical truths, then there will no longer be any place for the marvelous." The clarity of this attempted condemnation of logic will be complicated and undermined later in the essay. Perhaps it is already undermined, in a sense, by its own clinging to the language of a logical clarity, its insistence on the terms of causal argument, with hypothetical proposition ("it is probable that . . . ") and the assertion of a conclusion ("it is a fact that . . . "; "because of *x*, or because of *y*, a given fact is concluded"). This is already very far from the wide-eyed hesitation, marked by the initial motion of the pen in the first few lines of the essay.

But Takiguchi continues to assert that it is not philosophical thought, not logical reasoning, that he is reaching for and desires here: "I know that declarations like these will never amount to any kind of philosophical thought. And that is what I desire at present." Any kind of philosophical thought (*nanra no tetsugakuteki na shisō*) is a rather casual reference to philosophy, inserting the colloquialism *nanra* (any, what, whatever). And the *sore wo*—that is what I desire at present—for a moment makes us stop: does he or does he not desire philosophical thought, or is it the absence of thought that he says he desires at present? (The English reflects this ambiguity as well: "that is what I desire.") The desire occurs in the present moment (*ima*) of the writing, and its present tense seems to be emphasized by the speechlike colloquiality of the phrase ("any kind of philosophy").[38]

But in terms of the question of will and the possibility of writing, on the most explicit level, Takiguchi describes the necessity of the refusal of method in a way that recalls Breton's definition of Surrealism in the "First Manifesto." Breton writes that Surrealism is "dictated by thought, in the absence of any control exercised by reason, exempt from any aesthetic or moral concern."[39] An analogous refusal is constructed in the opening lines of "Shi to jitsuzai":

In the psychology of desire, which would like to see human actions more or less in perspective—outside of any consideration in the realms of logic, metaphysics, or even art—there is no kind of method at all which would let him confront this reality, except for perhaps the means of [visual] perspective.[40]

In a partial echo of Breton's formulation Takiguchi eliminates the logical, artistic and (this is his addition instead of the moral) the metaphysical. To see in perspective, to use the vantage point of perspective drawing (*tōshigateki hōhō*) seems a painfully inadequate recourse. Breton, too, rejects most given methods but, in a footnote to his "Second Manifesto of Surrealism," he alludes to the means of clairvoyance and metaphysics in his discussion of collaborative surrealist games and *cadavre exquis* (exquisite corpse). *Tōshi* can suggest not only the painter's perspective method but also "seeing through": the foretelling practiced by a diviner (clairvoyance) or the scientific vision of an x-ray. Throughout "Shi to Jitsuzai" Takiguchi privileges transparency and clarity in his description of the poem as a phenomenon of resistance between matter and spirit.

Yet we may recall also the effects of clairvoyance on the poet as they appear in Baudelaire's poem "La Voix" in *Les Fleurs du mal*:

Je vois distinctement des mondes singuliers,
Et de ma clairvoyance extatique victime,
Je traine des serpents qui mordent mes souliers[41]

I distinctly see singular [strange, marvelous] worlds
And, victim of my ecstatic clairvoyance
I trail serpents that bite at my heels

Clairvoyance leads to poetic, but also mad, vision to which one can fall victim: we recall the moment in Takiguchi's text when he says, "When through logical truths I enter into speech, there is no longer any place for the marvelous [strange]." This opposite voice warns against too much rationality, which makes speech possible but will drive away the *mondes singuliers*.

If the textual echoes of Breton remain veiled in these moments, such as in Takiguchi's refusal (of the realms of logic, metaphysics, and art), and in his suggestion of a last recourse in the quest for technique, one may follow those echoes another step into the sudden appearance of an image of the sunflower, *tournesol* (Japanese: *himawari no hana*).[42] Takiguchi writes, "I insist, together with the sunflower, on the idea that reflection [introspection], whatever we may understand by this term, has nothing in it that coincides with reality." For Breton, the sunflower first appears in the poem "Tournesol," written in 1923 and dedicated to Pierre Reverdy. Breton later decides that his writing of this poem was a premonition for his meeting with Jacqueline Lamba, and he describes it at some length in Section 4 of *L'Amour fou* (1937), marveling at the two meanings of the word in French: sunflower (plant that turns toward the sun) and the litmus paper that turns from blue to red in the presence of acid.

What does it mean, then, to "insist, together with the sunflower . . . that reflection [introspection] . . . has nothing in it that coincides with reality"? The speaking together is an odd double voice; Takiguchi uses the phrase as a preface to a refusal of the Platonic, a refusal of the opposition of the shadow (reflection) and the thing itself, with the hierarchy it creates. And yet, since Takiguchi does allude to Breton explicitly elsewhere, it is hard not to read this *himawari* (sunflower) as some kind of speaking together with Breton: "himawari to tomo ni rikisetsu"—I insist, emphasize, speak strongly, in part because I do not speak alone. It is a figure of "speaking with," and perhaps translation can be read as another form of this collaborative speaking.

Takiguchi's relation to Breton's texts is not a purely accepting one; there is resistance here too. If Takiguchi could not have read *L'Amour fou* yet (it had not yet been written), his essay nonetheless reflects similar fascinations: Takiguchi had read the "Second Manifesto of Surrealism," and he responds to that text's insistence on the "alchemy of the word" (*l'alchimie du verbe*, in allusion to Rimbaud) with an argument that calls upon chemistry, rather than alchemy, as the more promising means for the poet to break free of the poetry of the past and to create what he calls "a drama of incomparable violence": "This is where the science of the individual can come about (be created)." Takiguchi proposes a science of the individual, a personal science, and the French words appear: "Ce sont les conquérants du monde / Cherchant la fortune chimique personnelle" (They are the conquerors of the world / Seeking a personal chemical fortune). The words from the poem "Mouvements" in Rimbaud's *Les Illuminations* describe the voyagers, conquerors of the world, led "by unprecedented [extraordinary] lights and chemical newness" (*par les lumières inouïes / Et la nouveauté chimique*). This discovery, this chemical newness, Takiguchi counterposes to Breton's alchemy; Rimbaud's terms of the light of the unprecedented and "chemical newness" offer for Takiguchi a more promising path to approaching reality/actuality in writing.

But even this momentary solution is not a stable one. The essay "Shi to jitsuzai" was published in *Shi to shiron* with the mark "unfinished/incomplete" in parentheses at the end of its last line. After its polemic against alchemy, the text breaks off with a series of brief, direct declarations about poetry, which in themselves seem to mark a beginning rather than any kind of closure or denouement.

Poetry is not faith. Nor is it logic. Poetry is an act. An act that refutes all acts. This is the instant when the shadow of the dream resembled the shadow of the poem.[43]

If the goal is a resemblance, a faithful similarity (recalling again the terms of a translation) between poem and dream, then here the best one can hope for is a brief instant in which the shadow of one resembles the other's shadow. And this moment is reached not by logic, nor by faith, but by poetry as an act that refutes (repudiates, denies) all acts: a paradoxical moment in language that can allow one shadow to resemble another. Thus the poetic process for Takiguchi is by definition incomplete: the unfinished ending is itself deliberate, an act, symptomatic for Takiguchi of the way the dream narratives in his works and the language of poetic transcription will necessarily cut off before their moment of closure, before logic or reflection intervenes with a solution (or method) to dissolve the uncertainty they create.

If poetry puts one into contact with shadows, then (in terms of translation) it is interesting that Takiguchi repeatedly insists on the importance of the materiality of language, on the critical importance of attention to the contours and substance of the specific words used ("the exact contours of each word are of an extreme importance"), but at the same time, he emphatically denies the importance of maintaining or defining a distinction between Orient and Occident, between East and West. "I do not recognize the necessity here of clinging to the difference between the spirit of the Greeks and that of the Orient," he writes in an aside in this essay, using the term *sabetsu* (difference, distinction, also prejudice). He reiterates his emphasis on the importance of the languages in a supplementary answer to a questionnaire on Surrealism (many years later in March 1971, writing in French), in which he is asked to comment on his perception of the future of Surrealism.

Besides the essential question you have posed (about the future of Surrealism) I regret the fact that there is a very specific difficulty in language, in particular in the difference between those of the Orient and those of the Occident, and that difference in itself is not the principal problem—or rather, there is something essential in the future of Surrealist thought. The urgent necessity, but I do not conceal the difficulty, of realizing it [Surrealist thought] through discussion in a "manifest" and generalized language. What Liberty and community I believe in![44]

His desire here for some ideal of pure communication, of community, that would be attained through the medium of some manifest and generalized language, is countered by a deep recognition (accompanied by regret) about the very "specific difficulty" with which he has reckoned in his writings throughout his life. This ambivalence is one that marks many of Takiguchi's Surrealist writings, and the hesitation between these two impulses shapes the dynamic of the quest, there, for the encounter with writing, and with the actual. In tracing some of the threads of Takiguchi's encounter with Surrealism, or, to put it otherwise, of Surrealism's encounter with Takiguchi, one finds recognizable elements and terms of Surrealism cited, borrowed, and transformed through Takiguchi's appropriation of them and challenges to them. He wanted to transcend the boundaries of national language and of the traditional genres of literature. Late in his life he made a series of booklets that he called liberty passports, which he distributed among his friends and other artists. These contained fragments of Japanese, French, English, and German, written by himself and other poets, along with the names of the bearers, the date of issue, and stamps saying things like "valid permanently" or "date of issue lost." Marked with the name of no country, they invite the holder to voyage in some ideal, free realm. While the incompletions, the unresolved and fragmentary structures of much of Takiguchi's writing have at times been seen as a fault, like the passports, their openness has suggested the direction of a continuation and posed a challenge—taken up by the following generations of artists and writers, although still for the most part within Japan—toward the persistent, if hesitant, pursuit of "that act that refutes all acts," of that "instant when the shadow of the dream resembled the shadow of the poem . . ."

Thus, one sees clearly that Takiguchi's work, from its pursuit of the dream of writing and poetry to its critical hesitancies and its dance with Breton, explores the process of writing on the edge of immediacy or "actuality." At the same time it recognizes the difficulty or even impossibility of attaining or grasping that actuality. Writing, as a transcription, an instant or a shadow, has something in common with translation; Takiguchi's writings perform acts of translation or transcription and at the same time enact the philosophical or epistemological problems described by the words and ideas being translated. Moving toward and away from Breton at once, speaking with and yet beyond the ideas of Breton, Takiguchi condemns logic (as Breton does) and thus arrives at a contradiction—willing an access to something that transcends the logic of the will (of philosophical reasoning and the laws of the will). Yet he attempts to work toward this actuality nonetheless, or to dream its access. Both his poetic experiments and critical writings pursue these problems in ways that illuminate the overall workings of translation and poetic/cultural transmission.

Because memory, like Takiguchi's critical writings, involves a questioning and yet a desire for immanence or immediacy even in the midst of transcription, shadow, representation, reiteration, and aftereffects, it is useful to consider Takiguchi's writings as central elements and examples, as well as illuminating critical ideas for the present study. In a sense, his utopias have much to do with the notion of the past and the somehow utopian attempt to have access to the process of cultural interaction elaborated here. Concerned with questions that are elusive and yet nonetheless persist and survive over time, we find that Takiguchi comes to exemplify the paradox of the persistence and memory of these ephemeral poetic moments and flashes.

ETERNITIES AND SURREALIST LEGACIES

It's already more than half a century ago. Everyone has disappeared.
—Ema Shōko, June 19, 1998

When you opened your eyes from floor to ceiling nothing only dust and
not a sound only what was it it said come and gone was that it something
like that come and gone come and gone no one come and gone in no time
come and gone in no time . . .
—Samuel Beckett, *That Time*

And always
there is a yearning that seeks the unbound. But much
must be retained. And faithfulness is needed.
Forward, however, and back we will not look.
—Friedrich Hölderlin, "Mnemosyne"

THE EVOLUTION OF ETERNITY

In Japanese Dada, the notion of denying meaning in favor of non-
meaning was often identified with the Buddhist term *mu* (nothingness,
void). Tristan Tzara (1896–1963) already recognized the similarity between
Buddhist thought and his ideas of Dada, as in his statement in the 1922

Conférence sur Dada: "Dada isn't at all modern, it's rather a return to a quasi-Buddhist religion of indifference."[1] Although Tzara did not develop these ideas at length, Japanese Dadaist (and Zen Buddhist) Takahashi Shin-kichi (1901–1987) recollected that the connection was fundamental to his understanding of the movement:

[On reading Tzara's manifestos in Japanese translation], I recalled that, consider-ing Dada the same as Namu Amidabutsu, I used to scream, "Namu-Dada!" It can-not be doubted that Buddhism was absorbed promptly into the sagacious brain of Tzara. . . . His Buddhist background must have been Zen, because of his denial of verbal activity—his saying "thought without words" or "not counting on words" is in common with the Zen principle of no-word.[2]

In particular, Tzara's principle of nothingness ("DADA NE SIGNIFIE RIEN," the famous assertion in block type in the "Manifeste Dada 1918") was linked by Japanese Dadaists and later anarcho-nihilists (who created the magazine *Rien*,[3] from Tzara's *rien*) with the term *mu*, or "nothing," the "void." We recall Kitasono Katsue's elaboration of the "vacuum tube": the exploration of the principle of nothing or the void continued beyond the Dada movement in the work of Surrealists and later modernists.

Ōoka Makoto explicates the poetics of Nishiwaki Junzaburō in terms of such ideas of "nothingness" and draws convincing links between Nishi-waki's understanding of *mu* and his concept of "eternity," a term that Nishiwaki invokes repeatedly in his poetry before and after the war. How does this "eternity" of Nishiwaki's develop?[4] What is the relation between Nishiwaki's eternity (as a void, nothingness) and his vision of temporality, memory, and the understanding of the "real"?

Such questions about the changes in Nishiwaki's poetics lead one to certain larger questions concerning Surrealism in Japan. What happens to the Surrealist movement in Japan over time? Is the structure of memory, as explored above, related to this process of transformation, rearticulation, and revival of Surrealist thought in Japan in the postwar period? What is the relation between the Surrealists' notions of temporality (as articulated in their poetics) and these changes in Surrealism over time? Central to our notion of memory is the concept of the "gap" in consciousness (as in Freud's model of traumatic memory); we relate this also to the "horizon" or the "interval" as critical aspects of the recognition and return of memory within present consciousness. Memory creates a gap, horizon, or interval *within* the present moment. We trace the presence of a similar interval or horizon within the space of Japanese Surrealism (between European and Japanese poetic models, but also in the interval between meaning and meaninglessness, sense and nonsense, depth and surface, time and time-lessness). In the continued life of Surrealist thought in Japan after World War II, these horizons persist, ever more deeply integrated within the literary and artistic works.

Tzara includes among his definitions of Dada: "Dada: the abolition of memory."[5] Dada, for him, also invokes the abolition of the future and of prophesy. If Dada, as a process of negation, abolishes memory, prophesy, and the future, what happens to time in this realm of negation? Ōoka Makoto, in his analysis of Nishiwaki (outside of any reference to Dada) traces a related temporal problem in the link between negation (as "nothingness," *mu*) and eternity. According to Ōoka, the place of eternity and *mu* in Nishiwaki's poetics remains relatively unchanged over many years of his career. In the theoretical essay "Obscuro" (1933), for example, Nishiwaki writes:

> The poetry that tries to symbolize "eternity" develops, but it develops only in its methods, while the goal itself makes no progress at all. "Eternity" continues, forever unchanged.
>
> "Eternity" is a "nothingness of perception in the imperfect structure of the world of meaning." Or, to put it in plain terms, one might say that "it is the thing which is nothing at all." A perfect poetics is nothing more than a method for creating symbolizations that cannot symbolize [anything].[6]

Here, Nishiwaki identifies "eternity" with "the thing which is nothing at all" (which he places inside quotation marks). The aim of the "perfect poetics" is impossible: to symbolize, or to express in words and symbols, this "nothingness of perception" (*chikaku no kyomu*), and to create symbolizations that "cannot symbolize [anything]" ("nanimono o mo shōchō shiezaru shōchō," that symbolize nothing, where no symbolization is possible). One can make progress in a poetics that aims toward this goal, he claims, but one can never touch the goal itself, eternity. As he writes, "the goal itself makes no progress at all. Eternity itself continues, forever unchanged" (*Eien wa eikyū ni henka shinai*). He presents a temporal and linguistic paradox: on the one hand, poetry exists in time, it makes progress and develops (*shinpo suru*). But the goal of poetry, on the other hand, its aim of eternity and timelessness cannot be touched; it must exist outside of time and outside of any notion of progress.

This means that language succeeds, increasingly, in symbolizing or capturing this timeless space "in the imperfect structure of the world of meaning" (the gap in meaning or symbolization), and at the same time, as a part of this imperfect structure, language, by definition, must ultimately fail. Poetic language is a "method" that develops for creating "symbolizations" where nothing can be symbolized, in a place where even Nishiwaki's attempt to explain generates layers of terms in quotation marks (and the recurrent need to restate "in plain terms," to try once again to bring the explanation within the world of ordinary or simple "meaning").

Ōoka cites a later theoretical essay, "Poietes" (1959), in which Nishiwaki considers this problem and links the question of *mu* to Reverdy's formulation of the image:

The ultimate terrain of the poetic world consists of linking opposing elements and bringing them into harmony. That terrain is nothingness [*mu*]. The highest world of poetry is this world of nothing [*mu*]. Poetry's greatest freedom [*sharaku*, unconventionality, frankness] would be to symbolize this world of nothing. . . . The study of Zen perhaps involves this poetics of nothingness originating from Buddhism.[7]

One recalls Reverdy's formulation, reiterated by Breton and Nishiwaki, that the image is created not through a comparison but through bringing together and juxtaposing distant elements. Nishiwaki repeats a part of this formulation, naming it as the "ultimate terrain" or, more literally, the "pole" of the "world of poetry" (*shi no sekai no kyokuchi*). The idea that the world of poetry has "polar regions" and can be mapped in terms of positive and negative extremes (being or existence, *u*, and nothingness or emptiness, *kū*) is a formulation of the poetic world linking it (through Buddhist reference) to the joining of opposing elements, or the bringing of distant elements into harmony, that constituted Reverdy's understanding of the poetic image. Thus Nishiwaki's later articulation seeks to reconcile Buddhist with Surrealist poetics; it is striking, however, that now the link to Reverdy goes unspoken (need not, perhaps, be spoken) while the link to Zen and Buddhist thought, as a "poetics of nothingness," he chooses to name in explicit form.

Inoue Teruo, a poet and scholar of French literature,[8] writes of Nishiwaki that his poetry creates a world outside of time (an achronic world), a world unconcerned with temporal or historical constraints. In a space of deliberate erasure of temporal differences, memory also becomes problematic: how is it possible, in such a poetics, to recognize or construct memory? Inoue claims that, unlike the work of Baudelaire, Nishiwaki's poetry does not call upon the specificities of its historical situation, does not engage with questions of the social realities of its time; and yet, precisely in refusing to refer to them, Nishiwaki invokes in the reader the awareness of these events as an absence. In reference to the collection *Tabibito kaerazu* (No traveler returns; 1947) Inoue claims: "In the background of this mostly anachronistic landscape, which seems like a Chinese painting from the southern school, we know that some of the most violent historical events of the Showa period were whirling. Perhaps in this is a particular key to their reading."

The realm of the eternal evoked by Nishiwaki exists, in Inoue's view, precisely because of the historical and social forces whose oblivion it invokes—forgetting, or erasure, as the reverse side of recollection, of specific reference to historical moment or place. (Inoue refers to *Tabibito kaerazu*, published in 1947, and *Ushinawareta toki* [Lost time], from 1960, but one could extend this critique to Nishiwaki's earlier work as well.) Nishiwaki's poetry, written in modern Japanese poetic language, incorporating seamless paraphrases of Catullus and ancient sonnets, enacts an odd relation to social and historical time, in part through his continual process of revision and re-creation (reenactment) of his own notions of the infinite and of eternity. As Inoue describes:

The world of Nishiwaki's poetry is modern in its uses of language, and yet the landscape that unfolds there contains an achronic [timeless] myth that approaches the "zero" of eternity, rather than relating to a historical reality. [This landscape] may be considered as belonging to paganism. The eternity that appears at the end of *Ushinawareta toki* is antitemporal; it is a world that brings any interest in history to nought [*mu*]. Human beings, like the seeds of plants, exist merely as male and female attributes in a sad and desolate [*sabishii*] world. There we hear the whisper of the *dojin* [native, primitive], but we are surprised to see that the native has absolutely no interest in historical time or historical reality. A single peasant walks outside of modernity, outside of the contemporary world.[9]

Inoue contrasts this escape from historical time with the writings of Baudelaire, which profoundly influenced Nishiwaki and provided a point of reference for him. Baudelaire's depictions of the prostitute surrounded by bourgeois clients, the seductive landscape of the urban night, the bourgeois fever for riches and worldly gain, reflect, according to Inoue, an awareness of the profound changes taking place around him, a "new kind of consciousness" coming into being in the wake of events such as the July Monarchy and the revolution of 1848. Inoue sees these elements in Baudelaire's writing as part of a Judeo-Christian apocalyptic vision precisely linked to its historical moment and depending for its force on its relation to historical time.[10]

How, then, does this realm of the timeless eternal and of nothingness function in Nishiwaki's poetry? In a passage from *Tabibito kaerazu*, one finds an irruption of the questions of eternity and time, a philosophical meditation, in the midst of Nishiwaki's lines:

> Beginning at a certain time in the limitless past
> ending at a certain time in the limitless future
> the voyage of human life
> Any moment in this world
> is one moment in the time of eternity
> A single seed of grass
> is a dot in the space of eternity
> The existence of the limited is a fragment within limitless existence[11]

In the lines that precede these, Nishiwaki writes of the flow of existence in terms of an "eternal water mill," or a continual return to seed through the brief phases of flower and fruit, a metaphor that evokes a traditional poetics of ephemerality. His image of continual rebirth gains in complexity with its insistent repetition of *mi* (fruit, nut, kernel, core), a term written with the same character as *jitsu* (truth, reality, actuality, essence). According to the lines above, anything in this world must be seen as a part of the eternal: *eigō no jikan* (eternal time) and *eigō no kūkan* (eternal space). Parallel constructions expand the nuance of Nishiwaki's figures: at the beginning of two consecutive lines "mugen no kako no aru toki ni" (in the limitless past) and "mugen no mirai no aru toki ni" (in the limitless future, the infinite future) open out a kind of limitless expanse of time in which the brief phrase, the element of limit, can intervene: *jinmei no tabi* (the voyage of human life). Its seven-syllable form also, subtly, invokes the recollection of a tradition (a moment in the history) of poetic limits, a fragment of the rhythmic division of *waka* form. "Dot," "moment," and "fragment" are all evoked by the repeated term "one [single] part" (*ichibubun*) in Nishiwaki's lines. The emphasis is on the calculation of a single part or fragment of an eternal, infinite realm.

The single grain of grass seed is superimposed on more abstract con-

cepts (a moment in time, a fragment of existence) and becomes a meto-
nym for them. It is thus a question of more than merely seeds and flowers
when at the end of the stanza Nishiwaki writes:

> Young waterbirds fly off
> Seeking not the seed but the flower
> Yet the flower itself seeks the seed
> It is no more than a flower that exists for the sake of the seed

"A flower that exists for the sake of the seed" (*mi no tame no hana*): in this
landscape whose plants are framed as a part of the tradition of birds' memories (the poem asks, "kotori no tsuioku no dentō ka"; "is it the tradition of
small birds' memories"), the birds' names take their place beside the remembered plant names ("old plum tree, myrtle / evergreen oak, camellia
flower / bamboo grass" and "bush warblers, buntings") in a kind of catalogue of pointed specificity. Beyond evoking the particular species of plants
and birds, this list seems to bring before our eyes moments of the "particular" or limited universe that is to be understood as a small part or fragment in eternal space or time. The groups of birds that apprehend, or re-
member, along with the tradition of their memories, become symbols for a
larger realm: the names are like grains or seeds, moments or fragments of
existence, in the infinite space of language's possibilities. The poem dra-
matizes the expanse of these possibilities by the very rarity of the names it
specifies and their seeming lack of motivation or explanation—the arbitrariness of these particular details. The seed that is identified with the
"kernel, essence, core" (*mi* 實) can be read as a figure for the unmotivated
word, category, or idea, while the "flower" may be seen as the object one
wants and searches for ("seeking the flower," perhaps, of meaning, or coherence) that ultimately exists only for the sake of this seed, kernel, essence
of arbitrariness ("the flower exists for the sake of the seed")—the seed represented by the character that also means the "real" or "actual" (*jitsu*).

   In elaborating the contrast between flower and seed, Nishiwaki alludes to a tradition of aesthetic and metaphoric uses of the flower to describe an artistic blossoming (in contrast to the seed, which is related variously to the core of feeling in the heart, or to mastery of technique); yet the
terms he develops here and in his earlier poems overwrite these allusions
with their own complex matrix. He does not use precisely the terms of
the *Kokinshū* preface (which refers to "seeds" in the heart and "leaves of
words"); nor does he use *hana* (flower), for example, quite as Zeami em-

ploys it to describe the art of blooming and fading, as a critical principle of Noh dramatic performance. Nonetheless, his descriptions gain in richness through the resonance of a slight echo of these precedents in his lines. In his description of the flower and the seed in *Fūshikaden* (Style and the flower, 1400) Zeami, too, alludes to an earlier variant on this trope, quoting a Chinese Buddhist hymn:

> Before [an actor] can know the flower, he must know the seed. The flower blooms from imagination; the seed represents merely the various skills of our art. In the words of an ancient sage [Huineng]:
>
>> The mind-ground contains the various seeds,
>> With the all-pervading rain each and every one sprouts.
>> Once one has suddenly awakened to the sentiency of the
>>   flower,
>> The fruit of enlightenment matures of itself.[12]

In Zeami's use of this twenty-character Chinese poem, the seed is placed at the basis of skills of performance, and the flower becomes a "blooming of the imagination," a mature moment of art that grows out of it, comparable to Buddhist enlightenment. Possessing only the flower without the seed, a Noh actor (according to Zeami) would not have attained the "true flower" and his art would fade as quickly as it blooms. One senses here the connection between the "flower seeking the seed" or the "flower existing only for the seed," the principle elaborated in Nishiwaki's poem. Yet even as Nishiwaki plays into the aesthetic traditions that overdetermine the uses of the terms of flower and seed, he chooses the term *mi* (for seed, or fruit, rather than *tane*, or any of the other possible variants) in relation to *hana*, thereby setting up his own oppositional terms (not identical to Zeami's).[13] In the course of his long sequence of poems in *Tabibito kaerazu*, Nishiwaki performs the overwriting of the tradition into his own poetic vocabulary (deliberately including botanical names beyond the traditional poetic diction) so that one is forced to come to terms with his specific development of the metaphors of the flower and seed/fruit/essence. Thus, in poem 165 of *Tabibito kaerazu*, one sees Nishiwaki's transition from the use of *tane* 種 ("tane wa futatabi tane ni naru," seed becomes seed once again) to the pronunciation *mi* placed alongside the character for fruit (果 *ka*, which also means end, limit, completion; *hate*, the same character used by Huineng), arriving eventually at the *mi* that the poem settles on (*jitsu/mi*: seed, core, essence, actuality). The poem, in a brief expanse, passes through the tradition of this trope (as "the water flows, the wheel turns") before settling into its own space, like the departure of the young waterbirds on their search for the flower (for the flowers that seek the seed, that exist for the sake of the seed).

Walter Benjamin writes in the preface to the *Origin of German Trag- edy* that the "father of philosophy" was "not Plato but Adam," because he gave things their names.[14] This naming, central to the origins of philoso- phy for Benjamin, is also a crucial factor for Nishiwaki—in his collecting of details and names, as well as in his tracing and reenactment of a version of the history of those names. This history, then, becomes one manifesta- tion of the finite world that must be comprehended within the "limitless" expanse of language and eternity.

Nishiwaki's use of the term *mi* (with its undercurrent of *jitsu*, actual- ity), and the structure of his description of the "moment in the limitless past" and the "moment in the limitless future," seem to resonate within a mode of philosophical discourse or a "translated" mode, as opposed to the smoother, more traditionally "poetic" mode of the lines that touch on the "water birds," flowing water, or gardens. Nishiwaki was criticized by fellow avant-garde poets such as Kitasono Katsue for smoothing out his language in his later poetry into a more traditional style, for having lost his "mod- ernist edge." Yet in subtle ways these poems continue to hover between more traditional Japanese (and Chinese) poetic or allusive modes and a philosophical contemplation that retains links to Western philosophical questions of language, eternity, truth, and existence in memory.

At least in the case of this poem one cannot conclude that Nishiwaki comes down, finally, on either one side or the other (although by 1947, this division itself is problematic, a trace or lingering myth of a clear division that once was to have existed). The language of the poem, though clearly marked as modern, seeks to escape finite space or "real" location, as Inoue Teruo writes: "The landscape that unfolds there contains an achronic [timeless] myth that approaches the 'zero' of eternity." The "paganism" that Inoue identifies in Nishiwaki's words is neither "Eastern" nor "West- ern"—it evades Christian temporality or reference to apocalypse; yet, in the beginning of the poem the references to *tsuchi* (soil) and the return to seed ("seed returns to seed") do evoke the Biblical lines "man's origin is dust and his end is dust." The world of continual rebirth in the plants' metaphor contains its Buddhist aspect as well. Nishiwaki's poetic world

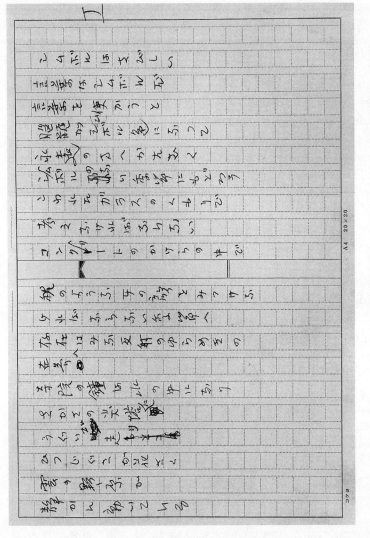

8. Nishiwaki Junzaburō, opening lines of *Eternitasu* (Aeternitas), handwritten manuscript courtesy of Kanagawa Museum of Modern Literature, by permission of Nishiwaki Jun'ichi.

creates its own fabric of woven allusions (with greater or lesser degrees of recognizability), and it is not, finally, a question of determining an allegiance to some vision of Eastern or Western poetics. Yet this question persists in the background, undeterminable but insistent, particularly due to the changes in Nishiwaki's vocabulary from its early clear alliance with (or some might even say, origins in) Western poetics (from Latin elegies to Surrealist love poetry) to his postwar reediting of his collection *Ambarvalia* in the smoother, more traditional poetic diction and style of the later version, retitled *Amubaruwaria*.[15] There could be several explanations for the fact that these modifications coincide chronologically with the war, and the change is not unilateral or universal. Yet the events that lie in the background of such a transformation may contain a key to their reading, even if one must only point out the absence of allusion to these changes in Nishiwaki's poetics within the poems themselves, and their insistence on the eternal continuity of space and time—their placement of the specificity of events and moments, objects and words of poetry, in relation to this larger continuum that the poems themselves seek to attain.

What is the relation of Nishiwaki's poetic theories to his poems? How is it possible to use his own writings about his attempt to symbolize "the highest possible realm of poetry," as embodied in the world of *mu* (nothingness), in order to understand the vision elaborated in his poetry? In the opening lines of his 1962 collection *Eterunitasu* (*Aeternitas*), he writes:

> Symbols are sad [lonely/desolate]
> Words are symbols
> When I use words
> My brain turns symbol colored
> and leans toward eternity
> Let me return to the season of no symbols
> I must think
> Through the mist on a broken glass

> Shimuboru wa sabishii
> kotoba wa shimuboru da
> kotoba wo tsukau to
> nōzui ga shimuboru iro ni natte
> eien no hō e katamuku
> shimuboru no nai kisetsu ni modorō
> kowareta garasu no kumori de
> kangaenakereba naranai[16]

From the foreign loan word *shimuboru* (symbol) Nishiwaki moves into the realm of poetic loneliness, sadness (*sabishii*); from words and symbols in the intellect (*nōzui*, brain) he slips into a poetic vocabulary of colors ("my brain turns symbol colored"), and this leads him into the realm of eternity ("and leans toward eternity"). He seems to write here about the process of poetic composition itself as a subjective experience ("When I use words"), simultaneously describing a poetics of the intellect and elaborating a subjective theory of poetry. The relation between Nishiwaki's *aeternitas* and the world of symbols is intimate, yet it passes through the "glass" of the poetic image (alternatively, "in [with] the cloudiness of broken glass, I must think," "Kowareta garasu no kumori de / kangaenakereba naranai"). While his thinking must pass through a mist, he "must think" not only with the "intellect" (already itself colored by symbols) but also with or through a poetic image, itself simultaneously a symbol, transparent, and an object, misted over and not susceptible to being seen through. Thus the mist (or frost) of broken glass becomes a symbol of "symbols," somehow sad and colored over like the clarity of the brain it tints and influences.

Ōoka Makoto writes of the paradoxical relation between Nishiwaki's poetry and theoretical writings:

The best writings on Nishiwaki's poetry are the poetic theories of Nishiwaki himself; and the opposite is also true [his own poems are the best comment on his poetic theories]. But this is not to say that each supplies a lack in the other. . . . His poems are themselves poetic theories and his poetic theories are themselves works of poetry. And yet it is not that the two are mirrors of one another. . . . What is the mirror trying to reflect? It is trying to reflect that thing called "eternity."[17]

A similar ambivalent reciprocity appears when one tries to understand the relation of Nishiwaki's poetry to Surrealist thought in Japan. Although, as mentioned earlier, Nishiwaki himself was central to introducing Surrealist thought in Japan and fostering the group of students who became known as Surrealists, his own relation to Surrealism was complex. In his attempts to resolve this difficulty, he often considered Surrealism as a part of the larger ("eternal") project of poetry, which he traced back through an aesthetics that incorporated Surrealism but also extended to aspects of the writings of Francis Bacon, Dryden, Pope, Coleridge, Apuleius, and Homer. He writes: "Today's Dadaism is firmly founded on classical aesthetic theory . . . the spirit of the pure art [of Surrealism] is a classical one."[18] Expounding with seriousness on the nature of poetry and its dangers, he also

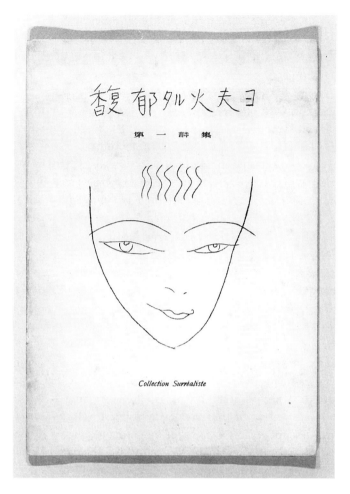

9. Cover of *Fukuikutaru kafu yo* (Ah, fragrant stoker). "Collection surréaliste," December 1927. Courtesy of Kanagawa Museum of Modern Literature.

revels in moments of irony; Nishiwaki's irony, present in both his poetry and critical writings, further complicates their relation and the comment they make on one another. Already in his contributions to the "Surrealist Collection" issue of *Fukuikutaru kafu yo* (Ah, fragrant stoker), one can observe the evolution of his idea of language pressing against its own limits, the search for "nothingness" and the "poles of the poetic world" that he elaborates in his later theories.

Even in the time between the first publication of the poem "Fukui-kutaru kafu yo" (1927) and its inclusion in "Le Monde moderne" section of *Ambarvalia* (1933), Nishiwaki made numerous small changes. The re-writing becomes more extreme in *Amubaruwaria* (1947), in which the poem appears for a third time, with many of the same images but a complete metamorphosis of poetic style—the poem is divided into twenty-six stanza sections, rather than its original prose-poem arrangement, and the diction is significantly changed. Yet even to examine the very first "layer" of transformations Nishiwaki made in this Surrealist poem, from its 1927 publication to the 1933 version, reveals central problems related to the striking change in his poetics, and his evolving relation to Surrealism.

In the 1927 version, Nishiwaki includes a preface that describes his concepts of pure poetry, of Surrealism, and the significance of the "fragrant stoker" of the title. The preface begins with the Latin sentence, "Cerebrum ad acerram recidit" (the mind sinks into the incense box [fragrance]). Resembling the opening to his *Surrealist Poetics* (*Chōgenjitsushugi shiron*, 1929), the preface goes on to describe "reality" as a function of the brain or intellect (*nōzui*). The breaking apart or abolition of the intellect becomes the means of access to the realm of the surreal. Nishiwaki writes: "The world of reality is no more than the mind. To break out of the mind is the goal of Surrealist art." The term *yaburu* (to break, rend, crush, defeat, shatter) is also used by Nishiwaki in describing the breaking down of custom for the intensification of the experience of reality. (In *Surrealist Poetics*, Nishiwaki describes reality as banal or monotonous, and it is habit or custom that must be broken to make reality exciting again: "shūkan wo yaburu koto wa genjitsu wo omoshiroku suru koto ni naru.")

The shattering of the mind is figured in the image of broken glass in the 1927 preface: "This is pure poetry. The mind becomes like an ultra-peach-colored glass. And poetry breaks the mind in this way. The broken mind is extremely fragrant, like a smashed tank of perfume."[19] In "pure poetry," the mind becomes "like an ultra-peach-colored glass" that poetry then crushes, releasing scent. This image seems to link to the Latin words of the opening: "the mind sinks into the incense box [fragrance]." What has changed from this broken glass, dyed ultra-peach color (again, neither transparent nor opaque), to the lament in the lines of *Eterunitasu* (thirty-five years later): "When I use words, my brain turns symbol colored" (nōzui ga shimuboru iro ni natte) and "I must think with the frost of broken glass"? The central question of the mind, its relation to words, and the emptying out of the mind to a state of transparency—images that were central to Nishiwaki's understanding of the project of Surrealist art—remain critical to his conception of poetry in *Eterunitasu* as well. The language and diction with which Nishiwaki constructs these images, however, have transformed radically, from "a thing like ultra-peach-colored glass" (*urutora-momoiro no garasu no gotoki mono*) to "with the mist of broken glass" (*kowareta garasu no kumori de*). On the most apparent level, Nishiwaki has moved closer to a conventional Japanese poetic diction: the later line does not have the mark (or "scent") of Japanese avant-garde poetics as embodied in the very awkwardness of such a term as *urutora-momoiro* (ultra-peach-colored) or the staggered rhythm of the continually repeated comparative link *no gotoki* (the mind is *like* glass, and poetry breaks it *as such*). There is a certain gentleness in the language of the later poem, which makes the earlier one appear more cerebral and hard-edged by comparison, even as both poems attempt to critique the cerebral aspect of reality, and (in the case of the earlier version) invoke the world of Surrealist art and sublime poetry to empty the mind or intellect, to break it (and later, to burn it: "Poetry is that which can combust the mind," "Mata shi wa nōzui wo nenshō seshimuru mono de aru").

With the disappearance of the *yo* from the 1933 title (which had made the title like an address to the fragrant stoker) and the editing out of its manifesto-like preface, the poetic world of Nishiwaki already begins to soften in its adamant tone. The search for the infinite, and for the void, remains strong in his later poems, but the shout ("fukuikutaru kafu yo!") has given way to a more cyclical sense of quest, like the movement from seed to flower to fruit. Unlike the preface of the earlier version, with its discourse on the nature of pure poetry, the 1927 poem itself undermines a narrative or discursive reading—it reflects a dispersed imagery that defies the attempt to read it in coherence. Typographically, the poem takes the form of many short prose paragraphs; instead of the open circle to end sentences that one finds in the second version in *Ambarvalia*, the first version has the closed period of a Western sentence, and the lines are printed horizontally from left to right. Thus it has a very different visual effect from the vertical lines, with Japanese punctuation as the poem appeared in *Ambarvalia*. One's first instinct upon reading the second version of "Fukuikutaru kafu" is to say, along with critics like Kitasono, that Nishiwaki has retreated from the strangeness of his own Japanese writing; he has tried to normalize the lines of his poem, to bring them closer to some kind of coherence or comprehensibility.

For example, in the 1927 version the last line reads: "kitaran ka" (Are you coming? [Is it coming? or not?]). The question is absolutely open, and one has no reason to believe that it should relate to the paragraph that precedes it, since none of the other paragraphs have any clear or certain relation to one another. The subject of the verb is not specified, and the invitation, if it is an invitation, or the speculation (it is coming, you are coming) has no antecedent, no certainty. Hence, when in the revised version Nishiwaki adds to it, "kitaran ka, hi yo" (Are you coming, fire? [Is the fire coming? Come, fire]), the pure openness of the invitation or question (and its resulting strangeness) is disturbed, pushed in the direction of coherence. The fire would evoke the fire that the "fragrant stoker" tends and stirs, that fire which in the preface would be identified with pure poetry, poetry that "combusts the mind." The "I" (*ware*) in the rest of the poem, then, through the addition of this single word, becomes more closely identified with the *kafu* (stoker). If in the last line of the poem, the lyric voice, ambiguous though it is, attempts to call upon the fire, then (given the poem's title) these words bring the poem full circle. After the difficult and complex images that intervene, a certain reassuring (if still delusive) sense of closure is achieved in the brief link back to the image of fire, and the directness of the address, "Are you coming? / Come, fire."

One would thus be tempted to conclude simply that Nishiwaki has moved in the direction of poetic closure; but considering the two versions together, one might as easily say that the very presence of the invocation of fire in the later version reinforces, or helps to construct, an increased sense of strangeness in the first version, in retrospect. In other words, one can appreciate the purity and openness of this first invitation ("kitaran ka") more fully if one is aware of the mention of the fire, as it limits the possibilities, in the second version. The explicit *yo* (*hi yo*) added to the ending seems to appear as the ghost of the *yo* lost from the title of the first version, and the poem, instead of invoking the person of the stoker, invokes the fire; the speaking subject becomes identified with the stoker. In other words, one might claim that the "empty space" in the first version signifies as strongly as it does now in part because of the existence of the later version; the later version allows the reader to experience actively the daring aspect, the risk taken, in the first version's silence. In a sense then, the 1933 version with its editions, or rather, the horizon between the two, *makes* the first version into a Surrealist poem, more explicitly and emphatically even than it was at first: it becomes a poem in touch with silences, with some kind of a void, a poem that can address the void shorthand.

One might pursue this question of legibility and the transformations in the poem's language within the words that precede the ending: "There is something reflected on the surface of a flower vase. It is the heel [footsteps] of Pietro [Pierrot?] who is returning from dinner. Deeply moved, I try to see this but [it is] too amaranth." A disorienting image, in which (the sound or sight of) Pierrot's heel is reflected in the surface of a flower vase; again, one finds clear and grammatically flowing sentences with a meaning that defies visualization. What would it mean for something (a vision? myself? being moved?) to be "too amaranth" (*amari ni amaranto de aru*)? Amaranth (French: *amarante*), a purplish flower, appears in the first edition of *Surrealist Poetics*, in an epigraph from Rimbaud.[20] In the 1933 version of "Fukuikutaru kafu," the image of the flower vase and Pierrot returning from dinner remains unchanged, but Nishiwaki edits the reaction: "amari ni amaranto no *me* de aru" (the *eyes* are too amaranth). In other words, although he adds only a single word, and the second version still does not explain what it would mean to be "too amaranth," it does reduce the ambiguity slightly: it is not the object seen nor the feeling of being moved that is "too amaranth," but only the eyes; the addition implies a viewer or observer of the scene.

Nishiwaki has moved one small but significant step away from the more open phrase, in the direction of a vision that would obey or imply some logical order. Does this addition reassure or make the line more "legible"? Only for a moment—while it seems to clarify the distinction between the observing subject and the odd vision he observes (Pierrot, the vase), it does not, in the end, change the disorienting vision itself. In other words, in his attempt to "translate" his earlier Surrealist vision into a more pointed poetic vision (by reinforcing the lyric subject ever so subtly as a category), he makes the first poem more radical in retrospect, now that one can see precisely how fleeting and tenuous its original images were by comparison. Part of the significance of this observation comes from the fact that nearly all the changes and additions move in this direction. A careful analysis reveals this process subtly at work in numerous instances in the revised version. In the line "When the makeup runs and gets into the eyes, I call the servant," one finds the term "servant" in the first version written with the single character *shimobe* (which can also be read *boku*, another term for "I"). The parenthetical reading (*shimobe*) that follows in katakana clarifies the reading, that it is not "I" but a servant. In the second version, the replacement of *shimobe* by the two-character term *jūboku* (also meaning servant) takes away that moment of ambivalence, the suggestion and subsequent erasure (by the reading in parentheses) of coincidence between the servant and the self. While it clarifies, it also effaces the uncertainty that enlivened the earlier line.

At another point, the earlier version reads, "Suddenly, an acacia flower! I drank eau de cologne, and yet—goodbye" ("Kotsuzentaru akashia no hana yo! Ware wa odokoron wo nomitari shikashisaraba"). In the later version the line becomes, "I drank eau de cologne. Farewell, oh death!" ("Ware wa odokoron wo nonda. Shi yo saraba!") The simplification of punctuation and action seems to make the phrase more definitive, and yet, in a sense, it moves the whole in the direction of dramatic parody. The clarification of death for the goodbye is perhaps less interesting because it is closer to being a simple "nonsense" image; does he die by drinking eau de cologne? By specifying "death" in the single short line, Nishiwaki lightens the strange resonance and sense of limitlessness in the earlier version. *Saraba* (goodbye, if so) seems to imply the cutting off of a relation: in the earlier line, is he breaking off relations with the flower by drinking its artifice (eau de cologne)? The first version contains the term *kotsuzen* (suddenly) and repeats the same character in the word *shikashi* (and yet); it seems to contain its own verbal logic, its own internal link (or automatism) through the repetition of the character. Changing this to *shi yo* (oh, death) eliminates this link, even while clarifying the break (as having to do with death).

What spurs Nishiwaki's drive to edit and impose limits on the language? One might consider the words "all too amaranth" (*amari ni amaranto*) which function so strongly in the first version in part because of the spare repetition of the sounds; the resonant term marking excess *amari ni* (too much, excessively) seems to be contained in the transcribed French term *amaranto* (amaranth), and the homophony overdetermines the phrase with the meaning "an excess of excess," the exceeding of something beyond. This excess, detached from any referent or antecedent (eyes, objects) radically opens the poetic field to the invitation that follows, itself without a clear object of address (*kitaran ka*, is it coming?). The impulse to construct limits on the meanings, to clarify the language of the poem, seems both an impulse of careful explanation and a painful attempt to approach some kind of limit, to curtail the excess. The effort is related to Nishiwaki's desire to "symbolize eternity," to contain (and control) in words that unsymbolizable, boundless space. At the same time, he seems to realize that the increase of language only renders that which he seeks farther away, as he writes in *Eterunitasu*: "When I use words / My mind turns symbol colored / and leans toward eternity . . . / Let me return to the season of no symbols." Paradoxically, the attempt to catch "eternity," to grasp timelessness in words, drives what he seeks elsewhere, if only, strangely, back more forcefully into the lines of his earlier Surrealist poem.

As if to emphasize the ever renewed quest for "eternity," the latest postwar edition of the poem (1947) ends with a new stanza not present in any of the earlier ones:

> The crack [crevice] in the soil
> dream of a meteorite
> fragment of eternity
>
> tsuchi no wareme
> inseki no yume
> eien no kakera [21]

Naming "eternity" explicitly, Nishiwaki clarifies the quest that pervaded the earlier poems as well; the effect, however, gives one the sense that perhaps the quest they explain ("dream of meteorite / fragment of eternity") is already fulfilled in the oblique touches that appear in the earlier poem. As the lyric subject (in the first version) tries to make his voice heard, he describes: "I kneel down, but eternity is so noisy" (*hizamazukitaredomo eikyū [tokoshie] wa amari ni kamabisushi*). Again, *amari ni* appears in relation to eternity; eternity is "all too noisy." Eternity, already hovering at the margins of the earlier version, amid the noise, becomes the central theme of the later poem, much quieted. And yet what emerges instead is an elaboration, in the interval between the two poems, of the relation of symbols and words to the self, and the articulation of this relation over time. Perhaps in spite of himself, Nishiwaki leaves a comment on change and temporality as much as on timelessness. In his very interaction with his own poetry over time, one can perhaps best observe his relation to time, to events, to cycles, to memory. Stretching toward eternity, he allows us to see better, through his changes, the Surrealist project that he finally abandons in his late poetry, but which seems to refuse to abandon him.

In this sense, then, perhaps the functioning of the past in memory can be compared to the pursuit of eternity in Nishiwaki's language. One recalls the description by Walter Benjamin in "Theses on the Philosophy of History": "The true picture of the past flits by. The past can be seized only as an image which just flashes up at the instant of its recognizability and is never seen again."[22] The past is recognizable only for a moment, and then, much as one might try to chase it, it is no longer available for recognition. Like the word "eternity" in the midst of a piece of (noisy) "automatic writing," it seems that eternity is not susceptible to control or revision, but appears for the duration of a flash, its instant of recognizability.

Margaret Cohen points out that Benjamin's vision of memory here, in which the past is recognizable for only a moment, approaches very closely Benjamin's definition of Surreality as well. Benjamin describes the "Now of *recognizability*, in which things put on their true—Surrealist—face."[23] Something that appears only for an instant, only at the moment it can be recognized, reveals its own Surrealist aspect. Surreality is framed here in terms of the "putting on" of a face (almost as if it were a mask, a costume): a "Surrealist face" becomes at once a kind of costume, a facial expression, and a revelation of the "true" or underlying way of things. The poem "Fukuikutaru kafu yo" describes many parts of a face (head, palate, mouth, neck, chin, forehead, eyes), such that this becomes a unifying element of the poem—almost as though Nishiwaki were himself in search of a moment of the "Surrealist face" of things. Perhaps one can employ a similar metaphor for the various layers and faces of Nishiwaki's Surrealist poetics, his multiple revisions and delvings in his search for the "flash" of the timeless, the moment of eternity within the ever-transforming, ever-limited expanse of time.

Eternity, like "Surreality," seems to be a flash, and the more Nishiwaki chases it, the more his historicity and temporal transformations are made explicit. Similarly, Surrealism (and its projects), while its particular faces change and it moves from one place to another, nonetheless has a paradoxical continuity or persistence through these transformations. There are many names and many faces of Surrealism in Japan, some of which have survived to gain recognition while others have been nearly forgotten. This study only begins to touch on the prominent figures of Japanese Surrealism and examines only a fragment of the works that could have been included under the rubric of these poetic ideas. Recorded in the journals that remain are the works of any number of others, each with differing views and expressions of what Surreality might mean and the ways in which its language might be employed.

ALLEGORIES OF FORGETFULNESS: TOMOTANI SHIZUE

European Surrealism has often been criticized for its hypermasculine milieu and its marginalization of women artists, even amid the pervasive representations of women in Surealist art and writings. More recently, scholars have delved into the contributions of the women associated with European Surrealism and discovered many fascinating unrecorded aspects of the movement. What follows represents only a brief "flash" or glimpse of the faces of two women associated with the Surrealist movement in Japan. In the course of my research I was struck by the near absence of women in critical works on the avant-garde movements and was intrigued by the few women who participated in these movements from their earliest stages. Tomotani Shizue in particular stands out as the one woman writer who was present at the very start, writing in *Ishō no taiyō* in 1929. Later, Ema Shōko and several others were associated with the journals *Madame Blanche* and *VOU*—Kitasono Katsue encouraged and included a more significant number of women writers in his coterie.

Although the following text only begins this alternative trajectory of analysis, I hope it may initiate a partial revision of the movement's legacies by considering how Tomotani and Ema elaborate their own perspectives on issues of eternity, dreaming, and forgetfulness. The performance they are engaged in with relation to European avant-garde elements seems to reflect, in my view, a particular and telling ambivalence about issues of inclusion and distance, nostalgia and remembrance.

Tomotani Shizue (1898–1991), born in Osaka, was one of the few early Surrealists who signed her work with her original name. After graduating from girls' school, she moved to Tokyo as a boarder in the house of the writer Tamura Ayako and continued her studies at Sakurai Private English School. She became associated with the magazine *Hansen* (Sailing ship), and in 1925 she collaborated with Hayashi Fumiko (1903–1951) to produce a privately published poetry collection *Futari* (Two of us).[24] Later in her career Tomotani became involved in the Futurist movement. She published several collections of poetry and a book of essays: *Umi ni nageta hana* (Flower thrown in the sea, 1940), *Aoi tsubasa* (Blue wings), *Hana to tettō* (Flower and steel tower), and others.[25]

On April 1, 1929, in the fifth issue of the Surrealist periodical *Ishō no taiyō* (The costume's sun), Tomotani published two brief texts entitled "Vaudeville" and "Tenshi wa ai no tame ni naku" (Angels cry for love). The group that produced *Ishō no taiyō* (six issues; November 1928–July 1929) was formed from two other groups of Surrealist writers in Tokyo, those who had produced the journal *Shōbi, majutsu, gakusetsu* (Rose, magic, theory) and the students of Nishiwaki Junzaburō who had collaborated on *Fukuikutaru kafu yo.* Thus the poets whose early writings are brought together in *Ishō no taiyō* include most of the later leaders of the Surrealist movement in Japan and the prominent poets within the avant-garde literary scene, including Takiguchi Shūzō, Kitasono Katsue, Nishiwaki Junzaburō, and Ueda Toshio.

"Vaudeville" retains a French (or English) title written in roman letters:

Vaudeville

[*Abana*] and [*fua-fua*] flow on for eternity
Moonlight illuminates red snow—women's feathered diadems
                    tangle in disarray
They fight brandishing shields of huge flowers
They will not be wounded, no matter what
Upon the backs of swans they sleep
Brilliant as flagships are the dreams they have[26]

The first two words of the poem, in katakana (suggesting foreign proper nouns, or onomatopoeic description), create an immediate mystery; the word *abana* (Urbana?) suggests the name of some foreign place (perhaps a river), and *fua-fua* sounds like a fanfare or the onomatopoeic term for something floating, fluffed in air; like the flowing sounds of a foreign tongue, these unreadable opening words seem to "flow on for [or toward] eternity" (*eigō ni nagareru*). The poem's descriptions seem to evoke actresses in a theatrical performance or night club burlesque, with their "feathered diadems." On the front cover of this issue is a burlesque or

10. Covers of *Ishō no taiyō* (The costume's sun). *Left*: February 1, 1929. *Right*: April 1, 1929. Reprinted (Tokyo: Tamura shoten) 1987, by permission of Hashimoto Akio.

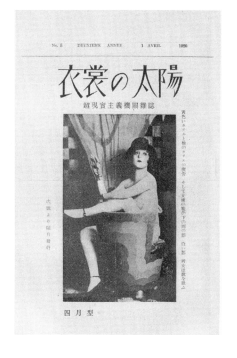

vaudeville dancer, in top hat and dark lipstick, bare shoulders, seated backward on a chair. The source of the image is unacknowledged, but the photograph is probably taken (without permission) from a French or German art magazine.[27]

The "they" who appear in every line of this poem other than the first are a conspicuously feminine and plural subject—*kanojo-tachi wa*, an odd-sounding term, so emphatic that it seems almost awkward in the grammar of the Japanese poem (particularly as it is repeated five times). The repetition of the term connotes a foreign poetic structure: the specificity of *kanojo-tachi* as a poetic subject suggests a translation of the French pronoun *elles*. One can sense in Tomotani Shizue's insistent use of this feminine plural the appeal she found in such an idea: the rhythm it creates breaks apart the smooth flow of her poetic phrase. Intrusive, it speaks of a poetic aim that would avoid smoothness, gentleness, subtly evocative imagery—this feminine plural protrudes, grammatically, from her lines (in a way that the English "they" cannot reproduce). The women depicted here seem to be out at night (the moonlight illuminates red snow, recalling a Toulouse-Lautrec Paris night scene); they wear feathered diadems (*umō no kammuri*) in a disarray (*midareru*) that carries an erotic suggestion; one might recall the term as used in the title of Yosano Akiko's collection of love tanka, *Midaregami* (Tangled hair) from 1901.

If we were to attempt to read the image of the fight that Tomotani evokes in the next few lines, we find that here the women appear as determined, struggling. The repetition of *kanojo-tachi* at the beginning of the line, though syntactically unnecessary for the meaning, underscores this subjective determination ("They fight brandishing shields of huge flowers / They will not be wounded, no matter what," "Kyodai na hana no tate wo furikazashi, kanojo-tachi wa tatakau / Kanojo-tachi wa kesshite fushō shinai"). But the fight they are engaged in is a theatrical one, with feathered costumes and flowers for shields. On the one hand, one can read this then as "not serious," as a fight taking place on theatrical grounds, a burlesque, a vaudeville; but perhaps, for a Surrealist poet, this may be the stage (among huge flowered shields, feathered diadems) upon which a battle with conventional modes of thought and language, of dress and acceptable modes of feminine behavior could take its proper place. The women dress in feathered clothes; they lash out and fight; they will not be wounded no matter what.

One might, however, see the women as remaining distant figures, stubbornly in the third person, at a certain remove: a collective, but not a "we" in which the speaker would explicitly be able to join. And the fight takes place through an intransitive verb: there is no direct object or enemy in the fight explicitly named. In the last two lines we see the sudden transition of the spectacle to sleep: "Upon the backs of swans they sleep" (*Kanojo-tachi wa hakuchō no se no ue ni nemuru*). Sleep, within Surrealist visions, has been associated with poetic creation—yet again one finds the ambiguity in the depiction of their role. "Brilliant as flagships are the dreams they have": they lead the battalions, their dreams are bright and splendid, in a loud, almost gaudy kind of dream; and the dreams are not "seen" (*yume wo miru*) as would be one of the expected expressions for dreaming, but possessed (*motsu*: have, hold, grasp, cling). Their brilliant dreams, as bright as flagships, push ahead in some figurative battle and will not easily be relinquished by this sleeping troupe. Still, the structure of the vision remains a dream, and what flows on "for eternity" remains illegible, something unknown and distant that cannot be grasped. The *kanojo-tachi* of the vaudeville may finally constitute an untouchable ideal for the implied speaker of the poem.

Rather than attempting to determine the place of these *kanojo-tachi* as at home or distanced in a foreign land (or deciding whether the theatrical stage upon which their fight takes place disengages it from danger, or places the danger in a different, performative realm) one can read the ambivalent desire of the speaker in this poem. Although the battle is fought with tousled diadems and flowered shields, it remains fundamental, encompassing the right to dream vivid dreams and to express them loudly and flagrantly (like the public dreaming of this sole woman poet in the all-male Surrealist magazine). And perhaps in breaking apart the syntax of her poetic language with foreign words (*abana*, "vaudeville") and grammatical constructions (the insistent naming of the feminine plural subject) this poem itself allows Tomotani to participate in the dream she is constructing.

A second poem in the same issue of *Ishō no taiyō*, opposite "Vaudeville," is the brief text of "Tenshi wa ai no tame ni naku" (Angels cry for love):

Even statues of alabaster gods may flow away like water
Hatred for destiny intoxicates me like opium
Because shellfish spew brine, are they unworthy of love?
No one remembers forever the instant of a beautiful sacrifice[28]

The poem opens with an image of gods in alabaster statues, suggesting Egyptian deities. Not only are the gods themselves not immortal here, but even their statues (or images), presumed to last forever, may (the poem claims) flow away, flow off, as swiftly as the waters. (*Sekka-sekkō no kami-gami no zō sae mo mizu no yō ni nagaresaru de arō*.) Thus the *unmei* (fate, destiny) implied in this context is the destiny of dying or of disappearing completely (even one's image) like water, without a trace. The speaker in the poem (*wata[ku]shi*) is intoxicated with hatred for this destiny: it intoxicates "like opium." The angel (*tenshi*) of the title is a recurring figure in *Ishō no taiyō*: one recalls the figure of a pencil-drawn top-hatted angel with an elongated eye, labeled *l'ange* by Kitasono Katsue in this issue, or the story by Fujiwara Sei'ichi which begins with the lines: "The angel set off the cannon. . . . Between the rose and the rose, like the nest of a small bird, was the white nest of the angel. . . . I eat the nest of angels."[29] The *ai* (love) for whose sake the angels cry in the poem's title also connotes a modern concept of "love" (this is not the *koi* or *iro* of traditional erotics). This *ai* returns in the third line: "Because shellfish spew brine / are they unworthy of love?" The lowly creatures emit (exhale, vomit, spit up) mere brine: does this make them unworthy of love? (And can this exhaling, this brine, be read as a figure for the poet's production?) Again in the lines is a resistance to the way the universe is ordered: not only shells but even gods made of alabaster will pass away ultimately—nothing lasts.

The closing line adds, "No one remembers forever the instant of a beautiful sacrifice" (*Utsukushiki kenshin no shunkan wo taremo eien ni kioku shinai no de aru*). The only thing that "flows on forever" in this poem is forgetfulness itself. In the last line, self-sacrifice, *kenshin* (also devotion, dedication, selflessness) is beautiful but does not guarantee that one will be remembered, at least not forever (the sacrifice lasts only an instant). If one were to read this within the context of the title, perhaps the selfless devotion of love is what the angels are crying for (or mourning), and, by extension, for the ephemerality of memory, for the great and small deeds and creatures forgotten. In terms of gender, this *kenshin*, which can also connote the mother's devotion to a child, or a self-sacrificing, devoted love (commonly associated with women), may be beautiful, the poem says, but will not ultimately be remembered—by anyone at all—although in these terms no cause, in a sense, is any more worthy than the shellfish spewing up brine. Nonetheless, there is the subtle possibility of protest suggested within the lines: the angels do, after all, "cry for love," and the speaker becomes drunk with abhorrence for fate.

The possibilities of protest are an issue in another poem by Tomotani, explicitly titled "Resistance" (*Teikō*). The poem was published in her first collection, *Umi ni nageta hana* (Flower thrown in the sea).[30] We encounter these lines: "All around me, / The clocks making an insipid sound of poverty, / Every single one of the old clocks, / I want to wrench them all apart with a violent twist." It may be possible, the poem suggests, after destroying all the clocks, to envision some way of being beyond time, beyond circumstance, as the poem continues: "I want to stand cold like a marble column / I want to fly through the pure white space like a brave cannonball / I want to become a huge reflecting mirror and read the electric waves from the beautiful stars." Having wrung apart the old clocks that make that unpleasant sound (literally *suna wo kamu oto*, the sound of chewing sand, which can allude to having nothing to eat), the speaker wants to stand eternal "cold like a marble column," to fly ("fly through the pure white space like a brave cannonball"), and then, in a third incarnation of self, neither present and still nor shooting bravely through space, she wants to become absorbing, open: "I want to become a huge reflecting mirror and read the electric waves from the beautiful stars." The repetition of the phrase "I want," the explicit desire (*tsumetaku tatteitai, tondeyukitai, yondeitai*), like the repetition of the term *kanojo-tachi* in "Vaudeville," places the speaker's desire—although its object changes from moment to moment—at the center of the poetic structure. More important, in the end, than the image of self desired at a given moment is, perhaps, the insistent presence of the desiring, demanding, subject.

In the poem "Tsuki" (Moon) published in the sixth and last issue of *Ishō no taiyō* (July 1929) the questions of love, transformation over time, and forgetfulness return in what seems at first glance a simple poetic fable:

Moon

In my last incarnation I was a jellyfish
The moon loved me   and I loved the moon

Now I am a hollyhock of the sun
The moon tries to wound me with its malevolent gaze

Gods, please change me again
This time into a five-colored bird

If you do I won't have to look at the moon anymore
And the moon may eventually forget me[31]

"In my last incarnation I was a jellyfish / The moon loved me   and I loved the moon": the poem opens in the rhythm of a children's story, idyllic. I and the moon become subject and object in a perfect and syntactically reciprocal, explicit love (*Tsuki wa watashi wo ai shi / watashi mo tsuki wo ai shiteimashita*). But this golden age is already in the past; from the first moment it is a previous incarnation (*zenshin*), and although the poem here broaches the theme of what seems to be a romantic love, the romance is here removed, at least on the explicit level, from the signs of gender (a moon and a jellyfish, a flower—hollyhock—and a sun and a moon in a love triangle).[32] "The moon tries to wound me with its malevolent gaze"; here the moon, anthropomorphized, tries to gain revenge for its lost love. As in "Angels Cry for Love," this allegory, too, ends with forgetfulness: "Gods, please change me again / This time into a five-colored bird / If you do I won't have to look at the moon anymore / And the moon will eventually forget me." The fable becomes about changing bodies, gazing and the breaking off of gaze ("I won't have to look . . . anymore"): the speaker's voice is humble and gentle, using the honorific verbs *itashimasu* and *nasattekudasai*, which hints at the possibility of a feminine speaker (although gender remains, finally, indeterminable). The story is deceptively simple, moving from one love to another, one imagined body to another, as it describes the pain of a betrayal, of a gaze withdrawn.[33] Tomotani's poems exist on the borders between a children's story, a tale of the uncanny, and lyric poetry.

Like the other Surrealists in Japan at this time, Tomotani deliberately chose not to situate her work among those movements that directly engaged political or social issues. Yet one can find an awareness of these movements in these writers' projects, even in their self-conscious pose as "minor" in relation to the literary mainstream, and in their allusions to the foreign as a source of inspiration. (As Nishiwaki writes on the opening page of the fifth issue of *Ishō no taiyō*, "We sing the praises of minor poets," with the words "minor poets" in English.)

The fresh oddness of Tomotani's language within the rather raw, unpolished poems (light, feather diadems of poems, still, perhaps, in tangles) reflects an experimentation in the rhetorical presentation of self, conveyed by the various bodies and incarnations of the speaker. Poetry becomes a space to express direct desires: *kanojo-tachi* appear, desire, fight, and per form, and the visual effect of this feminine plural on the page becomes strange to us in its repetition, making us notice the absence of the word in poetic language heretofore. The poems are at once outspoken and understated; for Tomotani, perhaps, and for the question of the place of women in Japanese Surrealism, as much is established through the very presence of her works in these earliest magazines (with her elaboration of place and signification and her use of the new, insistent expressions of desire) as would be accomplished through the language of an explicitly ideological battle.[34] At the same time, her implied elaboration of temporality and forgetfulness, although touched on earlier in the discussion of other poets and the encounter with the void, takes on a particular power when considered in relation to a poet whose inclusion in poetic remembrance is ultimately all the more tenuous. After World War II many of the women in Japan who wrote Surrealist or Surrealist-inspired poetry and gained recognition as modern poets often incorporated explicit or deliberately shocking sexual visions into their works. Yet here, in the earliest years, this first poet of the vaudeville *kanojo-tachi* (this lover of moons and destroyer of dull time) accomplishes her aims as much while floating on the backs of swans as in direct confrontation—her argument is elliptical but tenacious: "brilliant as flagships are the dreams they have."

EMA SHŌKO AND 'MADAME BLANCHE'

Beginning her career as a member of the coterie of Momota Sōji, with the journal *Shii no ki* (Chinquapin tree), Ema Shōko (1913–) went on to participate in many groups and magazines closely associated with Surrealism and post-Surrealist avant-garde poetics. She contributed work to the later issues of *Shi to shiron* (Poetry and poetics), *Shinryōdo* (New territories), *Madame Blanche* and *VOU* (edited by Kitasono Katsue), and *Shihō* (Prosody). Like Tomotani Shizue, Ema Shōko was one of the few women participating actively in the avant-garde poetic movements associated with Surrealism in the prewar period. In her work we notice again issues of transformation and nostalgia, even in a poetry that finds itself suspended between the familiar and the unknown. How does her work negotiate the realm, or suggest the layers of transformation, of the familiar recollection and the unknown (or foreign) in writing? How can remembrance become at the same time an encounter with the new?

In 1936 Ema published her first collection of poems, entitled *Haru e no shōtai* (Invitation to spring). In the postwar period, she was involved in the Futurist movement and became an editor of the magazine *Joseishi* (Women's poetry); in addition, she published volumes of poetry, children's stories, and translated a biography of Emily Dickinson. To consider how the work of Ema Shōko relates to Surrealist poetics, one might examine some of the early poems she published during the period when Surrealist thought was a prominent force in the periodicals for which she wrote. In *Madame Blanche* issue 7 (1933), for example, when she was only twenty years old, Ema published the poem "Haru" (Spring).[35] The poem treads a fine line between evoking a descriptive scene of spring (a legible, lyrical scene) and departing from the possibility of ordinary description, taking off from elements within the scene and entering a more abstract space of dream, art, or spirituality. The poem begins:

Spring
The shade in the rose-colored covered wagon rocks the window
   curtain facing out on the park. It was exactly a small heart.

With a "rose-colored covered wagon" (*bara-iro de aru horobasha*) and a "window curtain facing out on the park," the poem opens by suggesting a trip through the countryside in a wagon, a spring excursion. But instead of presenting the people inside the cart, or their perspective, the poem gives one to observe the cart itself, seen from the outside, with a rocking motion that makes it appear, perhaps, as "a small heart," a palpitation. The poem avoids a verbal link between the two phrases, however, and does not clarify that the wagon is "like" a heart, marking the metaphor as such. If indeed one is to read a link between the heart and the image of the wagon, the poem seems to aim for a literal transformation ("it was exactly a small heart"). The word *chōdo* (just, exactly) would seem to require the phrase *no yō ni* (like), but rather, it was "exactly" or "precisely" a small heart; it was none other than this; it was transformed. Because this is a poetic text, one could argue that the reader immediately infers the metaphorical aspect of the image; nonetheless, for a moment the poem seems to take its own description literally, since, by contrast, after this line the poem returns to the realm of explicit analogies (my emphasis):

In the middle of the green barley field it stopped suddenly, and then, *like* a hand that touched the window curtain, *like* a Dutch wall clock, *like* something one remembers, it began to move, the white fingertips joined as if in prayer.

On the level of description, the wagon has simply stopped suddenly and started up again. But an abundance of analogies intervenes, each marked with the (earlier absent link) *no yō ni* (like): like a hand [hands], like a clock, like a remembrance. In the surprise of the return to motion (a return that seems to mark the starts and stops of the poetic language itself, rocking, appearing in spurts), we see the traces of a human figure begin to emerge: "like a hand that touched the window curtain" marks a presence, perhaps, inside the covered wagon, visible only as the trace on the window curtain viewed from the outside. Is this the trace of the writer's hand, touching, through the poem, the window curtain? Is the window curtain, pulsing and moving, a figure for the poem itself, with the spring day and the writer's hand visible "through" it? The hand appears again—"the white fingertips joined as if in prayer"—and the wagon begins to move, leaving one uncertain whether the covered wagon itself is to be read in analogy to the "white fingertips," or whether one is observing white (gloved) fingers within the wagon or in the writing of the white page.

This scene could as easily occur in a landscape from a European nineteenth-century novel as take place in modern Japan, in the connotation of its details: the gloved "white fingertips," Dutch clock, the garden. This ambivalence persists in the striking exclamation a few lines later, with its first intervention of the figure of "I" (*watashi*):

Ah, there is the dear familiar [*natsukashii*] tree of grandmother, thrusting its dull lead-colored cane.—I lay a book called *Green Garden* face down on my knees. (A young composer died on just such an afternoon.)

Is the whole scene, from the heart to the covered wagon, part of a story the speaker is reading in an English book entitled *Green Garden*? (The title appears in the poem in English capital letters arranged vertically, creating the odd effect of a stacked column of roman letters suspended between the two languages.) Suddenly not only the "I" intervenes but, significantly at the same time, various self-conscious artistic modes appear: a book, musical composition. "Just such an afternoon" (*kono yō na gogo*): the description of the spring afternoon itself becomes an analogy (*kono yō*) for a moment that appears in parentheses—the recollection of a death of a young composer. Looking out on the scene (or writing the scene) of the garden and the spring afternoon, the figure of "I" turns the book face down on (her) knees: one is no longer reading, but through the interval of the moment of recognizing or recollecting the composer's death, the speaking subject seems to have taken the leap from reading (and writing) to dreaming, and the images depart into a disoriented space that seems to approach fantasy:

A stone staircase begins to dream. A faint cloud. That was also a small bird with cool feathers like the ice that still continued to sleep.—As I descend this staircase to the lawn, a splendid rite of spring is being performed at the lower reaches of the blue stream, a repainting of the paint on the bottom of a ship.

The "rite of spring," *haru no saiten*, the contemporary translation of Igor Stravinsky's 1913 composition title, seems to link obliquely with the mention of the composer (although Stravinsky did not die young). A stone staircase dreams, and a faint cloud appears that changes into a bird—and the bird's feathers are compared to ice, an ice seen as sleeping, thus returning the image full circle to the figure of the spring dream. Ema cuts the poem with odd dashes, as if to mark the transition between these (outdoor) spaces of the spring afternoon, the textual world inside the book, and the world of dreams.

What is occurring at the moment in "Spring" when the line breaks off with, "Ah, there is the dear, familiar tree of grandmother" (*a, are wa natsukashii obaasan no ki*)? The sudden recollection of the grandmother, in the form of the grandmother's tree, appears in the middle of the landscape. (The line could also be read, "There is the tree of dear grandmother"; the speaker's nostalgia could be evoked by the tree or by the thought of the grandmother.) Just before this line, the poem had floated off into a dreamlike metaphor: "yet this bottle of colored pattern in the hall of the mansion caved in with the weight of strong-scented flowers." Then, suddenly, after an ellipsis, the speaker or observer seems to return to the space of the landscape, or bring the landscape back from the unfamiliar, the unknown, into the realm of the familiar, recollected; and this return is marked by a moment of surprise, an invocation, "Ah, there it is, the dear, familiar tree of [my] grandmother." The familiar vision returns the observer/speaker to the present, to present objects (*a, are wa*), and to memory (*natsukashii*). The image that follows—"thrusting its dull lead-colored cane"—may obliquely suggest a pencil: the recollection of the grandmother (the tree of the grandmother) somehow brings the poem back out of the seemingly free realm of bottles of colored pattern and the weight of strong-scented flowers into what might imply the beginning of its own writing: the thrust of the pencil, the laying aside of the book *Green Garden* in order to come into touch with the visible garden from which the speaker begins her own dreams, recollections, and meditations.

The poem does not allow us to settle between the world of art and the world of natural landscape; neither does it allow us to settle as readers on a fixed location for the landscape at hand: it could be an English "green garden" with a covered wagon moving through it, gloved hands, and stone staircase, but could as well be a Japanese landscape with its mansion residence (*yashiki*), a familiar tree belonging to grandmother, the "spring dream." The image of the "bottle of colored pattern" caving in, or breaking, with the "weight of strong-scented flowers" again traces the border, on which the poem continuously hovers, between the artifice of pattern and created scent (fragrance in a bottle, or man-made patterns of color) and the natural world (the weight of strong-scented flowers). For the most part, Ema's language is not heavily weighted with the diction and vocabulary of classical poetry. It moves freely between the descriptive and the fantastical, the grounded world of the garden and the distant world of dreams. The moment of recognition of the grandmother's tree, however, as a recollection from the past (perhaps, also, the past of "grandmothers" writing, of earlier women writers, or memories of earlier landmarks in the poetic landscape), seems to ground or anchor this moment of writing as it bursts into metaphor—this moment serves as a pivot for the speaker's move from reading to writing, from observing to an active dreaming.

In the last line of the poem, the painting of the bottom of a boat and the "rite of spring" both occur at once, or can even be read as the same ritual (both are subjects of the verb *okonawareru*, "to be performed"). The rite of spring (which could be read as a figure for the composition of the poem "Spring" itself, the rite it performs) becomes both a festival in the present moment and an allusion to the earlier piece by Stravinsky. The poem again fluctuates between description and reference to the creative process: while painting the bottom of the boat seems a practical task, far removed from the realm of artistic creation, one may read it as yet another image of a grounding that remains ungrounded—a functional task that is also an act of painting, of covering over with layers. The bottom of the boat seems to suggest both a foundation, a lower limit, and a base that will float, rock, and become the vehicle for carrying the metaphorical images (like the carriage of the first line as well) away from the place where they begin. The painting of the bottom of the boat is a preparatory rite of spring, both the artistic product and the anticipation of its creation, like Ema's poem in its double motion—of anticipation and fulfillment, premonition and closure.

Further, "it was just such an afternoon" suggests a premonition of death—the recollection of a death and at the same time the implication of its repetition in this very afternoon: the carriage was itself a "small heart" that stopped moving and then started again, like a small death. White-gloved hands fold in prayer, and one is overwhelmed by the fragrance of strong-scented flowers, as at a funeral. Is this dreaming a sleep of death? Is the rite of spring also a sacrifice, as in Stravinsky's "Rite"? If so, it is a fertile one, not an ending but a "descent" into another realm (or dimension), to perform its own "splendid" ritual which leads to the anticipation of a continued voyage.

In another early work entitled "Vineyard" ("Budōen" or "Budōzono") from the October 1933 edition of *Madame Blanche*, Ema takes the vision of a landscape and the coming and going of language in yet another direction, further exploring the realm of dreams. Here, too, one views an unusual landscape, this one populated by birds, people, voices, and shadows, depicted as if in a constant process of transformation. Again, she surprises us with the continual metamorphoses in her use of poetic language; at first glance, her seemingly simple, fablelike, or fantastical sentences could almost prefigure the children's stories she was to write later in her life; yet, the simplicity of the language belies the complexity of the poetic images that emerge, describing both an "objective" (or exterior) landscape and a realm of dreams at once, in multilayered metaphors. Again, here, it is a question of discovering the fate of the "heart" ("all hearts") taken as an object in itself, seemingly detached from the people, minds, and relationships that belong to it. Meanwhile (as if oblivious to the fate of "all hearts") "people" come and go as part of the visible landscape, in mincing motions that "imitate birds":

Vineyard

Dreams, wrapped around people like capes, blow in the wind—happiness opens pupils, and one can hear the gentle voice of conversation here and there. In the end, all hearts like mirrors slid down. Between the lace threads of wind that untied themselves and wrapped around every tree trunk, people, imitating birds, continue to come and go in little mincing motions under the blue silk sky. The pigeon that flies out of a cloud, the watering can in the thicket, and the rattan chairs in the shadow of these trees—soon dusk rose from these, and the glistening leaves began to appear, jostling one another. But all we can hear at the moment is the sound of their touching one another, like silver coins.[36]

"Happiness opens pupils": happiness seems to exist as an abstract or disembodied entity in this landscape, like the hearts, pupils, and voices; the people are rather carefree, wrapped in the cloaks of their dreams, coming and going, "imitating birds." Dusk rises from the objects in the landscape, and the leaves seem to appear, glistening of their own accord, while the observer (or observers) hears them clinking together as if they had been transformed into the silver coins they visually resemble.

A certain causality is undermined in "Vineyard": the light at dusk does not cause the leaves to glisten—it simply rises over them, and they appear, in the act of glistening. Wind does not cause the leaves to jostle one another; these phenomena are suspended outside of a clear relation. Dreams and conversation do not cause happiness; happiness seems simply to appear, as another figure in the landscape. On the other hand, another sense of causality is constructed through the interaction and overlap of sounds: for example, the wind wrapping around the tree trunks is *miki ni maki-tsuite*, almost as if its wrapping were triggered by the similarity of sound of the word "trunk" (*miki*) and "wrap" (*maki*). Similarly, "dusk rose" seems to have a certain verbal overdetermination, in the aural link between *tasogare ga* (dusk) and *tachiagari* (rises). The poem hones its focus on sound: the gentle conversational voices, the sound of the clinking of the leaves.

The speaking subject, the composer, and other "people" (*hitobito*) appear, and parts of bodies are woven into the lines, but they remain neither explicitly feminine nor masculine. In the last line of "Vineyard," the speaker or observer becomes first person plural: "all we can hear at the moment is" (*watashi-tachi ga kiku koto ga dekiru no wa*). Certain objects might be coded as "feminine" (as well as European)—lace (*reesu*), perfume bottles—but such objects must be read in the context of their frequent appearance in the avant-garde poetry (of both men and women) in these journals; they become figures for poetic creation or suggestions of beauty and delicacy.

In a third poem from the same period, Ema touches obliquely on figures of a gendered voice. "Nezumi" (mouse) appeared in *Madame Blanche* issue 9 (September 1933):

Mouse
Lurking in the shade of scales lit up with summer
Feeding on a cluster of grapes, silver-
clothed, sometimes barefoot
Ah, worrisome diver
The traveler climbing up onto a coral island
can peek
at the sun sinking in the distance
Where laughter floats
Evening lace with a flutter
dangles from the ceiling
The hand that lifted the seaweeds
As if it had suddenly remembered
stopped moving the spoon
That is the voice of the princess Scheherazade. . . . [37]

The poem (unlike the prose-poem form of "Spring" and "Vineyard") is a (sonnetlike) fourteen-line verse divided into roughly equal short lines. Its last line seems to frame the scene of a narration: "That is the voice of the princess Scheherazade." The earlier image of the traveler enters a tale woven by that voice, and this framing is reinforced by the poem's structure. The grammatical enjambment of the sentences seems to make the poem alternate between a scene of a diver on a coral island (an idyllic summer landscape) and another scene of which the reader is made aware by the overlap of details like the ceiling (inside a room and a metaphor for the dangling lace of seaweed) and the hand that "stopped moving the spoon," as if it had suddenly remembered. Might the whole scene be read as a moment in an interrupted meal, when two people in a room are speaking, perhaps eating grapes, sharing "floating laughter"?

The emphasis in the poem is on the idyllic island landscape with the summer light, the "silver-clothed," barefoot figure of the diver (marked with the term *sensuifu*, in which *fu* designates the masculine), and a traveler peeking at the sunset.[38] The diver, however, is "worrisome" (*kizukawareru*; he provokes anxiety, worry, caring), perhaps, one might infer, because of the danger of his voyages into the deep. The term *kizukawareru* implies the figure of someone who worries (such as the speaker), which may be read in relation to the princess's voice that appears at the end of the poem. The figure of the diver, the island, the sunset, and the seaweed lead into an image of "evening lace," the paused hand holding the spoon, the voice of Scheherazade: does the whole vision take place in the space of the pause of a hand ("as if it had suddenly remembered") and the recognition of a voice?

The poem does not resolve this suggestion, however; it presents the various colors of a summer outdoor landscape and the vague evocation of an interior, the implication of gendered figures of the male diver and feminine narrator. One recalls that in the story of Scheherazade, her life depended on the possibility of continuing her tale; but here the tale becomes a brief moment of recognition in what seems like a pause in everyday life. Nonetheless, it is this recognition on which the rest of the poem, the rest of the poetic vision, depends. The poem does not explain the reason for its title, "Mouse": perhaps as a fleeting vision of impending night it, too, appears briefly from a crack and then is gone ("lurking in the shade"), or perhaps the wetness of the diver recalls the expression *nurenezumi* (wet rat) — but there is nothing to make one certain even of this. The poem's primary movement or gesture is, like the movement of the seaweed, a "fluttering," "dangling," which can serve as its focusing metaphor.

The language of the poem flutters (*yurayura to*) between possible visions: a summer island and an interior or domestic space (seaweed in a spoon, hand holding the spoon, ceiling, lace), a narrated moment and a silent space (sun sinking in the distance), a solitary traveler and an implied relationship. It flutters between light and shade, day and evening, masculine and feminine. In this sense, the poem activates the differences of gender as part of a passing back and forth, an oddly flickering vision within a frozen space of paused movement. It creates a flickering double motion like that of Ema's poems discussed above. In the opening line of "Vineyard" ("Dreams, wrapped around people like capes, blow in the wind— happiness opens pupils"), eyes are open, and yet one dreams; one is outdoors in a landscape, and also in an interior or emotional, spiritual realm (of the heart, dreams, happiness). In "Spring," one is outdoors in a garden, and at the same time the figural visions of a dream, a rite, and a heart come into play.

To discuss the poems of Ema Shōko in the context of Surrealist poetry, then, involves the overlapping of spaces of metaphor, fantasy, landscape, and the everyday, often all within a single line or series of images. She plays with language and yet does not break it. She layers her images one upon another until there is an overall effect at once of familiarity and strangeness, surprising moments of incomprehensibility and soothing, rhythmic gentleness: the "gentle voice of conversation" that "could be heard here and there," the clinking of leaves that touch like silver coins, or the voice of Scheherazade continuing her eternal tale. Of course, such images do not, in themselves, make the poem definable strictly as "Surrealist"; and yet, through their context, one can draw the link with Surrealist experiments in Japan. Ema's nonchalance perches on the boundaries between poetic traditions and styles. Her poems present their unexpected and at times baffling images as though they were a simple matter, not a violent upheaval or rite. (And yet, as in Stravinsky's "Rite of Spring," there are intimations of a sacrifice, of a possible death: the stopping of a heart, the fatal pause in Scheherazade's tale.)

Ema's original poetic vision, like the repainted bottom of the boat, may be an essential covering of "last year's" layer to prepare the vehicle for its new voyage. Her rewriting of the poetic tradition may be part of a process of poetic renewal, with its wavering, fluttering dream of the traveler's next destination. As such, her poetry also evokes pauses for a past remembered or nostalgia for something lost, recognized from the past—the recollection of the grandmother's tree, something "suddenly remembered" (*fu to omoidasareta yō ni*), "something recalled" (*omoidasareru yō ni*). Perhaps at the very moment of such remembering, one opens one's eyes ("happiness opens pupils") and the new dream takes flight.

PARADOXICAL LEGACIES: "I HAVE BREATHED TAKIGUCHI SHŪZŌ"

The dream hid in a pebble.
—Takiguchi Shūzō, "Suima"
(Drowsiness)

The influence of Surrealism persisted and was strengthened and transformed after the war. Of the avant-garde artistic movements that arose in the 1950s and 1960s, many traced their origins or precedents to prewar Surrealism. Nonetheless, they often took Surrealist thought for granted, incorporating it freely into their ideas and purposes. Takiguchi Shūzō, Kitasono Katsue, and Nishiwaki Junzaburō each fostered numerous disciples and followers among the young postwar artists, not only in the fields of poetry and fiction but also in dance, theater, the visual arts, music, and film.

The group Jikken Kōbō, or Experimental Workshop, was formed in the 1950s by young disciples of Takiguchi.[39] The Butoh movement in avant-garde dance (Ankoku Butoh, developed by Hijikata Tatsumi and Ohno Kazuo), while referring to its origins in Japanese folk culture and German Expressionist dance (Mary Wigman), incorporates a subversive, antilogical, improvisatory (automatic) approach that can trace Surrealism as an important precedent. Through Ankoku Butoh, the theatrical experiments of Kara Jūrō and Terayama Shūji take a part of their inspiration. For many artists of the postwar generation, the links with Surrealism were present but often no longer needed to be articulated; the form in which one adopted and re-created Surrealism became the important point (as an aesthetic, as a way of understanding the role of art in society, as a project for delving into the dark areas of the soul or unconscious). Many artists were struggling, as had the prewar Surrealists, with the question of how to reconcile or incorporate the signs of and allusions to a Japanese tradition into their art, and yet maintain the aspects and visions taken from "Western" art. As the artists observed the radical process of Americanization around them, some evoked a nostalgia for the Japanese countryside, for aspects of an "old Japan."[40] At the same time, artists and writers were reconsidering what Surrealism had been or still might be in Japan. Notably, the Wani (Crocodile) group of poets, which included Ōoka Makoto, Yoshioka Minoru, and Iijima Kōichi, formed a "Surrealist study group" for this express purpose.[41] Many writers incorporated experiments with "Surreal" scenes or episodes in their work. Works by writers as diverse as Ishikawa Jun ("Taka"), Shimao Toshio ("Yume no naka de no nichijō"), Kawabata Yasunari (Asakusa kurenaidan, "Kataude"), Satō Haruo, and Inagaki Taruho have been read in relation to a vision of the Surreal, of exploring the place of the surreal within the real.[42]

Often the presence or trace of Surrealist thought goes unspoken (and perhaps the very extent of the absorption of the ideas makes them more difficult to trace), but the prewar Surrealist writers long continued as important presences in the artistic world. One notes the continued (ever increasing) influx and translation of earlier Surrealist-related works from Europe and America. (Shibusawa Tatsuhiko was one writer active in this process and became known also as a writer of Surrealistic tales.) Marcel Duchamp had a strong influence on the postwar movement of conceptual art in Japan; a larger audience continued to discover the works of the Marquis de Sade, André Breton, Max Ernst, Paul Eluard, and others (to the point that their work became commercially viable).

Shimao Toshio (whose "Yume no naka de no nichijō," or "Everyday Life in a Dream," incorporates a fantastical ending many read as "Surrealistic") published a brief essay in 1958 on Surrealism in Japan, entitled "Hichōgenjitsushugiteki na chōgenjitsushugi no oboegaki" (Recollections of an un-Surrealistic Surrealism). Shimao comments:

> And yet again, one cannot call the daily life [that appears within one's dreams] "Surreal." Even if one brought in only those realities from our surroundings that are "invisible to the eyes," and even if they came to life in a form that did not merely lay bare these realities before our eyes, it would not mean that this expression had absorbed into itself the fear we have of what we cannot see. That fear will escape suddenly and remain vaguely detached, taking up a clear position on the outside. Our expanded daily life will be driven one step closer to crisis. This has been the extent of our understanding of the ways we can take possession of the larger expanse of reality. We have not, finally, succeeded in the attempt to grasp Surrealism fully.[43]

Shimao Toshio writes that "we" (in Japan) "have not, finally, succeeded" in opening Surrealism to its fullest possibilities. He looks back and finds that the Japanese Surrealist movement did not assimilate or grasp what for him, it seems in this essay, is essential to the Surrealist quest: to grapple with the "fear" that is caused by the things in this world that cannot be seen with the eyes, the realities that are outside of vision and therefore often outside of representation. He opens his essay by pointing out this fear of the unknown, the invisible, and noting people's desire to escape or deny all that seems to emerge from this realm of the unexpected, noting their desire to deny any connection to such things. And yet, he continues, the more one attempts to keep a clear boundary between the realm of the visible (known) and the invisible (unknown), that is, the more one attempts to separate them and save oneself from the fear of the unknown, the more one restricts the field of one's daily life and vision, as well as the possibilities for one's creative endeavors. (In the essay he calls this realm "the invisible," "me ni mienai mono," always in quotation marks, in a sense as though he, too, could not name it properly, or even retained a certain fear of it, and wanted to separate it from the main body of the text.) Those who do seek out the aspects of daily life not visible to the eye and who attempt to give them expression, he claims, do not necessarily succeed in touching the basis, the emotion, of fear that marks and in a certain sense identifies the truly unknown, the world that "we cannot see." Even in the attempt to express these elements, to expand one's reality to include them, the element of fear (that, presumably, would be assimilated in a "full" Surrealist grasp) escapes outside of one's expression, outside of the form that one has constructed.

According to this passage, if one succeeded in avoiding the most obvious expressions that would simply "make visible" the invisible, fear nonetheless retains its place beyond one's grasp. Furthermore, the realm of daily life (rather than expanding to include the unknown, fearful, invisible elements) is contracted, pushed or driven into a corner—driven one step closer to a dangerous realm of crisis. This, then, is his *oboegaki* (memorandum, note; also, memorial) on Surrealism in 1958, thinking back on what he considers to be the attempt and the shortcomings of what developed in Japan under the name of Surrealism. This pushing close to crisis marks the failure to "grasp" (*tsukamidasu*, as in 'empty the pockets of') what would have been promised by the Surrealist movement.

This condition of unrealized Surrealism in Japan is named by Shimao Toshio as an "irreplaceable condition" (*kakegae no nai jōtai*: cannot be substituted, the only one).[44] He implies that it could not, should not, have been any other way. This Surrealism reflects a kind of failure, but a failure that also constitutes a necessary or "irreplaceable" condition. Although one has not yet succeeded in assimilating the "fear," the fact of this failed state or circumstance in itself may function as more than a mere criticism; it becomes the analysis of a fundamental condition and thus suggests a future direction of pursuit. As the essay implies, the grasping of this fear, the full emptying out of the possibilities (and pockets) of Surrealism, would be no easy matter, but is an essential pursuit for the expansion of the realm of daily life and dreams.[45] What one did not succeed in was the "work of grasping Surrealism fully" (*tsukamidasu shigoto ni seikō shinakatta*)—this statement in itself implies that there is still a work (*shigoto*, task, mission, duty) that remains to be performed.

Another perspective for reconsidering the place of Surrealism in the postwar period is an article by the prominent avant-garde dancer Hijikata Tatsumi (1928–1986), founder (with Ohno Kazuo) of the Butoh movement. He discusses the work of Takiguchi Shūzō and thus establishes a relation to Surrealism through his writing (or rewriting) of Takiguchi. Hijikata weaves his voice into the developing legend of Takiguchi in a way that has as much to do with his own artistic projects as with the specific vocabulary of Takiguchi's work. Through this shift in the terms of the project, one can begin to observe the interval that opens between Surrealist-inspired work in the 1960s (and 1970s) and the projects of a prewar Surrealist. The essay, "Sen ga sen ni nitekuru toki" (When a line comes to resemble a line) opens with a declaration:

It's not that I usually live my life thinking about Takiguchi Shūzō. He is, rather, like air; up until now, there was no need to consider what meaning he might have. On the contrary, by not searching for meaning one is more likely to discover, as if by accident, what one is searching for—this is the manner [*ambai*] in which I have breathed Takiguchi Shūzō.[46]

Like many artists of the 1960s, Hijikata created his works in the "air" that Takiguchi Shūzō helped to create. He takes this air for granted ("It's not that I usually live my life thinking about Takiguchi"), and yet without it, he implies, it would not have been possible to become what he is, to do what he has done. Takiguchi's existence for Hijikata is both essential and "forgotten"; and through this image of air, Hijikata translates Takiguchi into the vocabulary and mythology that form the basis of his own art. In his dance Hijikata attempted to discover, as if by accident, the unspoken (taken for granted) aims of their common search and to bring them into the performative realm—through the breath, through the body and its improvisations, rather than through any technique or search for meaning.

The essay progresses in the form of thoughts and meditations sparked by moments in Takiguchi's writing. Not interested in a critical assessment of Takiguchi's contributions, Hijikata searches for what one can be brought to think, to discover, from the starting point of Takiguchi's words and work. In a later passage, Hijikata makes explicit his relations to Takiguchi and the form of their interaction with one another. At the same time, he expands the description into a meditation on dreams and objects:

Every time I dance, Takiguchi sends me a gift of a painting-like object. By now, I have accumulated many of them. In these objects like paintings, one might say, not that Takiguchi's hand has danced, but rather, that they are the materialization of the moment in which [his] hand has come to resemble a hand. Even that which is depicted [in them] comes to resemble this hand. Takiguchi's hand, having discovered the functioning of the dream, continuously violated the functioning of the simple hand of reality. His hand is perhaps eternally in the act of making a wager.

It is not that Takiguchi is attached to objects; rather, without a doubt, he has been spoken to by objects. These are not abandoned, clinging objects, nor vanishing objects sheltered by transcendent things. Objects [*mono*] here attempt to seize a spontaneous [automatic] dream. The dreams of Takiguchi Shūzō, which go even beyond this, seem truly to exist in actuality [*jitsuzai*].[47]

Here, Hijikata describes Takiguchi's painting-objects in terms of the image of the "hand" of Takiguchi and the relation of Takiguchi's hand to the objects around it and to dreams. Takiguchi's hand, according to Hijikata, "violated the functioning of the simple hand of reality" by having discovered "the functioning of the dream." In other words, Takiguchi's hand operates on a level that transcends the traditional causality of transcription. Rather than a painting that depicts an object or a hand that creates a painting resembling an object, here the usual order of resemblance is overturned: the hand itself comes to resemble a hand, or comes into its own, becomes more itself than it had been before through the process of making the painting. The objects depicted in the painting, the materialization of this moment of self-resemblance, thus come to resemble the hand.

According to Hijikata, Takiguchi does not address or seek out objects; rather, they seek him out, recalling the process explored in Francis Ponge's *Le Parti pris des choses*. Objects speak to Takiguchi and direct their address to him, like the objects that speak in Ponge's poems. The objects attempt to grasp the "spontaneous dream": of their own accord they reach out to grasp a dream (a dream that has to do with Takiguchi's dreaming function of the hand); the whole is a striking reversal of what would be the usual process of making a painting. In this sense, although Hijikata does not claim that "Takiguchi's hand is dancing," an element of dance exists (through Hijikata's description) in the performance of Takiguchi's hand in these works, and that element approaches the aims of Hijikata's dance, outside of technique and intention. Hijikata explores in this essay, as in his dance, the body's resemblance to itself through the functioning of the dream. With his body, Hijikata aims to attain the kind of "actuality" (*jitsuzai*) that Takiguchi describes in "Shi to jitsuzai" (Poetry and actuality)— "an act that refutes all acts." (He cites Takiguchi: "Poetry is not faith. Nor is it logic. Poetry is an act. An act that refutes all acts. This is the instant when the shadow of the dream resembled the shadow of the poem.") It is to this statement of poetic function that Hijikata refers when he writes of the hand: "The actuality of this dream—the shadow of the dream, is in fact the actuality of the hand that Takiguchi paints." Thus Hijikata draws the image of Takiguchi's hand itself, his body in the act of creating, into an understanding of Takiguchi's paradigm for the poetic process, the relation between poetry, actuality, and dream.

Hijikata thus does "breathe" Takiguchi: Takiguchi's formulations enter and become part of the air of Hijikata's project. Similarly, Takiguchi's precedents are incorporated into the body of Japanese avant-garde and subversive art: an interval opens between the way the works of the 1920s and 1930s were carried out and understood in their own time and the way that their language is appropriated and transformed in the postwar period. Hijikata, like many other postwar artists, may not have lived his life thinking about Takiguchi, Kitasono, Nishiwaki, and the other Surrealists, but if asked, postwar artists admit that without these artists their work would not have its current direction, even when at times that direction is a reconfiguration of what the earlier writers accomplished, or a critique of what they failed to achieve.[48]

In an essay on Marcel Duchamp from the 1960s, Takiguchi writes: "Words are anyway a result of our habitual usage over a long time, and they have formed a strong regime, more or less against the users."[49] Takiguchi continues to explore the processes that link objects and words, that make words age and then renew them in a process of objectlike use. Perhaps this image can provide a figure for what Surrealism comes to mean to various artists and writers in the 1960s and beyond, the legacy it left for them, for they never cease to grapple with the problems opened by Surrealism and to look back to the ways these questions were opened in the past—to criticize and experiment, with continued imaginative urgency. Surrealist thought, with its "habitual usage over a long time," becomes itself a kind of ready-made object available for later artists to appropriate, reclaim, destroy, violate, or reconstruct. Perhaps, too, it becomes an object that speaks, addressing the artist: through the process of appropriation and transformation, it may finally come more strongly to "resemble itself" than it ever had before. The difficulties faced by Surrealists in the prewar period and their aspirations have not disappeared—they have only been transformed and reconfigured, in works and movements that no longer bear the name of Surrealism, but will not fail to bear its mark.

PHYSICAL NOSTALGIAS

"As is often said, Butoh only happens once and leaves nothing be-hind," comments visual artist and designer Nakanishi Natsuyuki on the writings of Hijikata Tatsumi. "As is *often* said"—the rhetoric of singularity and presence follows Butoh like a shadow, like its missing trace. It is a trope, almost a cliché, of tracelessness and imminent physical presence. To evoke the continuities that nonetheless link this traceless Butoh with ear-lier avant-garde literary movements such as Surrealism, and to examine the rhetoric and ways of reading of the performative strategies of Butoh in the postwar period, it is useful to consider the (intricately related) question of nostalgia. This is not the nostalgia that has gained a bad name (in contem-porary theory) as a longing for return to a spurious origin, but rather an-other, more paradoxical nostalgia constructed in and through Butoh itself. As one example of a postwar movement in performance, what kinds of ideas and interpretations has Butoh generated and what readings and mis-readings has it invited (readings by its performers and collaborators as they create new works and by later writers)? Or in other words, what is the structure of Butoh's nostalgia?

The avant-garde dance movement of Butoh, or Ankoku Butoh (Dance of darkness) as Hijikata called it, began, according to his account, in 1956, and in 1959 he gave his first major Butoh performance, of "Kinjiki" (Forbidden colors, based on Mishima's novel by the same name). *Bu* is written with the character for dance (the same *bu* found in Kabuki) and *tō* means to step or tread. The term *butoh* was used since the Meiji period in Japan to designate foreign ballroom dance forms (ballet, fox-trot, tango) that were then coming into fashion.[1] The term *ankoku butoh* thus was in part a response to counter the perceived "lightness" of these Western dance forms, although the word *ankoku* was eventually dropped. Butoh originated also with the work of Ohno Kazuo (1906–), who studied dance in the 1930s with Ishii Baku (a pioneer of Western modern dance in Japan), and later with Eguchi Takaya (who had studied in Germany with Mary Wigman). There is a parallel history, then, that one might trace, alongside the development of Surrealism in the late 1920s and 1930s, of interactions and cultural implications of the exchanges that took place within the realm of dance. The important figures in this exchange were Ishii, Eguchi, Giovanni Rossi (who was hired by the Japanese Imperial Theater to teach classical dance and modern ballet; Ishii was one of his top students), and Ito Michio (who traveled to Europe and choreographed "dance-poems" to the poetry of Yeats).

Postwar Butoh as an avant-garde movement developed in the midst of the Anpo protests (the famous demonstrations against the renewal of the Japan-U.S. Security Treaty). A number of other important performance groups were active at the same time, from Suzuki Tadashi's Waseda Little Theater to Kara Jūrō's Situation Theater (Jōkyō Gekijō), Terayama Shūji's Tenjō Sajiki group, and Satō Makoto's Black Tent (Kuro Tento). Butoh can be considered also in relation to the movement of nostalgia for rural and marginal Japan in the 1960s and 1970s, sparked in part by the rise in popularity of the ethnological works of Origuchi Shinobu and Yanagita Kunio. Artists were interested in a new kind of return to Japan as a form of symbolic protest from the margins: in the words of Susan Klein, author of an important monograph on Butoh, they were trying to "soak up the Japaneseness of the periphery."[2] Third-generation Butoh groups such as Sankai-juku, whose work continues to seek, in part, an aestheticization of tradition, still enjoy significant popularity among European and American audiences. Many other dancers and groups might be considered in the context of such questions of tradition, including the tradition that Butoh itself has come to represent in dance: Hijikata's disciple Ashikawa Yōko, Takai Tomiko, Hijikata's widow Motofuji Akiko, Nakajima Natsu, Kasai Akira, Carlotta Ikeda, and well-known groups such as the former Byakko-sha, Maijuku, or Dai-Rakuda Kan. Such a discussion would open the question of Butoh's legacies, but for the moment, we shall return to the early 1960s to examine the early rhetoric of Butoh and nostalgia.

In 1963, the eccentric and engaging avant-garde sculptor Okamoto Tarō (who went to France in the 1920s and published a treatise on painting in French) wrote about Japanese tradition in one of his famous essays:

When I say "tradition," I think of it as the driving power that can break apart the old frameworks, and violently release what these frameworks contained—human vitality and potential. I use the word "tradition" in this revolutionary way. . . . Unlike convention, tradition should be something that comes to life within our daily existence and within our work. We should *discover and grasp the past in the vital passion of our own lives,* and view its value from the perspective of the present. . . . That is how it will become [what I call] tradition.[3]

The longing for tradition, in Okamoto's view, is a paradoxical but passionate desire for an active, living past, one to be discovered and grasped only from within "the vital passion of our own lives," in the physical and present moment. Tradition becomes a present, driving power: unlike convention, it is viewed by Okamoto as a force that releases human energy and possibilities from the cages of the "old frameworks."

Andreas Huyssen writes in another context, of the relation between nostalgia and utopia, that the "reconceptualization [of history] which problematizes history and story, memory and representation from any number of differing subject positions, may indeed be imbued with an element of nostalgia. Nostalgia itself, however, is not the opposite of utopia, but, as a form of memory, always implicated, even productive in it."[4] This kind of productive nostalgia that may be closely allied with utopian vision, a remembrance that looks toward the future, is a useful paradigm for considering the deliberate search for the known invisible in Butoh as well as in Surrealism's legacies. One can see in Butoh a complex negotiation with the meaning of the past and tradition. The utopian nostalgia expressed in Butoh, combined, at times, with despair, takes many forms—from Ohno

Kazuo's recurrent trope of the search for his mother, a dreamlike return to the womb also associated with the creation of the cosmos, to the search to embody the spirit of the ancestors. Both Ohno and especially Hijikata allude to northern rural Japan and farmers' bodies; childhood and rural mythology hold an important place in their work, and they later make use of Noh and traditional theatrical fragments. Yet these seeming turns toward the past have often been misread in essentialist terms as representing or expressing something "quintessentially Japanese"—the "Japanese imagination," or the "Japanese spirit." At other times, to counter this critical tendency, writers have focused on the influences and impact of Western dance forms in Butoh,[5] thus reaching the critical impasse of speaking about a pastiche of elements from "West" and "East" and failing to analyze the particular structure of Butoh's uses (and deliberate distancing of) these figurative "essences."

How does the language of Butoh function and yet resist codification or representational expression? How does it continually construct an expressive and imitable series of performative gestures and then violently resist their codification or repetition? Butoh, in my view, is structured around an iteration and citation based on longing or a complex structure of nostalgia. It depends upon reference to precisely those essences to which access is necessarily foreclosed. This longing, memory, and iteration are a source of remembrance within Butoh but also, and more centrally, of present passion (Okamoto writes, "We should discover and grasp the past in the vital passion of our own lives"). It is the discovery of something that is called "past" and identified with the figure of the past, but is, in a sense, misread as such. As a radically present or physically enacted nostalgia that nonetheless resists, precisely, being the representation *of* anything, it is dependent in part on this misreading, on this foreclosure of access, for its present, physical, imminent force.

If this hypothesis, which can only begin to be proposed here, is correct, and Butoh becomes a moment that invites misreading as a return to an absent past, then it is a phantasmatic recollection that at the same time enacts a refusal of this reading. Early Butoh also enacts, through what some would call its "breathtaking messiness," a refusal of wholeness and an emphasis on the fragment, an obvious rejection of the Western and *shingeki* (new theater) psychological realism of earlier twentieth-century theatrical forms; it performs instead a spiritual search that radically questions the boundaries of the body. It focuses on the physical materiality of the body and ultimately demonstrates the estrangement of the body from itself.

Mishima Yukio (1925–1970) was a close associate of Hijikata and other affiliated avant-garde artists—both Mishima and Hijikata posed for the important experimental photographer Hosoe Eikoh, for example, and Mishima wrote the calligraphy for stunning pastiche-like posters by designer Yokoo Tadanori advertising Hijikata's performances. Mishima wrote essays for the program notes of Hijikata's "Dance Experience no kai" performances, and in one entitled *Kiki no buyō* (Dance of crisis; 1960) he elaborated on the structure and aims of Butoh:

Avant-garde dance does not use toe shoes. Its purpose is the opposite of that of classical ballet: if the point of classical ballet is to attain a "balance that is constructed on top of crisis," one might say that the purpose of avant-garde dance is on the side of expressing the crisis itself. So avant-garde dance needs no artificial prerequisite for crisis like toe shoes. The very crisis and uncertainty of human existence must be made to appear vividly before our eyes, through the pure expression of the human flesh with little or no artificial prerequisite. It is inevitable that the requirement for actuality in dance takes on forms that may seem symbolic and difficult at first glance. The reason for this is that nothing (including words) is more adorned with our practical and customary purposes than the human flesh and its means of expression. Classical ballet takes advantage of such purposes to show the audience a false but beautiful dream; but if avant-garde dance does not manage to scrape off such concepts from the start, actuality will not be able to emerge. What seems to be difficult is but the dissonant sound of scraping off old paint. . . . Their performance is simple, plain, and very understandable.[6]

While continuing to rely on the oppositions of pure physical expression versus artifice, ballet versus avant-garde dance's actuality, Mishima can be seen to reiterate certain purposes present in prewar critical theories about experimental writing, such as Takiguchi Shūzō's essay on the relation between poetry and actuality, which emphasized notions of hesitating balance and a physical pausing of the writing hand just before attempting to reach the limit of the encounter with actuality.[7] Mishima speaks of a hesitancy, in contrast to the balanced state of classical ballet; without transcending customary purposes and practical habitual expressions, it will not be possible for "actuality" to emerge. His negative phrase places the crisis and actuality as the limit situation and implies that even transcending such customs does not guarantee actuality will necessarily appear. (Unlike Takiguchi's word *jitsuzai,* Mishima uses the English loan term, *akuchuaritii,* almost as if to estrange the word itself.)

At the same time, Mishima's idea of "expressing the crisis itself" or manifesting it, while relying on the idea of a pure human body with as little artificial prerequisite as possible, recognizes that the body/flesh itself and its means of expression are constructed, like language (and even more than language) within artifices of convention and habit: "Nothing (including words) is more adorned with our practical and customary purposes than the human flesh and its means of expression." This claim recalls the views of the early Surrealist poets about the difficulty of transcending the inherent conventionality of language, poetic form, and hence, of experience. The body, then, for Mishima becomes "covered" or "ornamented" within its own practical usefulness and the artifices of its customs to become, in a sense, invisible in its actuality as if it were covered with "old paint," its vitality trapped within an old framework. Thus the artifice of the body—even without such an extreme prerequisite as toe shoes—and the artifice of customary physical gestures become clear. The physical body itself, the pure expression of the flesh ("tada ningen no nikutai no junsui hyōgen"), becomes a horizon—as actuality was for Takiguchi and the Japanese Surrealists—of what cannot ultimately be accessed.[8] The attempt to reach the body's actuality, through crisis, needs to involve a dissonance, the sound of scraping off the old paint of habit and utility.

The next year, again writing in the program of Hijikata's Dance Experience performance, Mishima continued to discuss the relation between the body and everyday objects. According to the anecdote that begins the essay, Hijikata described to Mishima his fascination with the sight of a polio victim who, in trying to grasp an object, began by moving in the opposite direction from the object and took what seemed to be a long and meandering way toward it. Mishima begins with Hijikata's inspiration in order to observe the splitting open of the body within and through its relation to objects.

Butoh movement, related to [Hijikata's] observation, is useful in exposing the lies of our daily movements, the lies of our so-called "natural movements" or manners [*shizen no dōsa*] as trained and made habitual by social custom. When, for no particular reason, we reach out to grab the coffee cup or cigarette on our desk, what we are grasping (*begreifen*) is in fact the concept (*Begriff*) of the coffee cup and cigarette—we are inhabiting a world in which we are at peace with these things as concepts. What we consider to be natural movements are a momentary cheating on what is in fact a severe and terrifying relation between human beings and objects, conspiring to cover it over with a veil; thus, everyday movement becomes the performance of a kind of ritual conspiracy [of hiding the severity and terror of this relation]. A strange perversion is concealed in this; or rather, one might say that our everyday manners themselves are ceremonial, ritualistic, and the movements of avant-garde dance or the movements of the polio patient could perhaps be called, in the strict sense of the term, "natural movements."[9]

Mishima's observation defamiliarizes the opposition between the "ritualistic" and strange movements of Butoh and the so-called natural (assumed, everyday) movements of picking up the cigarette or coffee cup from one's desk. He makes the habitual motion itself a construction, a trained habit or fabrication whose making is under erasure. This view makes one's relation to objects, the grasping of objects, in fact a relation to concepts (he inserts the German word for concept, *Begriff*), a grasping of a concept (*begreifen*) rather than any kind of direct relation. *Begreifen* in German means to understand, to comprehend; at the same time the word *begreifen* contains the root word *greifen*, meaning to grasp in the physical sense of grasping an object. Bringing into play the notion of concept and the German word that combines physical movement and mental "grasp," Mishima links the structure of habitual movement to the conventionalized structure of a language. Here, the erasure of the construction becomes the inscription of preconception or custom, the conspiratorial deception that makes the movement of daily life "natural" and that of the polio victim or the Butoh dancer "unnatural." While still relying on oppositions, settling in the end into the opposition between naturalness and artifice, Mishima manages to undermine and point to the paradox of this opposition, especially by calling the formation of the "artifice" or "habitus" of everyday movement a form of "cheating," a "conspiracy" that is also an illicit liaison (*nareai*) and, literally, a perversion (*tōsaku*).

By pointing to the horizon between everyday movement and dance, by writing of seeking access to the inaccessible realm of bodily flesh, pure or natural physical movement—a direct expression of the crisis cited earlier involving the least artificial prerequisite of objects—Mishima makes clear another aspect of Butoh's nostalgic structure for a "beyond" of culture located in the flesh (*nikutai*) that nonetheless remains outside of the possibility of access. Hijikata narrates the process of arriving at the images of

11. Hijikata Tatsumi (above) and Ohno Kazuo, "Bara-iro dansu—Shibusawa Tatsuhiko no ie no hō e" (Rose-colored dance—toward the house of Shibusawa Tatsuhiko). Photo by Hosoe Eikoh, 1965.

dance through the encounter with one's experiences in a form that suggests a traumatic rupture: "When you encounter such experiences, things will emerge from your body of themselves," he narrates in a later speech entitled "Kazedaruma." "We don't have time to 'express' and 'represent.'" His body, as he tells of the process, transforms itself into and out of various objects through a violent process that moves beyond simple representation toward what Mishima called the "severity and terror" of the relation between human beings and objects. Hijikata describes and imagines fantastical transformations of the body:

I become a wicker trunk squashed into the shape of a pair of bellows, with my insides all splayed out, and I play around in that state. Just then, I see a horse standing still and I find myself wanting to cut it with a saw. . . . Or I cut a river, better if it is frozen, cut the river and bring it over here, and when I do that then very quickly, faster and faster my body begins to extend and enlarge. Like the sky, after all. Or if you think of it as a plate, then you can smash it to pieces. That's one single plate, a human-body plate; if you smash it to pieces then a riot might break out. The extension and expansion of the body, beyond and unconnected to such delusions, quickly continues to spread wider and wider.[10]

Hijikata imagines the body here as alternately container and contained, as wicker trunk that becomes a saw that cuts a river and then expands to become like the sky, metamorphosing into a plate, which one could break: a "human-body plate," continually expanding. This series of images suggests Hijikata's continual transformation of the body and its figures (and metaphors). The body becomes, exchanges itself for, and engages with objects in a continual process of expansion, rupture, and reconstitution.[11] He at once opens the boundaries of the body as the articulation of an interiority and as an object linked to the (impossible) returns of childhood and the countryside of Tōhoku, and linked as well to the crisis of relation to objects. In other words, the allusions to his native Tōhoku, his images of learning from rural Japanese farmers and from children, become a way of defamiliarizing the movements of everyday life and at the same time positing the space of an "other world," a utopian beyond (that is neither simplified or aestheticized but rather, in itself made strange) as an inspiration.

With his studio in Yokohama and his thrice weekly lessons, Ohno Kazuo even now leads students in a quest for dance that, in his view, begins in everyday life and so takes a different turn from Hijikata's images. "Butoh starts in the movements of the body in the everyday" ("nichijō no karada no ugoki," with the movements of the everyday body), he writes in "What Is a Lesson?"[12] Ohno's theories of dance, however, overturn the expectation that dance would be primarily about movement, about the acts and motions of the body: "In the last few years, one of my most striking realizations has been that it's not a good thing to move around too much. One has to move some, but there should be something like an interior movement, and if one holds back, holds back patiently, then at that moment, one's feeling can move ahead."[13]

The idea of restraining extraneous movement that is not motivated by an interior movement (in Ohno's vocabulary, by a movement of spirit—*tamashii*—or feeling) is linked by Butoh critic and contemporary haiku poet Nagata Kōi to the writings of Zeami on *senu tokoro* (time or space of not doing).[14] Nagata cites a section of Zeami's *Kakyō* (circa 1424). This passage is considered in some detail for what it implies about the structure of Butoh's nostalgia and longing, and the attempt to reach limits beyond artifice, custom, or physical habit. Zeami writes:

That which I call the *senu tokoro* [time or space of not doing] is the interval [between actions and representations]. . . . If one were to ask why people find these intervals (of not doing) interesting, it is because the player is not in the least restless or careless during these moments, but concentrates on assuring the connectedness of the performance. In the space between dances, when one ceases to sing, or when the acting and words or all other manner of things are paused, the actor keeps a concentration in the depths of his heart without relinquishing it. That interior feeling affects the sensation of the exterior and makes it interesting.[15]

In the intervals when the moving hand is stopped, or the voice ceases to make sound, the full tension of this deeper center of feeling (*naishin*) overflows onto the stage, lends its scent or effect (*soto ni nioite*) and because of this, according to Zeami, the fascination of these moments arises. In other words, these moments become not extraneous to the performance but central to it. At the same time, they become an open space for the investment or projection of tensions and longings in the performance, and a moment where the distinction between interiority and exteriority is undermined.

One recalls here the paradox that confronted the Surrealist writers, such as Breton and Takiguchi, centered around the problem of the will—the necessity of moving beyond logic and intention, yet the difficulty of willing or prescribing this movement toward the "beyond." A similar paradox of performative concentration considered by Zeami resonates with the ideas of dance expounded by Ohno even as they recall this Surrealist paradox. One's intention and concentration, according to Zeami (later in the same section) must not be visible to the outside or they will appear to be an artifice—*waza*, which means both a movement of the body in playing a role and also the appearance of conscious intent in acting. In other words, the moment will no longer appear to be *senu tokoro* (not doing), but precisely "doing."[16] So, for Zeami, one must hide this intention even from oneself in order to join the actions before and after the interval. Ohno's strongly antitechnical, anti-intentional idea of movement, as he describes it, is very close then to this particular moment in Zeami's ideas. Moving for its own sake is shunned: "Modern dance is too talkative and expresses too much. . . . If one holds back, holds back patiently, then one's feeling can move ahead."[17]

From this question of the paradox of intentionality and the avoidance of artifice, one might return to the question of memories and yearnings, and the specific kind of nostalgia that exists in Ohno's images. A central image of recollection in Ohno's work is his memory of his mother (associated with the womb and creation). He recounts in an interview:

When I was a child I was endlessly selfish toward my mother. I was selfish all the way up until my mother died. But my mother still gave everything for me. She always trusted me. Until my mother got sick and died, I took advantage of this and I was as selfish as it was possible to be. "Mother, I'm sorry" now I apologize all the time. It's become a habit. I realized that if you don't apologize right away you may never have the chance. "I understand how you feel, so it's all right," my mother says, comforting me instead. When my mother was dying, I stroked her head, her hair. Until the very end of the end, until she was gone. There was nothing else that I was capable of doing for her. As long as it was possible, I repeated, "Mother, please get well," and continued to stroke her hair.

A tiny child cries, wails, and slaps its mother with its little hands as if to chastise her, and the mother says, "I'm sorry, sorry, sorry," but still she looks happy. Until she died, in fact it was not me, but on the contrary my mother who stroked my head, and encouraged me. *More and more I have a feeling that I want to touch something* [just out of my grasp], I want to cherish and nourish that deep feeling.[18]

Ohno's relation to his mother is a paradoxical combination of gratitude and apology, and evokes a desire to reach something just out of his grasp. He describes a desire to cherish that feeling itself, the deep feeling of wanting to touch something (as, he implies, he did not know to cherish his mother before her death, at least not enough). From the place where Ohno holds that feeling of belated desire to comfort and encourage—the place of a desire that it is finally too late to fulfill—comes the sense of irreparable yet impossible loss, a missed connection from which the dance emerges. If one looks at the rehearsal and notes for Ohno's piece "Watashi no okaasan" (My mother), one sees both a literal seeking and love for an absence, and an association of the mother with the cosmos, the birth of the universe.[19] Later, in 1985, Ohno composed a piece inspired by his encounter with the Dead Sea. He writes: "Engulfed by painful feelings, I want to become a ghost, an apparition, I want to *borrow the form of an apparition* and meet other phantoms, and I must stretch out my hand to these phantoms and search out and discover where they are. Any apparition at all, it is the encounter that is the most important thing." Again, the hand reaches out to grasp something that has no substance and no definition, that is just out of reach. He continues, "A living ghost, a dying ghost, a ghost eternally in the process of dying"[20]—any ghost, between life and death, or most tellingly, in the state that is eternally in the process of dying, will effectively suit this grasp; but the search for such an encounter nonetheless remains paramount.

This fascination, the longing for the encounter with what is on the barest edge of possibility (the longing for crisis), like the longing in early twentieth-century Japanese poetry for the encounter with "actuality," has the structure in these postwar movements of a desire performed and incorporated in the physical movements of the dance, which is its experimental trial and both can and cannot "grasp" the object of this longing. Precisely in the sense that one "grasps" these entities as "concepts" one fails to grasp them in their "actuality," according to the implied logic of Butoh's nostalgia. The conscious quest for such an encounter is a paradox that requires a continual refusal and renegotiation between the dancer and the viewer: thus, while at times perhaps seeming to appeal to simple and originary essences, some of which are national, cultural, or traditional, the works overturn the structure of this very appeal, and continuously refuse to be reified into a structured or singular aesthetic vocabulary. At least, to the extent that they are not, Butoh, like Surrealism, can remain alive. Even the idea of the encounter itself must escape closure and remain within paradox. Ohno writes:

I cannot explain the word "encounter," and I do not want to. My dance is an encounter with humanity, an encounter with Life. But I cannot forget that we all sleep upon death, and that our lives are carried by the thousands of dead that came before us and whom we will soon join. If we decide intellectually/consciously what we wish to do, the dance we perform will be dead. A very small thing can make a very great work, a very small experience from life which we carry in our heart and allow to take form.[21]

Both Surrealism and the avant-garde performance forms of the postwar period—as one of the central (though not the only) places where Surrealism's legacy was carried on—have undergone many transformations, and some critics claim these movements have come too close to being formalized or conventionalized themselves as recognizable gestural vocabularies. Most of the prewar Surrealists and many early postwar performers

(Hijikata, Terayama) have died, and Ohno and many associated artists who are still alive and working must slip out each time from the naming and conventions that would transform them too thoroughly and too soon into objects of nostalgia. Thus Ohno and other avant-garde dancers have begun to refuse the term "Butoh" for their work, as this process of formalization begins to feel like a restriction. In the end, then, this very process of grasping and longing can run the risk of being too thoroughly conceptualized and grasped. Within an expanded notion of cultural memory as a constitutive part of creativity, however, one might imagine the possibility of further transformations and reverberations.

APPENDIX

The following reproductions are facsimiles of original Japanese texts, poems, and excerpts discussed in this volume. Numbers of the pages on which these texts are discussed or translated are given in parentheses after the legends.

囈語

窃盗金魚
強盗喇叭
恐喝胡弓
賭博ねこ
詐欺更紗
瀆職天鵞絨
姦淫林檎
傷害雲雀
殺人ちゆりつぶ
堕胎陰影
騒擾ゆき
放火まるめろ
誘拐かすてえら。

AI. Yamamura Bochō, "Geigo," from *Yamamura Bochō zenshū*, courtesy of Kanagawa Museum of Modern Literature (p. 19).

記號説

★

白い食器　花

赤い

白い　スプン　春の午後3時　白い

★

プリズム建築　白い動物

空間

★

青い旗

林檎と貴婦人　白い風景

花と樂器

★

白い窓

風

★

貝殻と花環

スリッパの少女

金糸鳥　緑の熱れる　汽船のある　肖像

★

温室の少年　遠い月

白い花

☆

人形と化粧　白い靴下　化粧のある暗い窓

白い美學　美學

☆

銅色立體人形　銀色立體人形

靜力學　花と鏡

★

白色建築

遠い郊外の空

巡り　★

屋上庭園　海岸

草をむしる少年　白い少年

空間 I

★

魔術する貴婦人の腕　魔術する貴婦人の腕　銀色の少年　魔術する銀色の少年

赤い鏡に映る　赤い鏡に映る

白い手と肩と花

空間　私

★

青い空

なにも見えない　なにも見えない

白い家

★

白い遠景

夜になると桃色の猫

願望

★

白い少年

遠い空

ヒヤシンス

窓

白い風景

☆

明るい生活と僕です
明るい思想と僕です
透明の快楽と僕です

透明の禮節と僕です
新鮮な食慾と僕です
新鮮な戀愛と僕です

青い過去の憶ひ出は
みんなイメーヂ壜に詰めてですてました

★

力學は暗い
植物は重い

★

花束と詩集
白い食器

白い
白い

黄色い

★

白い住宅
白い

桃色の貴婦人
青い空

★

トランペットの貴公子はみんな赤いネクタイをかけてゐる

★

夜会服 夜会服 夜会服 夜会服 夜会服 夜会服 夜会服
面白くない

A2. Kitasono Katsue, "Kigōsetsu" (Semiotic theory). Courtesy of Kanagawa Museum of Modern Literature (p. 22).

マックス　エルンスト　　MAX ERNST

夜の旅行者は
不可解な夜の手錠を
肉片のやうに
食ひ散らす

蜃のない夜牢に
ゴビ砂漠氣附で屆く
擬餌の手紙がある

言葉の雜詰を
飢えた永遠の島たちは
肉片と間違へるのだ

一夜
人間の贈物は
花の如く燃えてゐた

A3. Takiguchi Shūzō, "Max Ernst." Courtesy of Uchibori Hiroshi, by permission of Takiguchi Ayako. Photo: Y. Higashi (p. 27).

A4. Hagiwara Sakutarō, "Posutaa to shite no ishō." Courtesy of Kanagawa Museum of Modern Literature (p. 45).

● ポスタアとしての意匠

自然主義の文壇は、小説を科學的に畫くと稱した。最近の或る詩人等は、詩を機械學の方則により、メカニズムで書くと言つてる。かうしたアクセントの強い主張は、意匠の巧みなポスタアと同じやうに、確かに或る效果的な印象を人にあたへる。

だが本當のことを言へば、單なるポスタアの文學であり、幾智によつて誇張された修辭にすぎない。實際の創作としては、科學的の小説などとは何所もなく、メカニズムで作つた詩などとは一つもない。單に客觀的の態度で書いた小説や、趣味の外貌を機械的にした詩があるに過ぎない。かつて立體的の詩と稱した者は、馬鹿正直にも文字をピラミット形に印刷した。

先づ第一に、何故に現實を意識するのに、新しい方法が必要であるか？

西脇順三郎氏はその著書「超現實主義詩論」の第一頁で

「習慣は現實に對する意識力をにぶらす。傳統のために意識力が冬眠狀態に入る。故に現實がつまらなくなるので

ある。習慣を破ることは現實を面白くすることになる。意識力が新鮮になるからである。併し注意すべきことは習

慣傳統を破るために破るものでなく、詩的表現のために、換言すれば、詩の目的としてつまらない現實を面白くす

るため破るのである。」と記した。

實に言語同斷な暴論である。

これは單に超現實主義者に對する許す可からざる暴言であるばかりでなくて、現實に對して日夜增大して行く關心

を持つて居る現代人に對し、又殆んど壓倒的な威力を以て吾々を圍繞して居る現實に對して、西脇順三郎氏が極端な

認識不足を暴露したものであると共に、現實に直面する勇氣と力と正義と誠實とに缺けた人々の逃避を、最も尤もら

しく云ひ飾つたものである。

然るにこの不思議なる見方は、日本の超現實主義者の現實觀の一特徴となつた。

A5. Kanbara Tai, "Chōgenjitsushugi no botsuraku," excerpt. Courtesy of Kanagawa Museum of Modern Literature, by permission of Kanbara Ryō (p. 55).

シュルレアリストが持つ現實の世界に對する嫌惡を理解せよ。優れたる文學運動は通俗の價値に對する否定の新眞理を隱すものである。されば諸君はシュルレアリスムの眞理を理解せよ。現實世界の優秀のジューヌリスト達よ、シュルレアリスムの新しい眞理を理解せよ。新しい nihility の夢を理解せよ。正當に言へば藝術の法則に無智であるべし。現實世界は死の世界であり、又睡眠の世界である。睡眠の世界に夢を見る人人よ。諸君は存在してゐないのである。諸君は嫌惡すべき生物である。死せる創造のミューズなる者は睡眠の世界に睡眠する諸君に夢を與へるのである。夢を與へられた諸君は表現をなすのである。これは睡眠の世界に可能なるものであつて、睡眠してゐる人人のみの努力である。さうして諸君は表現をなすのである。その故で諸君は嫌惡すべき生物である。諸君は睡眠してゐる。諸君は夢を見てゐる。諸君は空想の世界にゐる。諸君は死の世界にゐる。諸君は知覺の世界にゐる。諸君は死に捕へられた者であり、死の世界の捕虜である。亡靈よ、語れ。亡靈よ、夢みよ。亡靈よ、祝福さるべし。諸君は死の國から出ようとする希望を持たないであらう。空想の世界から遁れようとする希望を持たないであらう。夢の國土から離れようとする希望を持たないであらう。諸君は睡眠の世界に永遠に睡眠することを欲するのか。表現の世界に永遠に表現することを欲するのか。諸君は永遠に存在しない人達である。

A6. Ueda Toshio, excerpt from "Watashi no chōgenjitsushugi" (My surrealism). Courtesy of Kanagawa Museum of Modern Literature (pp. 58–59).

●詩は正にほろびつつある

A7. Hagiwara Sakutarō, "Shi wa masa ni horobitsutsu aru," from "Shi ni tsuite no shō-essei." Courtesy of Kanagawa Museum of Modern Literature (p. 84–85).

詩 の 偶 像

ふるへる薔薇を拒絶する永遠の臓腑のために
そこに不可避的なる孤独がゐた
初夏の光りのネツトのなかに葡萄いろの高空と寂寞とを置いたのであつた
朗朗たる友のために また明快な訣別の日のために
崇高なる王のごとくすでに水晶の薔薇を祈禱する
その詩人の化粧せる瞳は死んでゐる

北 園 克 衛

A8. Kitasono Katsue, "Shi no gūzō." Courtesy of Kanagawa Museum of Modern Literature, by permission of Hashimoto Akio (p. 91).

Pélerin

飛鳥 融

僕の失ふ多くのもの・愛人・踊子・持物・名譽・そうして想出・皆さびしいことでした・「忙しくて忙しくて」そうして僕の若い年月を忘れてしまふ・友よ（有るものは失はれる）この一般的な眞理が僕に幸福の影を落すだらうか。さようなら・何も欲しない僕は何も失ひ度くない僕だつた。そして來る日も來る日も海邊には痛い太陽が續く

A9. Asuka Tōru, "Pélerin." Courtesy of Kanagawa Museum of Modern Literature (p. 95).

ETAMINES NARRATIVES

銅鑼と白薔薇とが協和音を構成するとつばさのある睡眠がさけびだす。そのなかには異常に青い草が繁茂する地方へ跳ねやる虹のやうに強靱な彈條がある。田舎は土龍のやうに美しいがその寒さにおのく掌は正確なので顔を蔽ふのに充分な引力を提供する。すべての音を發する物質と同じにあの睡眠も意志に屬してゐたのかしら？そこから頭腦が月のやうに細密な頭腦が見える。寒冷な鏡面には無數の神様が附着してゐる。この瞬間の噴水は花のごとく綺麗である。あふれる無用物をもつて花の意志をもつて新建築術をもくろむ葉卷色の嗟をした建築師の二つの眼は義眼である。そして彼の姓名がじだいに無機物に變化しつつあるのを意識してゐる。一すぢの黄金の光線は小鳥の發聲機官を衝きとほしたまふ。合理的なる午前七時よ。

瀧口修造

A10. Takiguchi Shūzō, "Etamines Narratives," part I. Courtesy of Kanagawa Museum of Modern Literature, by permission of Takiguchi Ayako (p. 109).

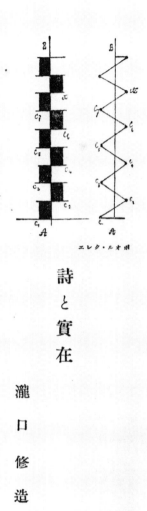

エレク・ル才ゼ

詩と實在

瀧口修造

それは正午、巨大な眼、僕のペンはピサの斜塔のやうに異様な均衡を保ちながら動き出す。僕の指たちは僕の意志の法則（sc.）に從つてこのペン軸を支へてゐる。僕の聲帯が、たとへば噴水が永遠的な姿態をその傍のナイオビの大理石像のそれと同じやうな效果を持つた時のやうに、もしも一つの意志の法則（sc.）に從つて振動するかのやうな不可避力を告白するならば、波紋に滿ちた僕の指たちは、僕の聲帯に向つて自負をもつて反抗するだらうか。人間の運動を多少とも透視畫的に視やうとする慾望の心理には、倫理的なものも、形而上學的なものも、美術的なものすらも缺除してゐる――唯一の現實への對立には人間はいかなる種類の方法をも有しない、唯一つ或る透視畫的方法があるばかりであるとするか？　人間はそれを最も重要な文化的發見の一つとして、現實處理法とする。或る人間はそれに

A11. Takiguchi Shūzō, opening lines of "Shi to jitsuzai" with illustration by Paul Klee. Courtesy of Kanagawa Museum of Modern Literature, by permission of Takiguchi Ayako (p. 112).

一六五

心の根の互にからまる
土の囁くはるかなる
土の永劫は静かに眠る

果を通り
花を通り
再び通りになる

人の運も再び人の運となる
姿女の花を通り
この永劫の水車
かなしげにとまる
水は流れめぐり
車はめぐり
また流れまはる

無限の過去の或時に始まり
無限の未来の或時に終る
人命の旅

この世のあらゆる瞬間も
永劫の時間の一部分
草の質の一粒も
永劫の空間の一部分
有限の存在は無限の存在の一部分
この小さい庭に
梅の古木さるすべり
樫 山茶花 笹
年中訪れる鶯 ほととぎす などの
小鳥の群慶の伴紹か限
すすき 薔薇
蓼 白く穂を出し

水車の隣りに茶屋があり
旅人のあんころ餅とか
この曼陀羅の里
若き水鳥の飛立つ
花を求めて質を求めず
質のための花にすぎぬ

A12. Nishiwaki Junzaburō, *Tabibito kaerazu* poem 165. Courtesy of Kanagawa Museum of Modern Literature, by permission of Nishiwaki Jun'ichi (p. 126).

序　文

Cerebrum ad acerram recidit. 現實の世界は腦髓にすぎない.
この腦髓を破ることは超現實藝術の目的である. 崇高なる藝術
の形態はすべて超現實主義である. 故に崇高なる詩も亦超現實
詩である. 詩は腦髓の中に一つの眞空なる砂漠を構成してその
中へ現實の經驗に屬するすべてのサンサシヨン, サンチマン,
イデ等をたゝき落すことによりて腦髓を純粋にせしむるところ
の一つの方法である. こゝに純粋詩がある. 腦髓はウルトラ桃
色のガラスの如きものになる. 詩はまた腦髓を斯くの如く破壞
する. 破壞されたる腦髓は一つの破壞されたる香水タンクの如
く非常に馥郁たるものである. こゝに香水商館的名譽がある.
吾々はも早やホコリツポイ葡萄をそのまゝ動物の如く食はない
然しそれをツブしてその汁をのむものである. 故に詩の成立價
値はシアンパン酒としての價値に他ならない. また詩は腦髓を
燃燒せしむるものである. こゝに火花として又は火力としての
詩がある. 吾々は現實の世界を燃料としてゐるのみであつて自
然人の如く燃料それ自身を享樂するものでない. 吾々はこの燃
料たる現實の世界をもやしてその中から光明及熱のみを吸收せ
んとするものである. 純粋にして溫かき馥郁たる火夫よ!

A13. Nishiwaki Junzaburō, preface to "Fukuikutaru kafu yo," 1927. Courtesy of Kanagawa Museum of Modern Literature, by permission of Nishiwaki Jun'ichi (p. 134).

アバナとフアーフアーは永劫に流れる

月光は紅い雪を照らし彼女たちの羽毛の冠は千々に乱れる

巨大な花の楯をふりかざし彼女たちは戰ふ

彼女たちは決して負傷しない

彼女たちは白鳥の脊の上に睡眠る

彼女たちは旗艦のやうに華やかな夢をもつ

Vaudeville

友谷静榮

天使は愛のために泣く

雪花石膏の神々の像さへも水のやうに流れ去るであらう

運命に對する嫌惡は阿片のやうに私を酔はせる

貝は鹽水を吐くことによつて愛に値しないであらうか

美しき献身の瞬間をたれも永遠に記憶しないのである

A14. Tomotani Shizue, "Vaudeville" and "Tenshi wa ai no tame ni naku." Reprinted (Tokyo: Tamura shoten) (pp. 142, 145).

月

私の前身は海月（くらげ）でした
月は私を愛し　私も月を愛してゐました

今では私は太陽の花葵です
月は意地悪な眼差で私を傷けやうといたします

神様私を轉身させて下さい
こんどは五色ノジュコになさつて下さい

さうしたら私は月を見ないですむでせう
月もやがて私を忘れるでせう

A15. Tomotani Shizue, "Tsuki." Reprinted (Tokyo: Tamura shoten) (p. 147).

春　　　　　　　　　　　　　　　　　　江間章子

薔薇色である幌馬車の翳が庭園に向つた窓掛けを搖すぶる。ちやうど小さい心臓であつた。それは青い麥畑の中でハタと止まり、かつてその窓掛けにふれた手のやうに、和蘭製の柱時計のやうに、想ひ出されたやうに、動き出し、白い指先は祈る姿で組まれ、けれど此の邸の廣間にある彩細模様の壜は香高い花の重みで崩壊れていつた。……あ、あれは懐しいお祖母さんの木、鈍い鉛色の杖をついて。――私は膝の上に GREEN・GARDEN なる書物を伏せる。（若い作曲家はちようど此のやうな午後死んでいつた。）石の階段は夢見る。仄かなる雲。それはなほ睡り續ける氷のやうに冷たい羽毛をもつた小鳥でゞもある。――この階段を踏んで芝生に降りると、青い河の下流では華やかな春の祭典、船底の塗具の塗換工事が行はれる。

A16. Ema Shōko, "Haru." Courtesy of Kanagawa Museum of Modern Literature, by permission of Ema Shōko (p. 150).

葡萄園

江間章子

夢はケープのやうに人々の姿をつゝみ風に吹かれて――幸福が瞳を開き、やさしい會話の聲があちらこちらに聞える。そして終ひに總ての心臟は鏡のやうに滑り落ちた。風のレースの糸がほぐれ、あらゆる幹に卷きついてゐるあいだ、なほ人々は小鳥たちを眞似て青い絹の空の下を小刻みに行つたり來たりする。雲から飛び出す鳩、叢の中の如露、それから木蔭の籐椅子等――まもなく此處から黃昏がたちあがり、そしてピカピカした葉つぱが押し合ひながら現はれはじめる。けれど今私たちが聞くことが出來るのはそれ等が銀貨のやうに觸れ合ふ音だけである。

A17. Ema Shōko, "Budōen" [Budōzono]. Courtesy of Kanagawa Museum of Modern Literature, by permission of Ema Shōko (pp. 154–155).

鼠

夏の光る鱗の甲にひそみ
薔薇の房を喰み、銀色の
衣裳でときどき裸足である
氣遣はれる潜水夫よ
旅人は珊瑚島にのぼつて
遙か太陽が沈み行くのを
垣間見る事が出來た
微笑の漂ふあたり
夜のレェスはゆらゆらと
天井から垂れる
海藻を持ちあげた手が
想ひ出したやうにふと
スプンを動かすのを止めて
あれはシエラツアド姫の聲だ……

江間章子

A18. Ema Shōko, "Nezumi." Courtesy of Kanagawa Museum of Modern Literature, by permission of Ema Shōko (p. 156).

REFERENCE MATTER

SELECTED CHRONOLOGY

This chronology is intended as a general reference for the reader and is by no means exhaustive. It cites certain major events relating to the development of Dada and Surrealism in Japan and provides contextual landmarks in world history and European Surrealism. Although some of these events were not discussed in the chapters above, they begin a chronological outline and may serve as suggestions for further research.

Most of the existing chronologies of Surrealism in Japan were compiled by Tsuruoka Yoshihisa and are to be found in *Nihon chōgenjitsushugi shiron* (Japanese Surrealist poetics), *Shururearisumu no tenkai* (The development of Surrealism), and "*Gendaishi no furontia*": *Modanizumu no keifu* (The frontier of contemporary poetry: The genealogy of Modernism). In addition to these references and original sources, I consulted the combined chronology in the exhibition catalogue *Nihon no shururearisumu, 1925–1945* (Japanese Surrealism, 1925–1945, Nagoya City Art Museum, 1990), 207–27.

# indicates events in European Dada and Surrealism
* indicates events in Japanese and world history

1889   Mori Ōgai publishes the collection of translated European poetry
       Omokage (Vestiges)

1905   Ueda Bin publishes *Kaichōon* (Sound of the tide), including translations
       of Baudelaire, Verlaine, and Mallarmé

1913   Yamamura Bochō composes "Geigo"
       Nagai Kafū publishes *Sangoshū* (Coral collection), including translations
       of Baudelaire, Verlaine, and Rimbaud

1916   #Tristan Tzara founds the Dada movement in Zurich

1917   Kanbara Tai publishes his first Futurist poems
       Hagiwara Sakutarō publishes *Tsuki ni hoeru* (Howling at the moon)

1918   *First World War ends

1920   Takahashi Shinkichi begins Dadaist writing, inspired by an article
        (August 15) in the newspaper *Yorozuchōhō* by Wakatsuki Yasuji, which
        provides information about the Dadaist movement in Europe and
        cites two of Tzara's manifestos
        *Japan becomes member of League of Nations

1921   Hirato Renkichi distributes the pamphlet "Manifesto of the Japanese
        Futurist Movement" to passersby in Hibiya Park, Tokyo
        Shiga Naoya begins serialization of the novel *An'ya Kōro*
        *Prime Minister Hara Kei [Takashi] assassinated by young ultranationalist
        *National Socialist German Workers' (Nazi) party formed in Germany
        #Nationalist writer Maurice Barrès found guilty of "crimes against the
        security of the spirit" in mock trial led by Dadaists

1922   Nishiwaki Junzaburō goes to England to study
        #André Breton and Tzara split, signaling the end of the Dada movement

1923   Takahashi publishes *Dadaisuto Shinkichi no shi* (The poetry of Dadaist
        Shinkichi)
        First issue of the journal *Aka to kuro* (Red and black) publishes anarchist-
        tending poetry and manifestoes
        *Great Kanto Earthquake (September 1)

1924   The journal *GE.GJMGJGAM.PRRR.GJMGEM* first published, edited by Kita-
        sono Katsue from second issue
        Yama mayu (Mountain silkworm) introduces Japanese readers to works
        by Baudelaire, Rimbaud, Jean Cocteau, and Yvan Goll
        First issue of the experimental poetry journal *A* published in Dairen,
        Manchuria, with contributions by Kitagawa Fuyuhiko
        and Anzai Fuyue
        The journal *MAVO* first published, edited by Murayama Tomoyoshi
        Takahashi publishes the prose piece *Dada*
        Dadaists and anarchists gather on the second floor of the Nantendō
        restaurant, later to become the Nantendō Gallery
        Sanka movement art exhibition, with Futurists and contributors to
        MAVO participating
        #The journal *La Révolution surréaliste* published in Paris, edited by
        Pierre Naville and Benjamin Péret
        #Breton's "First Surrealist Manifesto" published with *Poissons solubles*
        (Soluble fish)
        #Surrealist research center opens in Paris
        #Tzara publishes *Sept manifestes dada*, written 1916–1920

1925   Horiguchi Daigaku's collection of poetry translations *Gekka no ichigun*
        (Gathering by moonlight) introduces Japanese readers to the Surreal-
        ist poetry of Philippe Soupault and Goll

Nishiwaki returns from Europe
The journal *Bungei tanbi* first published
*Tokyo Broadcasting Station (precursor of NHK) begins radio broadcasting
*Universal male suffrage law passed in Japan

1926 Members of the Japanese Surrealist movement congregate at Nishiwaki's
home and at the Hakujūji cafe in Tokyo

1927 *Shōbi, majutsu, gakusetsu* (Rose, magic, theory) first published by
Fujiwara Seiichi, Kitasono (under the pen name Asaka Kenkichi),
Yamada Kazuhiko, Ueda Toshio, and Ueda Tamotsu
A Surrealist manifesto ("A Note") sent to Paris Surrealists by Ueda
Tamotsu, Ueda Toshio, and Kitasono in *Shōbi, majutsu, gakusetsu*
First issue of *Fukuikutaru kafu yo* (Ah, fragrant stoker) appears, edited by
Satō Saku, with works by Nishiwaki, Takiguchi Shūzō, Nakamura
Hisao, Ueda Tamotsu, and Miura Kōnosuke
"Etamines narratives" published by Takiguchi Shūzō
Akutagawa Ryūnosuke commits suicide
*Subway service opens between Ueno and Asakusa in Tokyo
*Successful publication of one-yen books, inexpensive series publications
of contemporary Japanese and world literature
#Breton, Paul Eluard, and Péret join the Communist Party

1928 First issue of *Shi to shiron* (Poetry and poetics; Haruyama Yukio, ed.,
with Nishiwaki, Kitagawa, Anzai, Takenaka Iku) publishes Louis
Aragon's "Textes surréalistes," translated by Ueda Toshio; second
issue includes translated poetry by Eluard and Aragon
First issue of *Ishō no taiyō* published by combined members of
Fukuikutaru kafu yo and *Shōbi, majutsu, gakusetsu*
Takiguchi publishes "Chikyū sōzōsetsu" (Theory of the creation of the
Earth) in *Shi to shiron*, no. 9
#Breton publishes *Nadja* and *Le Surréalisme et la peinture* (Surrealism and
painting)

1929 Kitasono publishes the collection *Shiro no arubamu* (White album)
Nishiwaki publishes *Chōgenjitsushugi shiron* (Surrealist poetics), which
concludes with a text by Takiguchi, "Dada yori shururearisumu e"
(From Dada to Surrealism)
In *Shi to shiron* nos. 3–6, many Dada- and Surrealism-related contributions and translations are printed, including Satō's translation of
Breton's "Deux manifestes Dada" (Two manifestoes of Dada) (no. 3),
Ueda Toshio's "Watashi no chōgenjitsushugi" (My Surrealism), the
translation of Breton's "First Manifesto of Surrealism" by Kitagawa
(no. 4), and Takiguchi's translation of Aragon's *Traité du style* (Treatise
on style)

Koga Harue writes the poem "Umi" (The sea)
The journal *Ciné* started by Nishiwaki and Yamanaka Chirū (Sansei)
The journal *Rien* first published
Kobayashi Hideo publishes "Samazama naru ishō" (Multiple designs)
Kawabata Yasunari begins publication of *Asakusa kurenaidan* (Scarlet
   gang of Asakusa)
#Breton publishes "Second Manifesto of Surrealism"

1930   The group producing *Shi to shiron* splits; Kitagawa and Kanbara
   withdraw
Shi: Genjitsu (Poetry: Reality) first published by splinter group from
   Shi to shiron; articles include "Chōgenjitsushugi no botsuraku" (The
   Fall of Surrealism) by Kanbara and "Chōgenjitsushugi bungaku no
   tachiba" (The state of Surrealist literature) by Iijima Tadashi
Shi to shiron (nos. 7–9): Breton's 1929 "Second Manifesto of Surrealism"
   translated by Hara Kenkichi (no. 7); "Nihon Chōgenjitsushugi shiron"
   (Japanese Surrealist poetics) by Ueda Toshio (no. 8)
Le Surréalisme international (Fujiwara Seiichi, ed.) publishes first and
   only issue
Nishiwaki completes the critical work *Shururearuismu bungakuron* (On
   Surrealist literature)
Takiguchi publishes *Chōgenjitsushugi to kaiga,* a translation of Breton's
   Le Surréalisme et la peinture (Surrealism and painting) and the essay
   "Dada to chōgenjitsushugi" (Dada and Surrealism)
L'Esprit nouveau (Kitasono Katsue et al., eds.) first issue contains articles
   by Satō, Sagawa Chika, Fujiwara, Haruyama, Kitasono, and transla-
   tions of Aragon, Eluard, Tzara, Péret, Henri Michaux, and Stéphane
   Mallarmé
Kobayashi Hideo's translation of Rimbaud's *Une Saison en enfer* published

1931   Haruyama publishes *Shi no kenkyū* (Studies of poetry)
Takiguchi's essay "Shi to jitsuzai" (Poetry and actuality) appears in *Shi to
   shiron* (no. 10)
Kitasono translates "Les Petites Justes" by Eluard
*Japanese invasion of Manchuria begins (Manchurian Incident)

1932   *Paris-Tokyo Shinkō Bijutsuten* exhibition includes works of Jean Arp,
   Joán Miró, Max Ernst, Yves Tanguy, and Francis Picabia for the
   first time in Tokyo
The journal *Madame Blanche* first published (Kitasono Katsue and
   Iwamoto Shūzō, eds.)
*Prime Minister Inukai Tsuyoshi assassinated, marking the end of party
   cabinet system

1933   *Kaiei* first issue published by Sagawa Chika and Ema Shōko

Nishiwaki publishes the collection of poems *Ambarvalia* in two parts, "Le Monde ancien" (The ancient world) and "Le Monde moderne" (The modern world)

Kitasono publishes *Ten no tebukuro* (The glove of heaven)

Takiguchi publishes the essay "Shururearisumu no dōkō" (Surrealist trends)

Tanizaki Jun'ichirō publishes *In'ei raisan* (In praise of shadows)

*Japan withdraws from the League of Nations

1934   *L'Esprit nouveau* publishes three more issues, then title changed to *Shigaku Bungaku Hyōron*, Haruyama Yukio
Hommage à Paul Eluard, Yamanaka Chirū, ed.
*Hitler becomes Führer of Germany

1935   *VOU* first published, edited by Kitasono
Yamanaka Chirū [Tiroux] poetry collection *Hiasobi / Jouer au feu* published
Takiguchi publishes *Shururearisumu bijutsu no Shindōkō* (New trends in Surrealist art)
Kawabata Yasunari begins serialized publication of *Yukiguni* (Snow country)
#Writer René Crevel commits suicide

1936   Haruyama Yukio publishes *Hana to paipu* (Flower and pipe)
Only issue published of the journal *L'Echange surréaliste* (Yamanaka Chirū, ed.)
*February 26 incident, a mutiny of some fourteen hundred Japanese troops, quelled with the intervention of the emperor
*Japan signs anti-Comintern pact with Germany
#*International Surrealist Exhibition* in London

1937   *Kaigai chōgenjitsushigi sakuhinten* (International Surrealist exhibition) organized in Tokyo by Eluard, Roland Penrose, Takiguchi, and Yamanaka (catalogue by Takiguchi and Yamanaka)
Arubamu shururearisto (Surrealist album), an essay and photograph collection, published by Yamanaka and Takiguchi on the occasion of the above exhibition
Takiguchi publishes illustrated poetry collection *Yōsei no kyori* (Fairy's distance)
The journal *Shinryōdo* (New territories) first published by editors Murano Shirō, Kondō Azuma, Haruyama Yukio
*Sino-Japanese war begins

1938   *VOU* (no. 22) special edition on Surrealism
Mita bungaku special issue on Surrealism

#Breton and Eluard publish *Un Dictionnaire abrégé du surréalisme* (An abridged dictionary of Surrealism)

1940   Arrest of members of Poetry Club, a Surrealist-communist group in Kobe opposed to the Sino-Japanese war
VOU publishes its intention to move toward more traditional poetry
#Walter Benjamin commits suicide
*Military alliance between Japan, Germany, and Italy signed

1941   Takiguchi and Fukuzawa Ichirō arrested; Takiguchi jailed for approximately nine months for leading avant-garde activities with revolutionary, communist, and leftist tendencies (special police internal report, 1941)
Kitasono publishes *Haiburau no funsui* (The fountain of the highbrow)
After a year of detention, Rien members released and sent to battle
*Japanese army occupies southern French Indochina
*Japan attacks Pearl Harbor
#Breton, Ernst, André Masson move to America; Aragon, Eluard, Robert Desnos go underground

1942   *First air-raid on Tokyo
*Japanese army occupies Philippines and Singapore

1944   Poets Fujiwara Seiichi and Morikawa Yoshinobu die fighting abroad

1945   *United States drops atomic bombs on Hiroshima and Nagasaki
Azuma Jun (formerly with *VOU*) goes to Nagasaki as a reporter following the dropping of the atomic bomb

1947   Nishiwaki publishes *Tabibito kaerazu* (*No traveler returns*) and *Amubaruwaria*
Kitasono's critique of the change in Nishiwaki's style appears in the journal *Arechi* (Wasteland)
*Japan Democratic party organized; first Diet meeting convened; Marshall plan

1948   *Liberal Democratic Party organized; General Tōjō Hideki and six others sentenced to death by hanging

1950   Yamanaka publishes *Shururearisumu no shi* (Surrealist poetry)

1958   Takiguchi visits Breton and Michaux in Paris

1962   Nishiwaki publishes the collection *Eterunitasu* (*Aeternitas*)

1966   Tsuruoka Yoshihisa publishes *Nihon chōgenjitsushugi shiron*

NOTES

PROLOGUE *What Is Called Surrealism*

1. For important writings on other ideological and poetic disruptions occurring at about the same time, along with discussions of their political implications, see Doak, *Dreams of Difference* on the Nihon rōman-ha (Japanese romantic school) and Miriam Silverberg's *Changing Song* on Nakano Shigeharu. Other collateral practices in prose fiction that would merit analysis along similar lines, by authors more centrally recognized in the literary canon of this period, might include works such as *Asakusa kurenaidan* by Kawabata Yasunari or *Shanghai* by Yokomitsu Riichi, among many others. For a discussion of the negotiation of the relation between reality and narrative transcriptions in modern Japanese literature, see also Tomi Suzuki, *Narrating the Self: Fictions of Japanese Modernity.* At the time of this writing, John Solt's book was available only in dissertation form, so I have cited that throughout. I have maintained Kitasono's own romanization of his surname, but have used the modified Hepburn system "Katue" for clarity of pronunciation. (The poet himself wrote "Katue.")

CHAPTER 1 *Introduction*

1. See, for example, the magazines *Fukuikutaru kafu yo, Shōbi, ajutsu, akusetsu, L'Esprit nouveau, Madame Blanche, VOU, Rien,* and many others. (A notable exception to this form is to be found in the thick, heavy volumes of *Shi to shiron* edited by Haruyama Yukio.)

2. Translations are mine unless otherwise noted.

3. Peter Bürger, *Theory of the Avant-Garde* (Minneapolis: University of Minnesota Press, 1992): 53. Bürger has written several other works in German on French Surrealism.

4. Bürger, *Theory of the Avant-Garde*, 53.

5. See, for example, the insert in the exhibition catalogue *"Gendaishi no furontia": Modanizumu no keifu ten* (Kitakami: Nihon gendai shiika bungakukan, 1994).

6. Maurice Blanchot, *The Infinite Conversation*, Susan Hanson, trans. (Minneapolis: University of Minnesota Press, 1993): 407.

7. Blanchot, *The Infinite Conversation*, 464 n. 1.

CHAPTER 2   *Distant Realities*

1. "L'image est une création pure de l'esprit. Elle ne peut naître d'une comparaison mais du rapprochement de deux réalités plus ou moins éloignées. Plus les rapports des deux réalités rapprochées seront lointains et justes, plus l'image sera forte—plus elle aura de puissance émotive et de réalité poétique." Pierre Reverdy, *Nord-Sud: Self-défense et autres écrits sur l'art et la poésie, 1917–26* (Paris: Flammarion, 1975): 73.

2. "Rapport établi entre un objet et un autre terme, dans le langage. V. allusion, image, métaphore." *Le Petit Robert: Dictionnaire de la langue française* (1987): s.v. *comparaison*.

3. Translation from André Breton, *Manifestoes of Surrealism*, Richard Seaver and Helen R. Lane, trans. (Ann Arbor: University of Michigan Press, 1972): 20–21. "Ces mots, quoique sibyllins pour les profanes, étaient de très forts révélateurs et je les méditai longtemps. Mais l'image me fuyait. L'esthétique de Reverdy, esthétique tout *a posteriori*, me faisait prendre les effets pour les causes. C'est sur ces entrefaites que je fus amené à renoncer définitivement à mon point de vue." *Les Manifestes du Surréalisme* (Paris: Le Sagittaire, 1955): 21.

4. It has been noted that Reverdy wrote his essay "On Images" after a debate with Breton (about an article by Georges Duhamel on the poetic image). See Gerard Bocholier, *Pierre Reverdy: Le Phare Obscur* (Paris: Champ Vallon, 1984): 131.

5. Breton, *Manifestoes of Surrealism*, 26.

6. "Profanus" is included in Nishiwaki Junzaburō, *Chōgenjitsushugi shiron* (Tokyo: Kōseikaku shoten, 1929): 9.

Nishiwaki's admirers claim that he is the first modern Japanese poet to transcend the boundaries of the Japanese language. They cite the recognition he received in England for his poetry in English and praise his new poetic diction in Japanese. Critics, however, have at times read his "strange" and "difficult" style of Japanese prose (combined with his prevalent interest in foreign works) as problematic, or even as a mask for a complex about having grown up in the provinces. Many cosmopolitan Tokyo Surrealists did trace their origins to the distant provinces of Japan. Whichever side one takes, it is clear that there is something critical at stake for Nishiwaki's writing in the theoretical question of bringing together distant elements. (As for the reception of his work abroad, Nishiwaki was nominated for the Nobel Prize in literature in 1962 along with Kawabata Yasunari, Tanizaki Jun'ichirō, and André Malraux. Kawabata received the prize in 1968.)

The first book-length critical study to introduce Nishiwaki's work in English takes this question of translation as a central theme. Hosea Hirata, *The Poetry and Poetics of Nishiwaki Junzaburō* (Princeton, N.J.: Princeton University Press, 1993).

7. "'Aihan suru mono o renketsu shite chōwa shitaru mono ga shi no honshitsu de aru' to iu setsu o shōkai shiyō to shita no da. Watakushi wa ima de mo." Nishiwaki Junzaburō, *Chōgenjitsushugi shiron* (Tokyo: Arechi shuppansha, 1954): preface.

8. Nishiwaki Junzaburō, *Chōgenjitsushugi shiron* (1954): preface.

9. On the terms of *achronie* in the work of Nishiwaki, see Inoue Teruo, "Nishiwaki Junzaburō to Baudelaire," in Nishiwaki Junzaburō, *Teihon Nishiwaki Junzaburō zenshū*, Kagiya Yukinobu, ed., app. vol. (Tokyo: Chikuma shobō, 1993–94): 586–96. See also my discussion in Chapter 4.

10. See Amagasaki Akira, *Nihon no retorikku* (Tokyo: Chikuma shobō, 1988): 146.

11. Nakanishi Susumu, "Nihon no sōzōryoku," paper presented at colloquium at International Center for Japanese Studies, Kyoto, Sept. 2, 1994.

12. See Yamamura Bochō, *Sei sanryō hari,* in *Nihon shijin zenshū* (Tokyo: Sōgensha, 1953).

13. Abe has incorporated this poem in his analysis "Baudelaire dans la poétique 'imagiste' de Hagiwara Sakutaro," part 2, *Proceedings of the Department of Foreign Languages and Literatures,* vol. 35, no. 2, College of Arts and Sciences, University of Tokyo (1987).

14. Abe, "Baudelaire," 3. We might recall in this context the form, for example, of the famous opening section of Sei Shōnagon's *The Pillow Book,* with its nominal associations beginning *Haru wa akebono.*

15. The first discovery of such links is attributed to the research of Bochō scholar Sekigawa Sakio.

16. This criterion is invoked in other contexts to valorize the work of certain members of Surrealist groups in Japan over others—Nishiwaki Junzaburō over Kitasono Katsue, for example, or Takiguchi Shūzō over Nishiwaki.

17. A highly illuminating text in this regard is Shoshana Felman and Dori Laub's *Testimony: Crises of Witnessing in Literature, Psychoanalysis, and History* (New York: Routledge, 1991).

18. Cited in Paul Eluard, *Selected Poems,* Gilbert Bowen, trans. (London: Riverrun Press, 1987): 10.

19. See Takiguchi Shūzō, "Takiguchi Shūzō jihitsu nenpu (Auto-chronology), reprinted in *Gendaishi techō* (Tokyo: Shichōsha): vol. 17, no. 11, "Takiguchi Shūzō" (Oct. 1974): 339. See especially entry under the year 1929. For an excellent description of the development and impact of the censorship and paper rationing that occurred with the approach of World War II, see the later chapters in Jay Rubin, *Injurious to Public Morals: Writers and the Meiji State* (Seattle: University of Washington Press: 1984).

20. For a description of publishers' struggles to produce journals, in particular

focusing on the efforts of private publisher Toba Shigeru (Bon shoten), see Uchi-bori Hiroshi, *Bon shoten no maboroshi* (Kyoto: Hakuchisha, 1992).

21. See also John Peter Solt, "Shredding the Tapestry of Meaning: The Poetry and Poetics of Kitasono Katue" (Ph.D. diss., Harvard University, 1989): 54–57, and translation in app.

22. Of the essays on *Kigōsetsu* noted by this reader, only that of Kitasono himself, "Shi ni okeru watashi no jikken" (My experiments in poetry), cites the poem nearly in full; *Kitasono Katsue zenhyōronshū*, Tsuruoka Yoshihisa, ed. (Tokyo: Chūsekisha, 1988): 620–60.

23. The term *jikken sareru* includes a range of meanings close to the French *expérience*, encompassing both the experiment (or test) and (lived) experience. In Japanese it also contains the sense of empirical demonstration or proof: "By writing poetry without meaning, one demonstrates the purity of poetry."

24. *Kitasono Katsue zenshishū*, Fujitomi Yasuo, ed. (Tokyo: Chūsekisha, 1983), 627. See also the discussion of this work in Solt, "Shredding the Tapestry of Meaning," 458.

25. He cites the opinion of Haruyama Yukio, who in *Shi no kenkyū* compares this poem to similar works by Ueda Toshio from around the same period. Haruyama was one of the first to interpret these works in relation to the ideas of formalism.

26. Solt, "Shredding the Tapestry of Meaning," 50. See also the expression of wonder at this phenomenon by Tsuruoka Yoshihisa in his introduction to *Shururearisumu no hakken* (Osaka: Yukawa shobō, 1979): 8–12.

27. Okada Takahiko, interview, June 28, 1994. Although the title seems on first glance to proclaim the work's experimental nature, according to Okada, Takiguchi may have selected this title in a humble uncertainty about these works' status as "poetry."

28. The idea of poetic convention takes on different and complex meanings in the poetic experiments of the individual Surrealist writers; yet most of them can be seen to be coming to terms with some vision of the "conventional" or "traditional" in language and poetics.

29. Etō Jun suggested this contextual reading. One might also recall the approach taken by the 1997 exhibition in the Musée d'Art Moderne in Paris, "Les Années 30" in which the art of each of the years of the 1930s was contrasted room by room with newspaper clippings, documentary photographs, and newsreels of the historical events of that year. The links were not "explained" by the curators, but their dramatic implications were left to the viewers. In November 1936, the year of the publication of *L'Echange surréaliste*, Japan signed the anti-Comintern pact with Germany. Earlier the same year was the famous "incident of February 26" (*ni-ni-roku jiken*), a large troop uprising in Akasaka barracks, an attempted coup d'état that required the emperor to intervene and bring them under control. This incident made an impression on Takiguchi, and he alludes to it briefly in his "Auto-chronology."

30. Takiguchi, "Auto-chronology," 243.

31. Breton, *Manifestoes of Surrealism*, 240–41.

32. One may further note that the term "Gobi" functions not only as the name of a desert but also as the term for "word endings," which for European poetry would mark the place of poetic rhyme. Here again we have the hint of a comment on poetic technique, and, in particular, foreign poetics.

33. One recalls the description by Satō Saku of the atmosphere within which he, Takiguchi, and the other Keio students gathered at the cafe Hakujūji to discuss poetry, surrounded by the growing numbers of "Marx boys" (young, politically engaged students involved in Marxism); their faces, he describes, always maintained a severe and serious expression. Interview, July 19, 1994. See also Satō Saku, "Daigaku jidai no Takiguchi Shūzō," *Taiyō*, no. 382, "Takiguchi Shūzō" (Apr. 1993): 55.

34. Uchibori, *Bon shoten no maboroshi*, 152.

35. See Takiguchi Shūzō, "Au Japon," in *Cahiers d'art*, vol. 10, no. 5–6 (Paris, 1935): 132.

36. Nishiwaki, *Chōgenjitsushugi shiron* (1929): 1–2. Translated also in Hirata, *The Poetry and Poetics of Nishiwaki Junzaburō*, 5.

37. Kagiya Yukinobu, *Shijin Nishiwaki Junzaburō* (Tokyo: Chikuma shobō, 1983): 60. Translated in Hirata, *The Poetry and Poetics of Nishiwaki Junzaburō*, 238 n. 34.

38. For a crucial response to related concerns about referentiality for contemporary critical theory, see Cathy Caruth, "The Falling Body and the Impact of Reference," in *Unclaimed Experience: Trauma, Narrative, and History* (Baltimore: Johns Hopkins University Press, 1996): 73–90.

Another key term that must be considered in understanding Nishiwaki's vision of "reality" is the related concept of *tsumaranasa* (boredom, triviality, monotony). This implies not only the supreme banality of the familiar, waiting to be defamiliarized (as it is commonly understood); its use is more closely related to Baudelaire's term *ennui* (see my discussion of *byt*, Chapter 3). An emphasis on the familiar in reference to the poetics of Shelley and Coleridge, an aspect also undoubtedly present in Nishiwaki's text, moves its interpretation in the direction of Blanchot's articulation of the "murmur" as an underlying flow of language without meaning.

Boredom may also be read as a part of Nishiwaki's pose, his cool stance, what is called (by his critics) his dandyism. In a flat voice he poses the question of boredom; he is also "posing while questioning," while laying claim to this question of boredom.

39. Another moment in which this becomes apparent is in the recollections by Tsuruoka Yoshihisa about Takiguchi's "auto-chronology" written for the *Gendaishi dokuhon* on Takiguchi's work. Tsuruoka, who edited this issue, recalls that he was originally designated to compile the chronology, but realized that he would have had to ask Takiguchi for all the information—this is the reason he gives for his de-

cision to ask Takiguchi to write the piece. Tsuruoka, *Shururearisumu no hakken*, 166.

40. Pamphlet inserted in the reprint edition of *Shōbi, majutsu, gakusetsu* (Tokyo: Nishizawa shoten, 1977).

41. Solt points out that it would have been difficult for readers of *Rose, Magic, Theory* to know that they were reading a Surrealist journal (although the issues contained translations from Aragon and Eluard, they only occasionally use the word "Surrealist").

42. My translation; the original title is in English, and the text contains no punctuation. Cited in Kitasono, "Recollections of *Rose, Magic, Theory*," insert in reprint edition of *Shōbi, majutsu, gakusetsu*; the capitalized words are spelled, in English and French, exactly as in the original text. Kitasono's translation, as he sent it, is no longer available; although this is one possible translation, the words of this paragraph are elliptical and open to several interpretations.

43. "L'opération surréaliste n'a de chance d'être menée à bien que si elle s'effectue dans des conditions d'asepsie morale, dont il est encore très peu d'hommes à vouloir entendre parler." In a later work, on the issue of objectivity and subjectivity, Breton writes: "Le surréalisme travaille à ce que la distinction du subjectif et de l'objectif perde de sa nécessité et de sa valeur, c'est à l'abri de tout délire." *Point du jour* (Paris: Gallimard, 1970). See also Henri Béhar, ed., *Les Pensées d'André Breton* (Paris: L'Age d'Homme, 1988): 313.

44. "La conscience objective des réalités et leur développement interne en ce que, par la vertu du sentiment individuel d'une part, universel d'autre part, il a jusqu'à nouvel ordre de magique." Cited in Claude Mauriac, *André Breton* (Paris: Editions Bernard Grasset, 1970): 38–39.

45. For example, the status of the coincidence (*hasard objectif*) is close to the kind of "indifference" or distance expressed in "A Note," the concept of something that can be experienced as necessary and yet escape one's grasp. In the lecture "Situation surréaliste de l'objet—Situation de l'objet surréaliste" (Surrealist situation of the object—Situation of the Surrealist object), Breton explains "the problem of *objective chance* [his italics], or in other words that sort of chance that shows man, in a way that is still very mysterious, a necessity that escapes him, even though he experiences it as a vital necessity." *Manifestoes of Surrealism*, 268.

In the same essay, in explaining the relation between the perception of the outside world and the ego, Breton speaks of "getting to the bottom [limit] of man's 'perception-consciousness' system," 272. He employs the terms of mechanization, but the debate here centers on the sense of mechanization as photographic technique, the blow that the invention of photography dealt to the sovereignty of "realist" painting, and the newly invented role for painting of "expressing inner perception visually." This is the sense in which Breton's writings on the dynamic between interior (perception/consciousness) and exterior (object/objectivity) reflect on the issue of mechanization.

46. Breton elaborates on Lautréamont's formulation in his 1935 lecture, "Surrealist Situation of the Object": "A ready-made reality, whose naive purpose seems to have been fixed once and for all (an umbrella), finding itself suddenly in the presence of another very distant and no less absurd reality (a sewing machine), in a place where both must feel out of their element (on an operating table), will, by this very fact, escape its native purpose and lose its identity; because of the detour through what is relative, it will pass from absolute falseness to a new absolute that is true and poetic: the umbrella and the sewing machine will make love. The way this procedure works seems to me to be revealed in this very simple example. A complete transmutation followed by a pure act such as love will necessarily be produced every time that the given facts—the coupling of two realities which apparently cannot be coupled on a plane which apparently is not appropriate to them—render conditions favorable." Translated in *Manifestoes of Surrealism*, 275.

47. Such a view is described, for example, in James Fujii, *Complicit Fictions* (Berkeley: University of California Press, 1993): 132.

CHAPTER 3 *On Memory and Doubt*

1. For a useful general outline of the history of translation and reception of French literature in modern Japan (which does not, however, address the question of influence as a theoretical or critical problem) see Nakamura Mitsuo, "The French Influence in Modern Japanese Literature," *Japan Quarterly*, Asahi shinbunsha, vol. 7, no. 1 (Jan.–Mar. 1960): 57–65. A curious early academic study, encompassing more general issues of cultural relations as well as literary relations (written contemporary with the development of Surrealist thought in Japan) is Nitobe Inazō et al., *Western Influences in Modern Japan* (Chicago: University of Chicago Press, 1931). The latter collection strongly supports assimilation, in particular of elements of Anglo-American culture: "Let us keep open house for foreign elements . . . and assimilate them to our utmost, thus accelerating the day on which we shall be able to cast off the slough of Chinese characters," 180. One finds there such praise of English tradition as: "The glorious lineage of English literature, in which Shakespeare is so conspicuously the greatest figure, surpassing *all the poets of the world*, as Mount Fuji is the most beautiful mountain on earth," 189; emphasis mine.

2. For example, such studies have considered the question of *japonisme* within French painting, images of the Orient in German philosophy and aesthetics, or the place of French literature within modern Japanese literature. The focus will tend to emphasize only one direction of a varied and complex relation. On the other hand, recent comparative essays that bring together a wide variety of perspectives under the rubric of "literary relations" include Cornelia Moore and Raymond Moody, eds., *Comparative Literature East and West: Traditions and Trends* (Honolulu: University of Hawaii; East-West Center, 1989) and Jean Toyama and Nobuko Ochner, eds., *Literary Relations East and West* (Honolulu: University of Hawaii; East-West Center, 1990).

3. Although other aspects of the question of influence deserve consideration, we shall confine our discussion for the moment to the most direct connection to our use of the concept of memory.

4. Recent studies have brought to bear this work of Walter Benjamin (on shock and consciousness in poetic writings) for an expanded understanding of European Surrealism. See Margaret Cohen, *Profane Illumination: Walter Benjamin and the Paris of Surrealist Revolution* (Berkeley: University of California Press, 1993); see also Hal Foster, *Compulsive Beauty* (Cambridge, Mass.: M.I.T. Press, 1993). In addition to his influential essays on cross-cultural reception, such as "The Task of the Translator" ("Die Aufgabe des Übersetzers"), in Walter Benjamin, *Illuminations,* Harry Zohn, trans. (New York: Schocken Books, 1968): 69–82, Benjamin also wrote an essay directly dealing with Surrealism, "Der Surrealismus: Die letzte Momentaufnahme der europäischen Intelligenz," in *Gesammelte Schriften,* vol. 2, *Aufsätze, Essays, Vorträge* (Frankfurt am Main: Suhrkamp Verlag, 1977): 295–310.

5. Sigmund Freud, *The Interpretation of Dreams,* James Strachey, trans. (New York: Avon Books, 1965): 312.

6. Sigmund Freud, *Beyond the Pleasure Principle,* James Strachey, trans. (New York: W. W. Norton, 1961): 27.

7. Freud, *Beyond the Pleasure Principle,* 28.

8. Those who have studied survivors' reactions to extreme circumstances and traumatic events write that "the event is not assimilated or experienced fully at the time, but only belatedly." The events return after the fact in the form of vivid and dramatic flashbacks, which are surprisingly literal: "Most analysts have remarked on the surprising literality and non-symbolic nature of traumatic dreams and flashbacks, which resist cure to the extent that they remain, precisely, literal." Cathy Caruth, Introduction to *American Imago,* "Psychoanalysis, Culture, and Trauma," vol. 48, no. 1 (Spring 1991): 8–11.

9. Harold Bloom, *A Map of Misreading* (New York: Oxford University Press, 1975): 19, and *The Anxiety of Influence* (New York: Oxford University Press, 1973): 70; cited in Peter de Bolla, *Harold Bloom: Towards Historical Rhetorics* (London: Routledge, 1988): 23.

10. Bloom, *A Map of Misreading,* 72.

11. Benjamin's understanding of the relation between a work and its translation functions in a similar way, placing the translation in the position of that which "completes" the work; one might extend this paradigm so that the good translator becomes a figure for the reader, and translation a paradigm for reading. See Walter Benjamin, "The Task of the Translator."

12. Platonic notions of writing also explore this anxiety on the part of the writer, the mistrust that comes from the knowledge that a text may fall into the wrong hands, may be susceptible to misreadings and "ill treated and unfairly abused," or would be "unable to defend itself." Plato, *Phaedrus,* cited in Zhang Longxi, *The Tao and the Logos* (Durham, N.C.: Duke University Press, 1992): 18.

13. *American Heritage Dictionary of the English Language* (1969).

14. Translation and explication of "Da Yu mo" with the help of Michael Puett. This compound has become a standard translation in both Japanese and modern Chinese for the European word "influence."

15. It recalls, perhaps incongruously, Wordsworth's lines that bring together the image of an echo with the effect of shock: "Redoubled and redoubled, concourse wild / Of jocund din; and when a lengthened pause of silence came . . . a gentle shock of mild surprise." William Wordsworth, "Prelude" (1850), in *The Prelude: 1799, 1805, 1850*, Jonathan Wordsworth, ed. (New York: W. W. Norton, 1979): 173.

16. *Kōjien* (Tokyo: Iwanami shoten, 1990) and *Kenkyūsha New Japanese-English Dictionary* (Tokyo: Kenkyūsha, 1974).

17. "Shi ni tsuite no shō-essei" appeared in vol. 5, June 1931. *Shi: Genjitsu* had split off from *Shi to shiron* in 1930. The multifaceted literary trend of naturalism in its early phases drew on the forms and ideas of European naturalist novelists (Zola, Maupassant, Flaubert, the brothers Goncourt). Beginning with Shimazaki Tōson's *Hakai* (Broken commandments, 1906) and Tayama Katai's *Futon* (1907), the naturalist writers' works were known for their confessional focus on the dirty underside of daily life and sexual desire. Their work is linked to the rise of *genbun'itchi* vernacular prose writing and the *watakushi-shōsetsu* ("I" novel). Hagiwara was later a member of the Nihon rōman-ha (the Japanese romantic school led by Yasuda Yojūrō) that attacked literary modernism and naturalism in part as manifestations of rational (Western) society.

18. Hagiwara Sakutarō, *Hagiwara Sakutarō zenshū*, vol. 5 (Tokyo: Chikuma Shobō, 1976):333.

19. When Hagiwara speaks of a poetics that follows the rules of mechanics, he can be understood to be referring to various contemporary poetic schools, such as the Futurists who concerned themselves with mechanism as an ideal for the eliciting of a sense of speed and inducing certain other effects in the poem. He dismisses Surrealists in a subsequent aphorism: "The group of Surrealists is not a real 'school of poetry.' This is because the basic principle of their dogma [*izumu*] is merely commentary on the most banal and universal considerations of a general poetics. I have no reason to oppose it here. Then again, however, I have no particular reason to applaud it either." *Hagiwara Sakutarō zenshū*, vol. 5: 333.

20. Later, Hagiwara traces this progress through a loss of the aural in modern poetry, and a too-prominent emphasis on the visual at the expense of musicality. Hagiwara's own poetry emphasizes this aural and rhythmic element, which also plays an important part in what he sees as the strength of Poe's writings.

21. One could find any number of such accusations in the pages of *Shi: Genjitsu*. We are more concerned here with the functioning of this kind of accusation than with the details of this particular rift between the members of *Shi to shiron* and the coterie of *Shi: Genjitsu*, which was nonetheless an important breaking point for Surrealist ideas.

It would be interesting to compare the kinds of resistances that the importation of European ideas provoked in the Taishō and early Shōwa periods to the reactions and fears provoked by cultural borrowing from the West during the middle decades of the Meiji period. For a concise and illuminating historical discussion of these responses, see Donald Shively, "The Japanization of the Middle Meiji," in Donald Shively, ed., *Tradition and Modernization in Japanese Culture* (Princeton, N.J.: Princeton University Press, 1971): 77–119.

22. Surrealism was not the only movement warped in this way, Tsuruoka claims; such a process could also be traced in the movements of Japanese naturalism (*shizenshugi*) and realism (*shajitsushugi*). Tsuruoka Yoshihisa, *Nihon chōgenjitsushugi shiron*, 2d ed. (Tokyo: Shichōsha, 1970): 32.

23. The reference is to Gaëtan Picon, brother of Pierre Picon; the latter is mentioned in the first manifesto of Surrealism. Gaëtan Picon published the reference and history *Surrealism, 1919–1939* (Geneva: Editions d'Art Albert Skira, 1977).

24. Tsuruoka, *Nihon chōgenjitsushugi shiron*, 64.

25. "Ce qui se passe dans le domaine de l'écriture n'est-il pas dénué de valeur si cela reste 'esthétique', anodin, dépourvu de sanction, s'il n'y a rien, dans le fait d'écrire une oeuvre, qui soit un équivalent . . . de ce qu'est pour le torero la corne acérée du taureau, qui seule—en raison de la menace matérielle qu'elle recèle—confère une réalité humaine à son art, l'empêche d'être autre chose que grâces vaines de ballerine?" Michel Leiris, *L'Age d'homme, précédé de "De la littérature considérée comme une tauromachie"* (Paris: Gallimard, 1986): 10. The text itself was written in 1930, and the preface appended in 1945.

26. Cited in Tsuruoka, *Nihon chōgenjitsushugi shiron*, 85.

27. This term can also be read as an indictment: Surrealist thought indicts the "emptiness" in his mind.

28. Tsuruoka, *Nihon chōgenjitsushugi shiron*, 86.

29. Iwaya Kunio, "Takiguchi Shūzō to André Breton," in *André Breton and Shūzō Takiguchi: The 13th Exhibition Homage to Shūzō Takiguchi* (Tokyo: Satani Gallery, 1993). Essay translation included in catalogue. The Satani Gallery sponsors homage exhibitions each year to document and commemorate various aspects of Takiguchi's career.

30. The emphasis is mine. Iwaya, "Takiguchi Shūzō to André Breton," 44.

31. Tsuruoka, *Nihon chōgenjitsushugi shiron*, 65.

32. "The Great East Asian War" is the translation of *dai tōa sensō*, the official Japanese designation (shortly after the Pearl Harbor attack) for Japan's acts of territorial and political expansion, with the ultimate aim of controlling not only China and Manchuria but also the Philippines, French Indochina, and the Dutch East Indies. The term thus refers to the period after the China war expanded into the Pacific phase of World War II.

33. The phrase *shiko no mitate*, translated as "your humble shield," is an ex-

pression by which a military man loyally promises to become like a powerful shield to resist the enemy. Tsuruoka, *Nihon chōgenjitsushugi shiron*, 65.

34. *Kitasono Katsue zenhyōronshū*, Tsuruoka Yoshihisa, ed. (Tokyo: Chūsekisha, 1988): 514. From *Kyōdo shiron* (Tokyo: Shōshinsha, 1944), the book of Kitasono's collected essays in which, during the war, he did advocate a traditionalist approach to poetry. This excerpt was first published in 1942.

35. One can compare, as Věra Linhartová has done, the split of the Japanese Surrealists over this issue to a similar split within the Parisian groups: "In 1930, the group attacked in Breton's Second Manifesto responded with 'Un Cadavre' and Aragon and Sadoul left for the sadly famous 'Congrès des écrivains.'" Věra Linhartová, *Dada et surréalisme au Japon* (Paris: Publications Orientalistes de France, 1987): 172.

36. The emphasis is mine. Kanbara Tai, "Chōgenjitsushugi no botsuraku," *Shi: Genjitsu*, no. 1 (June 1930).

37. Ueda Toshio, "Watashi no chōgenjitsushugi," *Shi to shiron*, no. 4 (June 1929): 1–18.

38. Clearly, Kanbara's critique is aimed at a larger group of Surrealists and at a general trend he perceives in their thinking about Surrealism. Yet one of the essays that provokes the attack can be seen as an exemplary formulation of the view of reality he criticizes.

39. Citations taken from Maurice Blanchot, *The Space of Literature*, Ann Smock, trans. (Lincoln: University of Nebraska Press, 1982), 167–8.

40. Blanchot, *The Space of Literature*, 163.

41. In 1954 Miyoshi (1902–1958) published a collection of essays entitled *Nihon oyobi nihonjin* (Tokyo: Kōbunsha, 1954).

42. Kanbara, "Chōgenjitsushugi no botsuraku," 31.

43. For an excellent discussion of this notion of *byt* in relation to the Surrealists and Mayakovsky, see Svetlana Boym, *Death in Quotation Marks* (Cambridge, Mass.: Harvard University Press, 1991): 156–65.

44. Translated in Boym, *Death in Quotation Marks*, 164.

45. Boym, *Death in Quotation Marks*, 154.

46. In Filippo Tommaso Marinetti's "La grande Milano tradizionale e futurista," Kanbara's name appears as Futurist comrade in "Tokio." His manifesto "Daiikkai Kanbara Tai sengensho" of 1921 is there considered the first avant-garde manifesto to appear in Japan.

47. Kanbara, "Chōgenjitsushugi no botsuraku."

48. *Kitasono Katsue zenhyōronshū*, 330.

49. See Tsuruoka's afterword in *Kitasono Katsue zenhyōronshū*.

50. Kitasono Katsue, "Chōgenjitsushugi no tachiba," *Shi to shiron*, no. 4 (June 1929): 172. Next to the word *essence* (*shinzui*) Kitasono appends the reading *temperamento* (temperament or psychological character), thus linking his view of art's

essence to the "psychological/spiritual revolution" that constitutes Surrealism as he describes it earlier in the same essay.

51. Maurice Blanchot, *The Gaze of Orpheus*, Lydia Davis, trans. (Barrytown, N.Y.: Station Hill Press, 1981): 21.

52. Blanchot, *The Gaze of Orpheus*, 22, 24.

53. Blanchot, *The Gaze of Orpheus*, 22.

54. To do so would be a simple return to the oppositional logic of his agreements and attacks.

55. "Chōgenjitsushugi shi to sono genkai," section 10, *Kitasono Katsue zenhyōronshū*, 331.

56. Tsuruoka, *Nihon chōgenjitsushugi shiron*, 66.

57. From Kitasono's essay "Chōgenjitsu shi to sono genkai," in *Kitasono Katsue zenhyōronshū*, 330.

58. *Kōjien* lists the English and German translations as the first definitions of these Japanese terms.

CHAPTER 4   *Poetry and Visuality, Poetry and Actuality*

1. Fenollosa, beginning in 1878, taught at Tokyo Imperial University and played an important role in advocating the preservation of traditional Japanese arts. He helped to found Tokyo School of Fine Arts (1889), and he translated numerous Noh plays. After his death, his widow gave Ezra Pound his numerous unpublished translations of early Chinese poetry and Noh dramas, which Pound revised and published to high acclaim. Pound translated Confucius while in jail for his wartime pro-fascist broadcasts and continued to translate ancient Chinese poetry after the war. For a study of Pound's interactions with Japanese avant-garde writers, see Kodama Sanehide, ed., *Ezra Pound and Japan* (Redding Ridge, Conn.: Black Swan Books, 1987); for his interactions with Kitasono, see John Peter Solt, "Shredding the Tapestry of Meaning: The Poetry and Poetics of Kitasono Katue (1902–1978)" (Ph.D. diss., Harvard University, 1989): chap. 5.

2. This passage and its implications for Pound's understanding of the Chinese script have been analyzed by various critics and Sinologists. A discussion of the problematic of phonetic versus ideogrammatic scripts is contained in Zhang Longxi's *The Tao and the Logos* (Durham, N.C.: Duke University Press, 1992): 24–27. Other readings of this problem (also cited by Zhang) are George A. Kennedy, "Fenollosa, Pound, and the Chinese Character," in *Selected Works of George A. Kennedy*, Tien-yi Li, ed. (New Haven, Conn.: Yale University Press, 1964); and Joseph N. Riddel, "'Neo-Nietzschean Clatter'—Speculation and/on Pound's Poetic Image," in Ian F. A. Bell, ed., *Ezra Pound: Tactics for Reading* (London: Vision, 1982).

3. Jacques Derrida, *Of Grammatology*, Gayatri Chakravorty Spivak, trans. (Bal-

timore: Johns Hopkins University Press, 1974): 92. See also Zhang, *The Tao and the Logos*, 24.

4. Rosalind E. Krauss, *The Originality of the Avant-Garde and Other Modernist Myths* (Cambridge, Mass.: M.I.T. Press, 1985): 93–94. See André Breton, "Le Surréalisme et la peinture," *La Révolution surréaliste*, no. 1 (July 1925): 26–30.

5. Krauss, *The Originality of the Avant-Garde*, 94.

6. Krauss, *The Originality of the Avant-Garde*, 112.

7. My translation from Ozawa Masao and Matsuda Shigeho, eds., *Kokinwakashū* (Tokyo: Shogakkan): 49. For an exposition in English, see Laurel Rodd and Mary Henkenius, *Kokinshū* (Princeton, N.J.: Princeton University Press, 1984): 35–47. See also McCullough, Helen C., *Brocade by Night: 'Kokin wakashū' and the Court Style in Japanese Poetry* (Stanford: Stanford University Press, 1985), chap. 5.

8. See also the discussion and hesitations around this word, *koto-ba*, in Martin Heidegger's dialogue on language with a "Japanese interlocutor," in which the possibility of making equivalences and translation in speaking of language is in question, and Heidegger's views on language are brought to bear on the Japanese term. Martin Heidegger, "Aus einen Gespräch von der Sprache," in *Unterwegs zur Sprache* (Pfullingen, Germany: Neske, 1959): 83–155; translated in "A Dialogue on Language," in *On the Way to Language* (San Francisco: Harper and Row, 1971): 1–54.

9. Hagiwara Sakutarō, "Shi wa masa ni horobitsutsu aru," originally published in *Shi: Genjitsu*, no. 5 (1931); reprinted in *Hagiwara Sakutarō zenshū*, vol. 5 (Tokyo: Chikuma Shobō, 1962): 335–36.

10. See Makoto Ueda, *Modern Japanese Poets and the Nature of Literature* (Stanford: Stanford University Press, 1983), for a discussion of this opposition in Hagiwara's poetics.

11. See "Shi no genri," in *Hagiwara Sakutarō zenshū*, vol. 3, 243–44, 258. See also Michiko Tsushima, "Hagiwara Translating Poe," paper presented at conference of the Institute for Japanese Studies, Berkeley, Dec. 21, 1993.

12. "Shiro no naka no shiro no naka no kuro," *Yū*, no. 8 (1975); reprinted in Kagiya Yukinobu, Shimizu Toshihiko, Fujitomi Yasuo, eds., *Nikakkei no shiron* (Tokyo: Libroport, 1987): 171–72. Translated in Solt, "Shredding the Tapestry of Meaning," 763–91.

13. "Shiro no naka no shiro no naka no kuro," 169–70, 180. The emphasis is mine. See also *Kitasono Katsue zenshashinshū* (Tokyo: Chūsekisha, 1992), which contains the full collection of available plastic poems, as well as photos of his work in book design.

14. For a full table of the poets who participated in each issue, see Uchibori Hiroshi, *Bon shoten no maboroshi* (Kyoto: Hakuchisha, 1992): 264–66. The magazine published seventeen issues from 1932 to 1935, at which point it was disbanded to form the *VOU* club.

15. "Pélerin," the title in French, would have an accent grave (*pèlerin*); I reproduce the original spelling from the pages of *Madame Blanche*.

16. Asuka Tōru along with Iwamoto Shūzō was a member of the coterie of the magazine *Hakushi* (White page), which later became *Madame Blanche*.

17. Michelle Loi, *Poètes chinois d'écoles françaises* (Paris: Librairie d'Amérique et d'Orient Adrien Maisonneuve, 1980): 7, 61–62.

18. Loi, *Poètes chinois*, 59.

19. "Takiguchi Shūzō jihitsu nenpu" (Auto-chronology), reprinted in *Gendaishi techō* (Tokyo: Shichōsha), vol. 17, no. 11, "Takiguchi Shūzō" (Oct. 1974): 339.

20. Takiguchi Shūzō, "Shururearisumu no shiron ni tsuite," in *Collection Takiguchi Shūzō*, vol. 11 (Tokyo: Misuzu shobō, 1991): 32.

21. André Breton, *Manifestoes of Surrealism*, Richard Seaver and Helen R. Lane, trans. (Ann Arbor: University of Michigan Press, 1972): 10.

22. For example, see two poems from the *Ise monogatari*:

Kimi ya koshi ware ya yukikemu omohoezu / yume ka utsutsu ka nete ka samete ka (Did you come to me? / Was it I who went to you? / I am beyond knowing. / Was it dream or reality? / Was I awake or asleep?)

Suruga naru utsu no yamabe no utsutsu ni mo / yume ni mo hito ni awanu narikeri (Beside Mount Utsu / in Suruga province / I can see you / neither when I am awake [in reality] / nor, alas, even in my dreams.)

Translated in Steven Carter, *Traditional Japanese Poetry* (Stanford: Stanford University Press, 1991): 79; Helen C. McCullough, *Classical Japanese Prose* (Stanford: Stanford University Press, 1990): 42.

23. "Superposition d'images de catalogue . . . il saisit l'occasion de me glisser ses cartes postales . . . " André Breton, *Les Manifestes du surréalisme* (Paris: Le Sagittaire, 1955): 10.

24. The translated passage is from Breton, *Les Manifestes du surréalisme*, 12: "Le rationalisme absolu qui reste de mode ne permet de considérer que des faits relevant étroitement de notre expérience. Les fins logiques, par contre, nous échappent. Inutile d'ajouter que l'expérience même s'est vu assigner des limites. Elle tourne dans une cage d'où il est de plus en plus difficile de la faire sortir. Elle s'appuie, elle aussi, sur l'utilité immédiate, et elle est gardée par le bon sens." Takiguchi's text is from his essay "Shururearisumu no shiron ni tsuite," 32.

25. Takiguchi Shūzō, "Etamines narratives," originally published in *Yama mayu* (parts 1–3) and *Fukuikutaru kafu yo* (parts 4–6); reprinted in *Takiguchi Shūzō no shiteki jikken 1927–1937* (Tokyo: Shinchōsha, 1967): 12–16.

26. "Dōsen to shirobara to ga kyōwa-on o kōsei suru to tsubasa no aru suimin ga sakebidasu." "Etamines narratives, 1," In *Yama mayu*. no. 22 (July 1927): 1.

27. Iwanari Tatsuya, "'Takiguchi Shūzō no shiteki jikken 1927–1937' ni tsuite no 2, 3 no memo," *Gendaishi techō*, vol. 17, 94. As a rupture with the lyricism of

his earlier poetry, this work caused much discussion among the contributors to *Yama mayu*. See Věra Linhartová, *Dada et surréalisme au Japon* (Paris: Publications Orientalistes de France, 1987): 167.

28. "Subete no oto o hassuru busshitsu to onaji ni ano suimin mo ishi ni zoku shiteita no kashira?" "Etamines narratives, 1," 1.

29. Maurice Blanchot, *The Space of Literature*, Ann Smock, trans. (Lincoln: University of Nebraska Press, 1982): 178.

30. "Etamines narratives, 3," in *Yama mayu*. no. 25 (Jan. 1928): 2.

31. If the "sleep" with wings, the sleep which may or may not belong to the will, has no sleeper to attend to or possess these dreams, these narratives, how then does inspiration function?

32. At the same time, his translations reflected as much his own changing attitudes toward poetry and poetics as they did the "original intention" of the texts; hence perhaps his need to retranslate *Le Surréalisme et la peinture* as his understanding of Surrealism changed with the years.

33. Takiguchi Shūzō, "Shi to jitsuzai," in *Shi to Shiron*, no. 10 (Jan. 1931): 1.

34. Takiguchi, "Shi to jitsuzai," 1.

35. It is not "I" that writes: it is the organs of the body, a material process through them that bypasses the "I" (speaker) completely.

36. From "De l'héroïsme de la vie moderne," in "Salon de 1846." Charles Baudelaire, *Oeuvres complètes* (Paris: Editions Robert Laffont, 1980): 687.

37. Takiguchi, "Shi to jitsuzai," 1–2.

38. This is the first time in the essay that the "I" appears as a subject that knows and desires—only in order to desire "that": "that is what I desire at present" (mata boku wa ima sore o hossuru), an object whose nature we deduce primarily from its context.

39. "Dictée de la pensée, en l'absence de tout contrôle exercé par la raison, en dehors de toute préoccupation esthétique ou morale." Breton, *Les Manifestes du surréalisme*, 26.

40. Takiguchi, "Shi to jitsuzai," 1.

41. Baudelaire, *Oeuvres complètes*, 117.

42. Věra Linhartová discusses this allusion, with different conclusions and in different terms, in *Dada et Surréalisme au Japon*, 170.

43. Takiguchi, "Shi to jitsuzai," 5.

44. *Gradiva*, no. 2, "Symbolisme, surréalisme, poésie" (Nov. 1971): 36. "Quelle Liberté et quelle communauté en laquelle je crois!"

CHAPTER 5　*Eternities and Surrealist Legacies*

1. "Dada n'est pas du tout moderne, c'est plutôt le retour à une religion d'indifférence quasi-bouddhique." Tristan Tzara, *Oeuvres complètes* (Paris: Flammarion, 1975): 420. Translated in Tristan Tzara, *Seven Dada Manifestos and Lampister-*

ies, Barbara Wright, trans. (London: Riverrun Press, 1992): 108. He goes on to link it briefly to Daoism as well, with the claim, "Dchouang-Dsi [Zhuangzi, circa 300 B.C., author of the Daoist work named for him] was as dada as we are," 110. However brief, these allusions reveal that Tzara was already aware of the links that would be extended and pursued by the Japanese artists of the avant-garde, who did not see these connections as particularly surprising but rather as apparent ones. Ko Won elaborates the connections between these references of Tzara to Buddhist and Daoist thought and the writings of Japanese Dadaist Takahashi Shinkichi in Ko Won, *Buddhist Elements in Dada* (New York: New York University Press, 1977); see esp. 84–85. This citation from Tzara is also cited and discussed, along with the uses of the terms for "nothingness," in Věra Linhartová, *Dada et surréalisme au Japon* (Paris: Publications Orientalistes de France, 1987): 35, 41.

2. Takahashi Shinkichi, article in *Tokyo shinbun,* May 9, 1970; cited in Ko, *Buddhist Elements in Dada,* 87.

3. *Rien* (pronounced "rian") appeared for nineteen issues (Mar. 1929–June 1937); it included poetry, fiction, theoretical essays, and criticism and explored questions of Marxism, proletarian literature, and Surrealism.

4. Further, what is the relation between Nishiwaki's vision of eternity and that of Takiguchi? One might consider Takiguchi's image of the "eternal birds" (*eien no toritachi*) and the association in his work between bird images and eternity or the future. For example, in "Miroir de miroir: kagami no kagami": "long ago, the bird with pebble ears fell in the mirror in the woods; owl of the eternal future solitude." In *Ishō no taiyō,* no. 6 (July 1929): 18–19.

5. "Manifeste Dada 1918," in the section "Dégoût dadaïste"; Tzara, *Oeuvres complètes:* 367. "DADA; abolition de la mémoire: DADA; abolition de l'archéologie: DADA; abolition des prophètes: DADA; abolition du futur."

6. Nishiwaki Junzaburō, "Obscuro," in *Yōroppa bungaku* (Tokyo: Daiichi shobō, 1933). Cited in Ōoka Makoto, *Chōgenjitsu to jojō: Shōwa jūnendai no shiseishin* (Tokyo: Shōbunsha, 1967): 271.

7. Nishiwaki Junzaburō, "Poietes," *Mugen,* Murano Shirō, Kusano Shinpei, and Kitagawa Fuyuhiko, eds., no. 1 (1959).

8. Inoue is a former student of Nishiwaki, contributor to the avant-garde poetry magazine of the 1960s, *Doramukan,* and professor of French at Keio University.

9. Inoue Teruo, "Nishiwaki Junzaburō to Baudelaire: Sono shiron o chūshin to shite," in Kagiya Yukinobu and Niikura Toshikazu, eds., *Nishiwaki Junzaburō zenshū bekkan* (Tokyo: Chikuma shobō, 1983): 587, 596. Since the publication of *Ushinawareta toki,* the term *dojin* has come to be considered discriminatory language (*sabetsu yōgo*) and so only rarely appears in published materials, or it is accompanied by notes from the editors.

10. Inoue, "Nishiwaki Junzaburō to Baudelaire," 595–96.

11. From poem 165, *Tabibito kaerazu* (Tokyo: Tokyo shuppan, 1947): 135–36.

12. Translated in J. Thomas Rimer and Yamazaki Masakazu, *On the Art of the Nō Drama* (Princeton, N.J.: Princeton University Press, 1984): 30. The words of the "ancient sage" are quoted from the Chinese sage Huineng (638–713), as translated in Philip Yampolsky, *The Platform Sutra of the Sixth Patriarch* (New York: Columbia University Press, 1967): 178.

13. In the *Kokinshū* and in Zeami's text, the term for seed is *tane*; Huineng's hymn comes closest to Nishiwaki's usage, with his linking of three terms, which (in Zeami's Japanese readings) become *hana* (flower), *tane* (seed), and *mi* (fruit, but written with the character *ka* or *hate*, different from Nishiwaki's *mi*).

14. Cited by Hannah Arendt in the introduction to Walter Benjamin, *Illuminations*, Harry Zohn, trans. (New York: Schocken Books, 1968): 49.

15. *Ambarvalia* (1933) was reedited and published along with *Tabibito kaerazu* in 1947. Kitasono Katsue's scathing critique of the change in Nishiwaki's style appeared in the February 1947 edition of the journal *Arechi* (Wasteland, titled after T.S. Eliot's poem): see "*Tabibito kaerazu* e no tegami: Kaze o hiita bokujin" (A letter to *No traveler returns:* The shepherd who has caught a cold), reprinted in Murano Shirō, Fukuda Rikutarō, and Kagiya Yukinobu, eds., *Nishiwaki Junzaburō kenkyū* (Tokyo: Yūbun shoin, 1971): 113–22.

16. Nishiwaki Junzaburō, *Eterunitasu*. (Tokyo: Shōshinsha, 1962.) Translated (with slight differences from my version) in Hosea Hirata, *The Poetry and Poetics of Nishiwaki Junzaburō* (Princeton, N.J.: Princeton University Press, 1993): 119.

17. Ōoka Makoto, *Chōgenjitsu to jojō*, 270.

18. Nishiwaki Junzaburō, "Esthétique foraine" in *Chōgenjitsushugi shiron* (Tokyo: Kōseikaku shoten, 1929); see also Hirata, *The Poetry and Poetics of Nishiwaki Junzaburō*, 37, 39.

19. Preface to *Fukuikutaru kafu yo: Collection surréaliste*, no. 1 (Tokyo: Ōokayama shoten, 1927).

20. Niikura Toshikazu, *Nishiwaki Junzaburō zenshi in'yu shūsei* (Tokyo: Chikuma shobō, 1982): 167; Hirata, *The Poetry and Poetics of Nishiwaki Junzaburō*, 224 n. 27. In another poem by Rimbaud, "Ce qu'on dit au poète à propos de fleurs" (What one says to the poet concerning flowers) one finds the lines: "Le Lys qu'on donne au Ménestrel / Avec l'oeillet et l'amarante" (The lily you give to the Poet / With the pink and the amaranth). This poem can be read in part as a parody of the Parnassian poets' use of exotic plant names; here one may find a precedent for Nishiwaki's catalogues of plant names as well, which, through his interest in Rimbaud, gains a parodic nuance. Arthur Rimbaud, *Rimbaud: Complete Works, Selected Letters*. Wallace Fowlie, ed. (Chicago: University of Chicago Press, 1966): 105–7.

21. From the revised poem, "Fukuikutaru kafu: Seimei no haretsu" (Fragrant stoker: The rupture of life), *Amubaruwaria* (1947) in *Teihon Nishiwaki Junzaburō zenshū*, vol. 1: 125.

22. Benjamin, *Illuminations*, 255.

23. Margaret Cohen, *Profane Illumination: Walter Benjamin and the Paris of Surrealist Revolution* (Berkeley: University of California Press, 1993): 41 n. 49.

24. The publication of *Futari* was financed by a contribution from an anarchist student acquaintance. Hayashi Fumiko writes of this venture and of her relation with Tomotani in the following scene in *Hōrōki* (Chronicles of a Vagabond, 1927):

> I visit my friend Shizue Tomodani at her boarding house in Dangozaka. We talk about starting a literary magazine called *Futari*, "Two of us." I am uneasy about this plan, unable to raise even ten yen myself, but surely Shizue would help in some way. The lives of rich people seem so mysterious to me, I don't know what to say.
>
> On Tomodani's invitation we go together to the public bath. Our two small naked bodies are reflected in the morning light of the mirror. We look like sculpture by Maillol, two frolicking cats. . . .
>
> I write poems, but I won't be a success. I will starve and shrivel up. I wonder if my life would be easier if I were beautiful . . . Tomodani is a pretty woman. She radiates self-confidence. Her skin is dark, but has the aroma of wild fruit. My naked body looks like a plump boy's. Nothing but fat. [. . .]
>
> Tomodani dusts the nape of her neck with thick white powder. Her dark skin grows pale as a cloud. I haven't used powder for a long time; I stand in front of the mirror like a boy and start to do calisthenics. How funny it would be to run out the door just as I am and walk to the main road.

Translated by Elizabeth Hanson in Yukiko Tanaka, ed. *To Live and to Write* (Seattle, Wash.: Seal Press, 1987): 113–14. In this work Hayashi also mentions being intrigued by Dadaist poetry.

25. Tomotani lived with the poet Okamoto Jun and then with the poet Ono Tōzaburō during this period. Later she married Ueda Tamotsu (brother of Ueda Toshio), an active figure in the Surrealist movement and eight years her junior. At that time she changed her name to Ueda Shizue.

26. From *Ishō no taiyō*, no. 5 (Apr. 1929): 14. Also included in this issue are the translation of a manifesto of Surrealism by Yvan Goll, a poem of Takiguchi dedicated to Paul Eluard, and poems and prose by Kitasono, Ueda Toshio, Nishiwaki, Yamada Kazuhiko, Miura Kōnosuke, and others.

27. Alongside the photo is a line from a story by Ueda Toshio, which appears in the issue, telling of the narrator's encounter with an actress: "And the shadow of rain under the actress's shoes White shadow She sings a song."

28. *Ishō no taiyō*, no. 5: 15. Printed in four vertical lines without punctuation.

29. Fujiwara Sei'ichi, "Bavardage du Coq," *Ishō no taiyō*, no. 5: 23.

30. Ueda Shizue (Tomotani Shizue), *Umi ni nageta hana* (Tokyo: Sanwa shobō, 1940). The poem in its entirety appears as follows:

Resistance

All around me,
The clocks making an insipid sound of poverty,
Every single one of the old clocks.
I want to wrench them all apart with a violent twist.
And then,
I want to stand cold like a marble column.
I want to fly through the pure white space like a brave cannonball.
I want to become a huge reflecting mirror and read the electric waves from
   the beautiful stars.

31. *Ishō no taiyō*, no. 6 (July 1929): 21. "Five-colored bird" is a translation of *no-jiko*, a kind of Japanese bunting.

32. One might compare, in this aspect, the poem Tomotani published on the facing page, entitled "We" ("Watashi-tachi," a title that invokes the rare first-person plural):

We

Simple angels
Oh grass, trees! birds! insects!
I know your heart's true form
Oh gentle air
Down quilt of clouds
In the shadow of white-thorned flowers I dream

My angel Oh my dove
Today again there was a needle in your letter
but I forgive you
We, filled with errors
We, filled with caresses
that tomorrow you will probably regret

Here, too, there are the intimations of a love poem (one might easily categorize this work as such), and yet again the marks of gender are, for the most part, absent: the intimate address is to angels, to objects in nature (grass, trees, insects, air, dove, spoken to in the familiar form, *omae-tachi*). Only at the last moment does the lover become human (*anata*), sending a "letter" (itself a metaphorical image, containing a "needle"), and the verb form, as in the poem "Tsuki," becomes honorific: "Ashita anata wa kōkai nasaru darō" (Tomorrow you will probably regret [them]).

33. The allegorized characters of the moon and *watashi* recall the form of the fantastic stories and prose poems of Inagaki Taruho, in particular in *Issen ichibyō monogatari* (One thousand one-second tales; 1923). The self and the personified

moon in those stories become the protagonists in a series of continual transformations and struggles. In one tale entitled "When My Friend Turned into the Moon," Inagaki writes:

> One evening as I was walking with a friend   I spoke disparagingly of the moon   My friend was silent so I asked "Well, don't you think so?   As I spoke I turned to the side   He was the moon   I ran away but the moon came chasing after me

The absence of punctuation and the simplicity of the narration contribute to the feeling of the unexpected, of the odd unpredictability of the lines. Inagaki's work later turned to focus on questions of homosexuality: perhaps in the earlier work as well, the use of fantasy protagonists whose gender remains unspecified allows him, as it does Tomotani, a certain freedom to explore relationships in terms that might otherwise have been difficult to make acceptable. Inagaki Taruho, *Issen ichibyō monogatari* (Tokyo: Shinchōsha, 1969): 34.

34. Because her work is so rarely considered, I include here translations of two other poems from *Umi ni nageta hana*, to further indicate the direction of her subsequent work.

I Have Sunk Deep into Sadness

Like the plates and bowls,
On the bright kitchen shelf,
Jostling one another like thunder[clouds]
They all seem so happy.
In the smell and light
Of new furniture
Flitting about like honeybees.

Faces like warm cakes.
My words, yellow and peach colored
Are scattered all about
Together with their satisfied smiles.
Eyes and heart
filled with them,
I have sunk deep into sadness.

Forehead like the Woods

It was a cloudless moonlit night.
The open field had the majesty of a palace courtyard.
The roof of every house glistened sharply like steel,
and every wall concealed a beautiful dark shadow.

We were lucky the road was frozen.
Pale moonlight swelled the faint ripples on its surface into waves.

My forehead was dark green like a forest.
My heart was heavy [with cares] to the point of crumbling.
Many times I restrained myself from speaking with him.
Had he been a valiant officer
or a pitiable cook, it would have made no difference.
Like a single naked tree
His soul reflected in my eyes.

35. Ema Shoko, "Spring," *Madame Blanche* (Tokyo: Librairie Bon), no. 7 (June 1933). The pages of *Madame Blanche* are not numbered.

36. This is a translation of the poem in its entirety. From *Madame Blanche*, no. 10 (Oct. 1933).

37. This is a translation of the entire poem. *Madame Blanche*, no. 9 (Sept. 1933).

38. A female diver in this period would be called *ama*.

39. Among the group's most famous members are Takemitsu Tōru, Yuasa Jōji, and Akiyama Kuniharu.

40. The transformed meanings of Surrealism were in part related to a changed relation of postoccupation Japan to European and American cultural influences: particularly significant was the 1960 uprising of artists, students, and intellectuals to protest the renewal of the U.S.-Japan Security Treaty. Many artists and intellectuals, within a culture rushing headlong into Americanization, called upon a Japanese symbolic tradition and attempted reevoke that spiritual ground. (See Okamoto Tarō's alternative view of tradition in the Epilogue below.) Before the war, such evocations of tradition might have been immediately susceptible to co-optation by an imperialist rhetoric of Japan; after, they become one of the possible directions for inspiration of an experimental or subversive art.

41. Formed in 1959, the group was associated with the journal *Wani*.

42. Regarding Inagaki, one of the strongest cases can be made for the relation between his work and the Futurist movement. For an excellent assessment of Inagaki's work and its relation to Futurism, see the recent work by Shigeta Mariko, *Taruho/Miraiha* (Tokyo: Kawade shobō shinsha, 1997).

43. Shimao Toshio, "Hi-chōgenjitsushugiteki na chōgenjitsushugi no oboe-gaki," *Eiga hihyō*, no. 8 (Feb. 1958); reprinted in *Shimao Toshio zenshū*, vol. 13 (Tokyo: Ōbunsha, 1982): 212.

44. The significance of this phrase ("irreplaceable condition") is also discussed in a reading of Shimao Toshio's essay by Tsuruoka Yoshihisa in *Nihon chōgenjitsushugi shiron* (Tokyo: Shichōsha, 1970): 233–34.

45. Parts of his work attempt to explore beyond the realms of everyday life, to delve into the world of the "everyday" as a dream and the dream or fantastical event as part of the everyday. Allowing the distinction between these two worlds to blur, he opens up the boundary that has been so rigidly constructed between them.

46. Hijikata Tatsumi, "Sen ga sen ni nitekuru toki," *Gendaishi techō* (Tokyo:

Shichōsha), "Takiguchi Shūzō" (1974): 243–47. Reprinted in Hijikata Tatsumi, *Bibō no Aozora* (Tokyo: Chikuma shobō, 1987): 122–29.

47. Hijikata, "Sen ga sen ni nitekuru toki," 124.

48. One cannot overestimate the importance of these writers as a center of artistic activity and encouragement for young, aspiring postwar artists. The composer Takemitsu Tōru of the group Jikken Kōbō (Experimental Workshop) reminisces: "The greatest force behind the solidarity of our group was clearly the presence of the poet Takiguchi Shūzō. . . . The creative teaching of Takiguchi was more important in opening our minds and cementing the bond between us than the creative activities we actually carried out . . . I can never forget meeting the person whom I can truly call my spiritual teacher . . . " *Jikken kōbō to Takiguchi Shūzō: The 11th Exhibition Homage to Shūzō Takiguchi—Experimental Workshop* (Tokyo: Satani Gallery, 1991): 192. Takiguchi was forty-eight when the group was formed; most of its members at the time were in their twenties.

49. Takiguchi Shūzō, "Toward Rrose Sélavy: A Marginal Note to *To and From Rrose Sélavy*," translated by Takiguchi in Takiguchi Shūzō, ed., *To and From Rrose Sélavy: Maruseru Dyushan goroku / Selected Words of Marcel Duchamp* (Tokyo: Bijutsu shuppansha, 1968): 2–4.

EPILOGUE   *Physical Nostalgias*

1. The kanji compound of *butoh* (舞踏) can be found already in the Chinese classic *Shu Jing*, but its use to refer to Western dance forms began in the Meiji period (1868–1912) in Japan. In modern Chinese, *butoh* or *wu dao*, is not the common colloquial word for dance but can still be used to refer to certain kinds of artistic dance forms.

2. See Klein's analysis of Butoh, *Ankoku Buto: The Premodern and Postmodern Influences on the Dance of Utter Darkness*, Cornell East Asian Papers no. 49 (Ithaca, N.Y.: Cornell University Press, 1988), for an enlightening discussion of Butoh's history and an analysis of representative works.

Marilyn Ivy's *Discourses of the Vanishing* (Chicago: University of Chicago Press, 1995), on nostalgia and its uses in postwar Japan from an anthropological/sociological perspective, is also relevant in this context in that it considers the way in the 1970s and 1980s the objects of a certain nostalgia were reconstructed as tourist attractions, exoticized as a tradition that could be revisited at particular rural sites.

An exhibition organized by Alexandra Munroe entitled *Scream Against the Sky* (1995; Solomon R. Guggenheim Museum, San Francisco Museum of Modern Art, and Yokohama Museum of Art) introduced developments in Japanese postwar visual arts to the American audience. The exhibition displayed a video of Hijikata's peformance "Revolt of the Flesh," Takiguchi's liberty passports, and other important postwar works. See the catalogue, Alexandra Munroe, *Japanese Art after 1945: Scream Against the Sky* (New York: Harry N. Abrams, 1994).

3. The emphasis is mine. Okamoto Tarō, "Dentōron no atarashii tenkai," in *Nihon no dentō*, vol. 4, *Okamoto Tarō chosakushū* (Tokyo: Kodansha, 1980), 176.

4. Theodor Adorno also writes of this simultaneous forward and backward movement: "Longing in artworks, which aims at the reality of the nonexistent, takes the form of remembrance." Theodor Adorno, cited in Andreas Huyssen, *Twilight Memories: Marking Time in a Cultural Amnesia* (New York: Routledge, 1995): 85, 88.

5. One could allude, for example, to the clear impact on Butoh of European modern and expressionist dance, from Mary Wigman and tangos and waltzes onward, citing the fact that one of Ohno's major works, "Admiring La Argentina," is an homage to the flamenco dancer Antonia Mercé, whom Ohno saw dance at the Imperial Theater in Tokyo as early as 1929. But, in my view, either of these routes would be missing the point.

6. Mishima Yukio, "Kiki no buyō," in "Hijikata Tatsumi Dance Experience no kai" (program notes, July 1960), reprinted in *Mishima Yukio zenhyōronshū*, vol. 4 (Tokyo: Shinchōsha, 1989): 161–62.

7. At the point of beginning to write, Takiguchi states, the "pen, maintaining an odd equilibrium like the tower of Pisa, begins to move." Here, too, it is a question of an odd or precarious balance that leads, hesitantly, toward expression. See the section "'Etamines Narratives': Experiments in Actuality" in Chapter 4.

8. Takiguchi writes of the relation between the poem and actuality, in the best case, as a momentary resemblance of two shadows.

9. Mishima Yukio, "Zen'ei buyō to mono to no kankei," in "Hijikata Tatsumi Dance Experience no kai," reprinted in *Mishima Yukio zenhyōronshū*, 163–64.

10. In the play between "single plate" and "human-body plate," Hijikata seems to be led by the play of sounds; in *hitosara*, *hito* can mean single or human (hence the new word body-plate, using the kanji for person). Hijikata Tatsumi, "Kazedaruma," in *Gendaishi techō* (Tokyo: Shichōsha), vol. 28, no. 6, special issue, "Butō, shintai, gengo" (May 1985): 73. For a collection of excerpts from Hijikata's writings, essays on Hijikata, homages, and reliable chronologies of his work, see Motofuji Akiko, et al. *Hijikata Tatsumi butō taikan: Kasabuta to kyarameru* (Tokyo: Yūshisha, 1993). See also the anthology of Hijikata's collected writings, *Hijikata Tatsumi zenshū*, 2 vols. (Tokyo: Kawade shobō shinsha, 1998).

11. Hijikata, in the same essay, tells a story of his fascination with the small children in his village in Akita, who were tied to pillars in the house while their parents went to work in the fields. He observed the strange movements the children made: "One of them was feeding something to his own hand. What a strange thing thing to do! . . . So the child was treating his hand as if it weren't his own hand; he was treating it like an object, not his own hand, although it was a part of his body." And he describes his father, a carpenter, with his hands resting on a table: "He worked so much, that when he rested his hands on the table, and

looked at them, they looked like a planing tool or some carpenter's tool. Those hands were his own body and yet not his own body." "Kazedaruma," 73.

12. See Ohno Kazuo's collection of writings, notes, and essays, including critical essays on his work, *Goten, sora o tobu: Kazuo Ohno butoh no kotoba / The Palace Soars Through the Sky: Kazuo Ohno on Butoh* (Tokyo: Shichōsha, 1989): 26. These essays and the pieces that follow were written over a number of years but compiled in the late 1980s, and thus, like Hijikata's "Kazedaruma," they reflect a retrospective view of Butoh more than, for example, the contemporary program essays by Mishima. Nonetheless, they are useful in illuminating the rhetoric and practices of Butoh that had developed over several decades.

13. Ohno Kazuo, "Keiko to wa," in Ohno, *Goten, sora o tobu*, 26.

14. Nagata Kōi, "Ohno Kazuo to Zeami," cited in Ohno, *Goten, sora o tobu*, 312.

15. The quoted section is "Mannō o isshin ni tsunagu." Nagata cites a modern translation; this is my translation from Zeami's text. Nose Asaji, ed. *Zeami jūrokubushū hyōshaku*, vol. 1 (Tokyo: Iwanami shoten, 1963): 375–76.

16. "Kayō naredomo, kono naishin ari to, yoso ni mietewa warukaru beshi. Moshi mieba, sore wa waza ni naru beshi. Senu ni te wa aru bekarazu." Zeami Motokiyo, "Kakyō," in Nose, ed., *Zeami jūrokubushū hyōshaku*, 376.

17. Ohno Kazuo, "Keiko to wa" in Ohno, *Goten, sora o tobu*. At the same time, Ohno's movements can be very flamboyant, extravagant.

18. Emphasis mine. From "Sei to shi no sakai o koeru butō," interview with Tsuruyama Yūji, in Ohno, *Goten, sora o tobu*, 73. Again and again in this interview Ohno emphasizes reaching limits and pushing against the boundaries of the possible, even in relation to his mother.

19. "Watashi no okaasan" was composed in 1981. Motif notes in Ohno, *Goten, sora o tobu*, 123–28.

20. "Shikai: Uinna warutsu to yūrei," in Ohno, *Goten, sora o tobu*, 147.

21. Ohno, *Goten, sora o tobu*. A recent publication transcribes Ohno's improvised images and words from tapes of his workshops: see *Ohno Kazuo: Keiko no kotoba* (Tokyo: Fuirumu aatosha, 1997).

BIBLIOGRAPHY

A (Dalian [Dairen], China: A-sha). Nos. 2–35 (Dec. 1924–Dec. 1927).

Abe Yoshio. "Baudelaire dans la poétique 'imagiste' de Hagiwara Sakutarō," part 2. *Proceedings of the Department of Foreign Languages and Literatures.* Vol. 35, no. 2. College of Arts and Sciences, University of Tokyo, 1987.

———. *Hito de nashi no shigaku.* Tokyo: Ozawa shoten, 1982.

———. "Un malentendu: T. E. Hulme et une poétique 'surréaliste' au Japon." Claudio Guillen, ed. *Proceedings of the 12th Congress of the International Comparative Literature Association, New York, 1982.* Vol. 2, *Comparative Poetics.* New York: Garland Publishing, 1985: 293–99.

———. "Nihon no modanizumu." In Kawamoto Kōji, *Uta to shi no keifu.* Tokyo: Chūōkōronsha, 1994.

———. "Poésie d'avant-garde au Japon de 1923 à 1939." *Nichifutsu bunka* (Tokyo), no. 37 (Mar. 1979): 20–41.

Aeba Takao, ed. *Shimao Toshio kenkyū.* Tokyo: Tōjusha, 1976.

Aka to kuro. Nos. 1–5 (Jan.–June 1923).

Amagasaki Akira. *Nihon no retorikku.* Tokyo: Chikuma shobō, 1988.

André Breton and Shūzō Takiguchi: The 13th Exhibition Homage to Shūzō Takiguchi. Tokyo: Satani Gallery, 1993.

Art Vivant. No. 33, "'MAVO' no jidai." Tokyo: Seibu bijutsukan (1989).

Asai Kiyoshi et al. *Kenkyū shiryo gendai nihon bungaku.* Vol. 7, *Shi.* Tokyo: Meiji shoin, 1980.

Balakian, Anna. *André Breton: Magus of Surrealism.* New York: Oxford University Press, 1971.

Baudelaire, Charles. *Oeuvres complètes.* Paris: Editions Robert Laffont, 1980.

Bédouin, Jean-Louis. *La Poésie surréaliste.* Paris: Editions Seghers, 1964.

Behar, Henri, ed. *Les Pensées d'André Breton.* Paris: L'Age d'Homme, 1988.

Benjamin, Walter. *Gesammelte Schriften.* Vol. 2, *Aufsätze, Essays, Vorträge.* Frankfurt am Main: Suhrkamp Verlag, 1977.

———. *Illuminations,* Harry Zohn, trans. New York: Schocken Books, 1968.

———. *Reflections,* Edmund Jephcott, trans.; Peter Demetz, ed. New York: Schocken Books, 1978.

Blanchot, Maurice. *The Gaze of Orpheus*, Lydia Davis, trans. Barrytown, New York: Station Hill Press, 1981.
———. *The Infinite Conversation*, Susan Hanson, trans. Minneapolis: University of Minnesota Press, 1993.
———. *La Part du feu*. Paris: Editions Gallimard, 1949.
———. *The Space of Literature*, Ann Smock, trans. Lincoln: University of Nebraska Press, 1982.
Bloom, Harold. *The Anxiety of Influence*. New York: Oxford University Press, 1973.
———. *A Map of Misreading*. New York: Oxford University Press, 1975.
Bocholier, Gerard. *Pierre Reverdy: Le Phare obscur*. Paris: Champ Vallon, 1984.
Boym, Svetlana. *Death in Quotation Marks*. Cambridge, Mass.: Harvard University Press, 1991.
Breton, André. *L'Amour fou*. Paris: Gallimard, 1937.
———. *Communicating Vessels*, Mary Ann Caws and Geoffrey Harris, trans. Lincoln: University of Nebraska Press, 1990.
———. *Les Manifestes du surréalisme*. Paris: Le Sagittaire, 1955.
———. *Manifestoes of Surrealism*, Richard Seaver and Helen R. Lane, trans. Ann Arbor: University of Michigan Press, 1972.
———. *Nadja*. Paris: Gallimard, 1964.
———. *Oeuvres complètes*, vols. 1 and 2. Paris: Gallimard, 1988.
———. *Point du jour*. Paris: Gallimard, 1970.
———. *Le Surréalisme et la peinture*. Paris: Gallimard, 1928.
Browning, Gordon Frederick. *Tristan Tzara: The Genesis of the Dada Poem or from Dada to Aa*. Stuttgart: Akademischer Verlag Hans-Dieter Heinz, 1979.
Bungaku. Nos. 1–6 (Mar. 1932–Dec. 1934).
Bürger, Peter. *Theory of the Avant-Garde*. Minneapolis: University of Minnesota Press, 1992.
Carter, Steven. *Traditional Japanese Poetry*. Stanford: Stanford University Press, 1991.
Caruth, Cathy. *Unclaimed Experience: Trauma, Narrative, and History*. Baltimore: Johns Hopkins University Press, 1996.
———, ed. *American Imago*, "Psychoanalysis, Culture, and Trauma," vol. 48, no. 1 (spring 1991).
———. *Trauma: Explorations in Memory*. Baltimore: Johns Hopkins University Press, 1995.
Cendre (Tsu: Asagi shobō), Kitasono Katsue, ed. Nos. 1–7 (Jan.–Oct. 1948).
Chadwick, Whitney. *Women Artists and the Surrealist Movement*. London: Thames and Hudson, 1985.
Cohen, Margaret. *Profane Illumination: Walter Benjamin and the Paris of Surrealist Revolution*. Berkeley: University of California Press, 1993.

Crevel, René. *L'Esprit contre la raison et autres écrits surréalistes.* Paris: Société Nouvelle des Editions Pauvert, 1986.

de Bolla, Peter. *Harold Bloom: Towards Historical Rhetorics.* London: Routledge, 1988.

de Man, Paul. *The Resistance to Theory.* Minneapolis: University of Minnesota Press, 1986.

Derrida, Jacques. *Of Grammatology,* Gayatri Chakravorty Spivak, trans. Baltimore: Johns Hopkins University Press, 1974.

Doak, Kevin Michael. *Dreams of Difference: The Japan Romantic School and the Crisis of Modernity.* Berkeley: University of California Press, 1994.

Ebara, Jun. "Japon," and other entries. In *Dictionnaire général du surréalisme et de ses environs.* Paris: Presses Universitaires de France and Office du Livre, 1982.

———. "Si cette pierre philosophale n'existait pas . . . Le surréalisme au Japon." *Opus international.* No. 19–20, "Surréalisme international." Paris (Oct. 1970): 86–89.

L'Echange surréaliste. Tokyo: Bon shoten, 1936.

Eluard, Paul. *Selected Poems,* Gilbert Bowen, trans. London: Riverrun Press, 1987.

Ema Shōko. *Ema Shōko zenshishū.* Tokyo: Hōbunkan shuppan, 1999.

———. *Haru e no shōtai: shishū.* Tokyo: Vou Kurabu, 1936.

L'Esprit nouveau (Tokyo: Librairie Kinokuniya). Nos. 1–6 (Oct. 1930–Feb. 1935).

Felman, Shoshana, and Dori Laub. *Testimony: Crises of Witnessing in Literature, Psychoanalysis, and History.* New York: Routledge, 1991.

Foster, Hal. *Compulsive Beauty.* Cambridge, Mass.: M.I.T. Press, 1993.

Freud, Sigmund. *Beyond the Pleasure Principle,* James Strachey, trans. New York: W. W. Norton, 1961.

———. *The Interpretation of Dreams,* James Strachey, trans. New York: Avon Books, 1965.

Fujii, James. *Complicit Fictions.* Berkeley: University of California Press, 1993.

Fujitomi Yasuo. *Kitasono Katsue.* Tokyo: Yūseidō, 1983.

Fukuikutaru kafu yo (Tokyo: Ōokayama shoten). No. 1, "Collection surréaliste" (1927).

Fukuikutaru kafu yo—seitan hyakunen: Nishiwaki Junzaburō sono shi to kaiga. Yokohama: Kanagawa kindai bungakukan, 1994.

GE.GJMGJGAM.PRRR.GJMGEM (June–Dec. 1924).

Gendaishi dokuhon (Tokyo: Shichōsha). "Nishiwaki Junzaburō" (Sept. 15, 1985).

Gendaishi dokuhon (Tokyo: Shichōsha). "Takiguchi Shūzō" (Oct. 1, 1985).

"*Gendaishi no furontia": Modanizumu no keifu ten.* Kitakami: Nihon gendai shiika bungakukan, 1994.

Gendaishi techō (Tokyo: Shichōsha). Vol. 28, no. 6, "Butō, shintai, gengo" (May 1985).

Gendaishi techō (Tokyo: Shichōsha). Vol. 37, no. 2, "Nishiwaki Junzaburō yomi-naoshi" (Feb. 1994).

Gendaishi techō (Tokyo: Shichōsha). Vol. 17, no. 11, "Takiguchi Shūzō" (Oct. 1974).

Gradiva. No. 2, "Symbolisme, surréalisme, poésie" (Nov. 1971).

Guillén, Claudio. *The Challenge of Comparative Literature.* Cambridge, Mass.: Harvard University Press, 1993.

Hagiwara Sakutarō. *Ao neko.* Tokyo: Nihon Kindai Bungakukan, 1969.

———. *Hagiwara Sakutarō zenshū.* 15 vols. Tokyo: Chikuma Shobō, 1975–78.

———. *Tsuki ni hoeru.* Tokyo: Kanjōshisha, 1917.

Haruyama Yukio. *Shi no kenkyū.* Tokyo: Kōseikaku shoten, 1931.

———. "Totsuzen-ha Taruho no koto." *Gensō bungaku* (Tokyo: Gensō bungakukai shuppansha). No. 3, "Taruho" (Dec. 1987): 176–79.

Heidegger, Martin. "A Dialogue on Language." In *On the Way to Language.* San Francisco: Harper and Row, 1971: 1–54.

———. "Aus einen Gespräch von der Sprache." In *Unterwegs zur Sprache.* Pfullingen, Germany: Neske, 1959.

Hijikata Tatsumi. *Bibō no Aozora.* Tokyo: Chikuma shobō, 1987.

———. *Hijikata Tatsumi zenshū.* 2 vols. Tokyo: Kawade shobō, 1998.

Hirata, Hosea. *The Poetry and Poetics of Nishiwaki Junzaburō.* Princeton, N.J.: Princeton University Press, 1993.

Hon no techō (Tokyo: Shōshinsha). Vol. 9, no. 4, "Takiguchi Shūzō." (Aug. 1969).

Horie Nobuo. *Yamamura Bochō no bungaku.* Tokyo: Tsukuba shorin, 1994.

Horiguchi Daigaku. *Gekka no ichigun.* Tokyo: Daiichi shobō, 1925.

Huyssen, Andreas. *Twilight Memories: Marking Time in a Cultural Amnesia.* New York: Routledge, 1995.

Iijima Kōichi. *Nihon no shūrurearisumu.* Tokyo: Shichōsha, 1963.

———. *Shururearisumu to iu dentō.* Tokyo: Misuzu shobō, 1992.

Inagaki Taruho. *Issen ichibyō monogatari.* Tokyo: Shinchōsha, 1969.

Inoue Teruo, "Nishiwaki Junzaburō to Baudelaire: Sono shiron o chūshin to shite." In Kagiya Yukinobu and Niikura Toshikazu, eds., *Teihon Nishiwaki Junzaburō zenshū,* vol. 13. Tokyo: Chikuma shobō, 1993–94.

Ishikawa Jun. *Ishikawa Jun zenshū.* Tokyo: Chikuma shobō, 1989.

Ishō no taiyō (Tokyo: L.E.S.-sha). Nos. 1–6 (Nov. 1928–July 1929). Reprint *Fukkokuban "Ishō no taiyō,"* with *Fukuikutaru kafu yo* and *Le Surréalisme international.* Tokyo: Tamura shoten, 1987.

Ivy, Marilyn. *Discourses of the Vanishing.* Chicago: University of Chicago Press, 1995.

Iwamoto Shūzō. *Iwamoto Shūzō shi shūsei.* Yokohama: Blue Canyon Press, 1989.

Iwaya Kunio, ed. *Shibusawa Tatsuhiko bungakukan.* Vol. 11, *Shururearisumu no hako.* Tokyo: Chikuma shobō, 1990.

Jackson, Earl, Jr. "The Heresy of Meaning: Japanese Symbolist Poetry." *Harvard Journal of Asiatic Studies*, vol. 51, no. 2 (Dec. 1991): 561–99.

————. "The Metaphysics of Translation and the Origins of Symbolist Poetics in Meiji Japan." *Publications of the Modern Language Association of America*, vol. 105, no. 2 (Mar. 1990): 256–72.

Janeira, Armando Martins. *Japanese and Western Literature: A Comparative Study*. Rutland, Vt.: Charles E. Tuttle, 1970.

Japon des Avant-Gardes 1910–1970. Paris: Editions du Centre Georges-Pompidou, 1986.

Jean, Marcel, ed. *The Autobiography of Surrealism*. New York: Viking Press, 1980.

Jikken kōbō to Takiguchi Shūzō: The 11th Exhibition Homage to Shūzō Takiguchi—Experimental Workshop. Tokyo: Satani Gallery, 1991.

Joan Miró to Takiguchi Shūzō: The 10th Exhibition Homage to Shūzō Takiguchi. Tokyo: Satani Gallery, 1990.

Jouffroy, Alain, ed. *Pour un temps: Ecritures japonaises*. Paris: Editions du Centre Georges-Pompidou, 1986.

Kagiya Yukinobu. *Shijin Nishiwaki Junzaburō*. Tokyo: Chikuma shobō, 1983.

————, Shimizu Toshihiko, and Fujitomi Yasuo, eds. *Nikakkei no shiron*. Tokyo: Riburopōto, 1987.

Kakuta Toshirō. *Nihon kindaishi*. Tokyo: Shinchōsha, 1968.

Kanada Hiroshi. *Tabibito tsui ni kaerazu: Nishiwaki uchū no ichiseiun kara*. Tokyo: Chikuma shobō, 1987.

Kanbara Tai, "Chōgenjitsushugi no botsuraku." *Shi: Genjitsu*, no. 1 (June 1930).

Keene, Dennis. *The Modern Japanese Prose Poem*. Princeton, N.J.: Princeton University Press, 1980.

————. *Yokomitsu Riichi: Modernist*. New York: Columbia University Press, 1980.

Kennedy, George A. *Selected Works of George A. Kennedy*, Tien-yi Li, ed. New Haven, Conn.: Yale University Press, 1964.

Kikuchi Yasuo. *Aoi kaidan o noboru shijintachi*. Tokyo: Seidosha, 1965.

Kin-gendaishi yōgo jiten. Tokyo: Shin jinbutsu ōraisha, 1992.

Kitagawa Tōru. *Shiteki retorikku nyūmon*. Tokyo: Shichōsha, 1993.

Kitasono Katsue. *Haiburau no funsui*. Tokyo: Shōshinsha, 1941.

————. *Kitasono Katsue zenhyōronshū*, Tsuruoka Yoshihisa, ed. Tokyo: Chūsekisha, 1988.

————. *Kitasono Katsue zenshashinshū*. Tokyo: Chūsekisha, 1992.

————. *Kitasono Katsue zenshishū*, Fujitomi Yasuo, ed. Tokyo: Chūsekisha, 1983.

————. *Shiro no arubamu*. Tokyo: Kōseikaku shoten, 1929.

————. *Ten no tebukuro*. Tokyo: Shunjū shobō, 1933.

Klein, Susan Blakeley. *Ankoku Buto: The Premodern and Postmodern Influences on the Dance of Utter Darkness*. Cornell East Asian Papers no. 49. Ithaca, N.Y.: Cornell University Press, 1988.

Ko Won. *Buddhist Elements in Dada.* New York: New York University Press, 1977.

Kodama, Sanehide, ed. *Ezra Pound and Japan.* Redding Ridge, Conn.: Black Swan Books, 1987.

Koga Harue. *Koga Harue shigashū: Ushi o yaku.* Tokyo: Higashi shuppansha, 1974.

Kōjien. Tokyo: Iwanami shoten, 1990.

Kojima Noriyuki and Arai Eizō, eds. *Shin nihon bungaku taikei.* Vol. 5, *Kokin wakashū.* Tokyo: Iwanami shoten, 1989.

Krauss, Rosalind E. *The Originality of the Avant-Garde and Other Modernist Myths.* Cambridge, Mass.: M.I.T. Press, 1985.

Kristeva, Julia. *La Révolution du langage poétique.* Paris: Editions du Seuil, 1974.

Kudoh Miyoko. *Sabishii koe.* Tokyo: Chikuma shobō, 1994.

Leiris, Michel. *L'Age d'homme, précédé de "De la littérature considérée comme une tauromachie."* Paris: Gallimard, 1986.

Linhartová, Věra. *Dada et surréalisme au Japon.* Paris: Publications Orientalistes de France, 1987.

Liu, Lydia He. *Translingual Practice: Literature, National Culture, and Translated Modernity—China, 1900–1937.* Stanford, Calif.: Stanford University Press, 1995.

Loi, Michelle. *Poètes chinoises d'écoles françaises.* Paris: Librairie d'Amérique et d'Orient Adrien Maisonneuve, 1980.

Lower, Lucy. "Poetry and Poetics: From Modern to Contemporary in Japanese Poetry." Ph.D. diss., Harvard University, 1987.

Madame Blanche (Tokyo: Librairie Bon). Nos. 1–17 (May 1932–Aug. 1934).

Marinetti, Filippo Tommaso. *La grande Milano traditionale e futurista: Una sensibilità italiana nata in Egitto.* Milano: A. Mondadori, 1969.

———. *Marinetti: Selected Writings.* R. W. Flint and Arthur A. Coppotelli, ed. and trans. New York: Farrar, Strauss, and Giroux, 1971.

Mauriac, Claude. *André Breton.* Paris: Editions Bernard Grasset, 1970.

MAVO. Nos. 1–6 (July 1924–Aug. 1925).

McCullough, Helen C. *Brocade by Night: 'Kokin wakashū' and the Court Style in Japanese Poetry.* Stanford: Stanford University Press, 1985.

———. *Classical Japanese Prose.* Stanford: Stanford University Press, 1990.

Michaux, Henri. *Plume, précédé de Lointain intérieur.* Paris: Gallimard, 1963.

Mishima Yukio. *Mishima Yukio zenhyōronshū,* vol. 4. Tokyo: Shinchōsha, 1989.

Miyoshi Jūrō. *Nihon oyobi nihonjin.* Tokyo: Kōbunsha, 1954.

Moore, Cornelia, and Raymond Moody, eds. *Comparative Literature East and West: Traditions and Trends.* Honolulu: University of Hawaii; East-West Center, 1989.

Motofuji Akiko, Tsuruoka Yoshihisa, and Tanemura Suehiro, eds. *Hijikata Tatsumi butō taikan: Kasabuta to kyarameru.* Tokyo: Yūshisha, 1993.

Munroe, Alexandra. *Japanese Art after 1945: Scream Against the Sky.* New York: Harry N. Abrams, 1994.

Murano Shirō, Fukuda Rikutarō, and Kagiya Yukinobu, eds. *Nishiwaki Junzaburō kenkyū.* Tokyo: Yūbun shoin, 1971.

Nadeau, Maurice. *Histoire du surréalisme suivie de documents surréalistes.* Paris: Editions du Seuil, 1964.

Nakamura Mitsuo, "The French Influence in Modern Japanese Literature," *Japan Quarterly* (Tokyo: Asahi shinbunsha), vol. 7, no. 1 (Jan.–Mar. 1960): 57–65.

Nakanishi Susumu. "Nihon no sōzōryoku." Paper presented at colloquium at International Center for Japanese Studies, Kyoto, Sept. 2, 1994.

Nakano Ka'ichi. *Modanizumu shi no jidai.* Tokyo: Hōbunkan, 1986.

Nihon no shiika. Vol. 25, *Kitagawa Fuyuhiko, Anzai Fuyue, Kitasono Katsue, Haruyama Yukio, and Takenaka Iku.* Tokyo: Chūōkōronsha, 1969.

Nihon no shururearisumu, 1925–1945. Nagoya: Nagoya City Art Museum, 1990.

Nihon shijin zenshū, vol. 23. Tokyo: Shinchōsha, 1967.

Niikura Toshikazu. *Nishiwaki Junzaburō hen'yō no dentō.* Tokyo: Tōhō shobō, 1994.

———. *Nishiwaki Junzaburō zenshi in'yū shūsei.* Tokyo: Chikuma shobō, 1982.

Nishiwaki Junzaburō. *Ambarvalia.* Tokyo: Shii no kisha, 1933.

———. *Atelier* (Tokyo). Vol. 7, no. 1, "Chōgenjitsushugi kenkyū" (Jan. 1930): 1–74.

———. *Chōgenjitsushugi shiron.* Tokyo: Kōseikaku shoten, 1929.

———. *Chōgenjitsushugi shiron.* Tokyo: Arechi shuppansha, 1954.

———. "Poietes." *Mugen*, Murano Shirō, Kusano Shinpei, and Kitagawa Fuyuhiko, eds., no. 1 (1959).

———. *Shururearisumu bungakuron.* Tokyo: Tenjinsha, 1930.

———. *Tabibito kaerazu.* Tokyo: Tokyo shuppan, 1947.

———. *Teihon Nishiwaki Junzaburō zenshū.* 12 vols. Tokyo: Chikuma shobō, 1993–94.

———. *Yōroppa bungaku.* Tokyo: Daiichi shobō, 1933.

Nitobe Inazō et al. *Western Influences in Modern Japan.* Chicago: Chicago University Press, 1931.

Nose Asaji, ed. *Zeami jūrokubushū hyōshaku*, vol. 1. Tokyo: Iwanami shoten, 1963.

Ohno Kazuo. *Goten, sora o tobu: Ohno Kazuo butoh no kotoba / The Palace Soars Through the Sky: Ohno Kazuo on Butoh.* Tokyo: Shichōsha, 1989.

———. *Ohno Kazuo: Keiko no kotoba.* Tokyo: Fuirumuaatosha, 1997.

Okamoto Tarō. *Okamoto Tarō chosakushū.* 9 vols. Tokyo: Kōdansha, 1979–80.

Ōoka Makoto. *Chōgenjitsu to jojō: Shōwa jūnendai no shiseishin.* Tokyo: Shōbunsha, 1965.

——— and Thomas Fitzsimmons, eds. *A Play of Mirrors: Eight Major Poets of Modern Japan.* Rochester, Mich.: Katydid Books, 1987.

———, Hinatsu Kōnosuke, Nakano Shigeharu, Miyoshi Tatsuji, Yano Hōjin, and Sangū Makoto, eds. *Nihon gendaishi taikei.* 13 vols. Tokyo: Kawade shobō, 1974–76.

Ōtaka Orio, ed. *Furansu bungaku to watashi.* Tokyo: Heibonsha, 1985.

Ozawa Masao and Matsuda Shigeho, eds. *Kokinwakashū.* Tokyo: Shōgakkan, 1983.

Peterson, Elmer. *Tristan Tzara: Dada and Surrational Theorist.* New Brunswick, N.J.: Rutgers University Press, 1971.

Picon, Gaëtan. *Surrealism, 1919–1939.* Geneva: Editions d'Art Albert Skira, 1977.

Ponge, Francis. *Le Parti pris des choses.* Paris: Gallimard, 1942.

Reverdy, Pierre. *Nord-Sud: Self-défense et autres écrits sur l'art et la poésie, 1917–26.* Paris: Flammarion, 1975.

———. *Pierre Reverdy Selected Poems,* Timothy Bent, ed.; John Ashbery, Mary Ann Caws, and Patricia Terry, trans. Winston-Salem, N.C.: Wake Forest University Press, 1991.

La Révolution surréaliste (Paris). Nos. 1–12 (1924–29). Reprint *La Révolution surréaliste: Collection complète.* Paris: Editions Jean-Michel Place, 1975.

Richter, Hans. *Dada: Geijutsu to han-geijutsu,* Haryū Ichirō, trans. Tokyo: Bijutsu shuppansha, 1966. Japanese translation of *Dada: Kunst und Antikunst.* Köln: M. DuMont Schauberg, 1964.

Riddel, Joseph N. "'Neo-Nietzschean Clatter'—Speculation and/on Pound's Poetic Image." In Ian F. A. Bell, ed., *Ezra Pound: Tactics for Reading.* London: Vision, 1982.

Rien. Nos. 1–19 (Mar. 1929–June 1937).

Rimbaud, Arthur. *Rimbaud: Complete Works, Selected Letters,* Wallace Fowlie, ed. Chicago: University of Chicago Press, 1966.

Rimer, J. Thomas, ed. *Culture and Identity: Japanese Intellectuals During the Interwar Years.* Princeton, N.J.: Princeton University Press, 1990.

———, and Yamazaki Masakazu. *On the Art of the Nō Drama.* Princeton, N.J.: Princeton University Press, 1984.

Rodd, Laurel, and Mary Henkenius. *Kokinshū.* Princeton, N.J.: Princeton University Press, 1984.

Rubin, Jay. *Injurious to Public Morals: Writers and the Meiji State.* Seattle: University of Washington Press, 1984.

Sato Hiroaki. *Ten Japanese Poets.* Hanover, N.H.: Granite Publications, 1973.

Satō Saku. *Baudelaire oboegaki.* Tokyo: Kōdansha, 1949.

———. *Chisei no bungaku: Gendai furansu no bungaku.* Tokyo: Kawade shobō, 1956.

———. *Chōgenjitsu to shi: Furansu bungaku to nihon bungaku.* Tokyo: Shichōsha, 1981.

———. *Gendai furansu bungaku no tenbō.* Tokyo: Karuchaa shuppansha, 1985.

———. *Seidō no kubi.* Tokyo: Shichōsha, 1987.

Sawa Masahiro. *Nishiwaki Junzaburō no shi to shiron.* Tokyo: Ōfūsha, 1991.

Schwartz, William Leonard. *The Imaginative Interpretation of the Far East in Modern French Literature, 1800–1925.* Paris: H. Champion, 1927.

Shibusawa Kōsuke. *Shi no kigen o motomete.* Tokyo: Shichōsha, 1977.
Shi: Genjitsu (Tokyo: Musashino shoin). Nos. 1–5 (June 1930–June 1931).
Shigeta Mariko. *Taruho/Miraiha.* Tokyo: Kawade shobō shinsha, 1997.
Shihō (Tokyo: Librairie Kinokuniya). Nos. 1–6 (Aug. 1934–Jan. 1935).
Shimao Toshio. *Shimao Toshio zenshū.* 17 vols. Tokyo: Shōbunsha, 1982.
Shinchō. Vol. 91, no. 8, "Nishiwaki Junzaburō seitan hyakunen." (1994).
Shinryōdo (Tokyo: Aoi shobō). Nos. 1–56 (May 1937–Jan. 1942).
Shirakawa, Yoshio, and Uno Kiichi, "1920/1960: Les Avant-gardes au Japon et le parti des assassins." *Canal* (Paris), no. 35–36 (Jan.–Feb. 1980): 4–6.
Shi to shiron (Tokyo: Kōseikaku shoten). Nos. 1–14 (Sept. 1928–Dec. 1931).
Shively, Donald, ed. *Tradition and Modernization in Japanese Culture.* Princeton, N.J.: Princeton University Press, 1971.
Shōbi, majutsu, gakusetsu (Tokyo: Retsusha), Asaka Kenkichi (Kitasono Katsue), ed. Nos. 1–4 (Nov. 1927–Feb. 1928). Reprint *Shōbi, majutsu, gakusetsu.* Tokyo: Nishizawa shoten, 1977.
Shururearisumu dokuhon 2 (Tokyo: Shichōsha). "Shururearisumu no tenkai" (May 1, 1981).
Shururearisumu o meguru sakka-tachi. Toyama: Toyama Kenritsu Bijutsukan, 1997.
Shururearisumu no dokuhon. Vol. 2, *Shururearisumu no tenkai.* Tokyo: Shichōsha, 1981.
Silverberg, Miriam. *Changing Song: The Marxist Manifestos of Nakano Shigeharu.* Princeton, N.J.: Princeton University Press, 1990.
Solt, John Peter. "Shredding the Tapestry of Meaning: The Poetry and Poetics of Kitasono Katue (1902–1978)." Ph.D. diss., Harvard University, 1989.
———. *Shredding the Tapestry of Meaning: The Poetry and Poetics of Kitasono Katue (1902–1978).* Harvard East Asian Monographs, no. 178. Cambridge, Mass.: Harvard University Asia Center, 1999.
Stryk, Lucien, trans. *Triumph of the Sparrow: Zen Poems of Shinkichi Takahashi.* Chicago: University of Illinois Press, 1986.
Suleiman, Susan. *Risking Who One Is.* Cambridge, Mass.: Harvard University Press, 1994.
Le Surréalisme international (Tokyo: Fujiwara Sei'ichi). No. 1 (1930).
Suzuki, Tomi. *Narrating the Self: Fictions of Japanese Modernity.* Stanford: Stanford University Press, 1996.
Taiyō (Tokyo: Heibonsha). No. 382, "Takiguchi Shūzō" (Apr. 1993).
Takagi Ichinosuke, Gomi Tomohide, and Ōno Susumu, eds. *Nihon koten bungaku taikei.* Vols. 4–7, *Man'yōshū.* Tokyo: Iwanami shoten, 1957–62.
Takahashi Shinkichi. *Afterimages.* London: London Magazine Editions, 1971.
———. *Dada.* Tokyo: Naigai shōbō, 1924.
———. *Dadaisuto Shinkichi no shi.* Tokyo: Chūō bijutsusha, 1923.
———. *Dada to zen.* Tokyo: Hōbunkan, 1971.

———. *Shinkichi shishō.* Tokyo: Hangasō, 1938.

———. *Takahashi Shinkichi shishū.* Tokyo: Nansō shoin, 1928.

———. *Takahashi Shinkichi shishū.* Tokyo: Kadokawa shoten, 1957.

———. *Takahashi Shinkichi zenshū.* 4 vols. Tokyo: Seidosha, 1982.

Takiguchi Shūzō. "Au Japon." *Cahiers d'art* (Paris). Vol. 10, no. 5–6, "Surréalisme" (1935): 132.

———. "Baiser à l'absolu" and "L'Étoile scellée se perpétue." *Opus international* (Paris). No. 19–20, "Surréalisme international" (Oct. 1970): 85–86.

———. *Collection Takiguchi Shūzō.* Tokyo: Misuzu shobō, 1991–95.

———. *Shururearisumu no tame ni.* Tokyo: Serika shobō, 1974.

———. *Takiguchi Shūzō no shiteki jikken, 1927–1937.* Tokyo: Shinchōsha, 1967.

———. *Yohaku ni kaku / Marginalia.* Tokyo: Misuzu shobō, 1982.

——— and Joan Miró. *Tezukuri kotowaza: Joan Miró.* Barcelona: Ediciones Poligrafa, 1970.

———, ed. *To and from Rrose Sélavy: Maruseru Dyushan goroku / Selected Words of Marcel Duchamp.* Tokyo: Bijutsu shuppansha, 1968.

Takiguchi Shūzō to sono shūhen. Osaka: Kokuritsu Kokusai Bijutsukan, 1998.

Tamagawa Nobuaki. *Dadaisuto Tsuji Jun.* Tokyo: Ronsōsha, 1984.

Tanaka, Yukiko, ed. *To Live and to Write.* Seattle, Wash.: Seal Press, 1987.

Terayama Shūji. *Gensō toshokan.* Tokyo: PHP kenkyūjo, 1982.

———. *Shintai o yomu: Terayama Shūji taidanshū.* Tokyo: Kokubunsha, 1983.

Thunman, Noriko. *Nakahara Chūya and French Symbolism.* Stockholm: University of Stockholm, 1983.

Toyama, Jean, and Nobuko Ochner, eds. *Literary Relations East and West.* Honolulu: University of Hawaii; East-West Center, 1990.

Tsukahara Fumi. *Kotoba no avangyarudo: Dada to miraiha no nijusseiki.* Tokyo: Kōdansha, 1994.

Tsuruoka Yoshihisa. *Nihon chōgenjitsushugi shiron.* 2d ed. Tokyo: Shichōsha, 1970.

———. *Shururearisumu no hakken.* Osaka: Yukawa shobō, 1979.

Tsushima, Michiko. "Hagiwara Translating Poe." Paper presented at conference of the Institute for Japanese Studies, Berkeley, Dec. 21, 1993.

Tyler, William Jefferson. "The Agitated Spirit: Life and Major Works of the Contemporary Japanese Novelist Ishikawa Jun." Ph.D. diss., Harvard University, 1981.

Tzara, Tristan. *Oeuvres complètes.* Paris: Flammarion, 1975.

———. *Seven Dada Manifestos and Lampisteries,* trans. Barbara Wright. London: Riverrun Press, 1992.

Uchibori Hiroshi. *Bon shoten no maboroshi.* Kyoto: Hakuchisha, 1992.

Ueda, Makoto. *Modern Japanese Poets and the Nature of Literature.* Stanford: Stanford University Press, 1983.

Ueda Shizue. *Aoi tsubasa.* Tokyo: Kokubunsha, 1957.

————. *Hana to tettō.* Tokyo: Shichōsha, 1963.

————. *Umi ni nageta hana.* Tokyo: Sanwa shobō, 1940.

Ueda Tamotsu. *Shōchōshugi no bungaku to gendai.* Yokohama: Ueda Shizue, 1977.

Variété (Tokyo: Sansaisha). Nos. 1–6 (1933–June 1934).

VOU. Nos. 1–30 (July 1935–Oct. 1940).

Wordsworth, William. *The Prelude: 1799, 1805, 1850,* Jonathan Wordsworth, ed. New York: W. W. Norton, 1979.

Yama mayu. Nos. 1–36 (Dec. 1924–Feb. 1929).

Yamamura Bochō. *Sei sanryo hari.* In *Nihon shijin zenshū.* Tokyo: Sōgensha, 1953.

————. *Yamamura Bochō zenshū.* 4 vols. Tokyo: Chikuma shobō, 1989–90.

Yamanaka Chirū [Tiroux]. *Hiasobi / Jouer au feu.* Tokyo: Bon shoten, 1935.

————. *Shururearisumu shiryō to kaisō 1919–1939.* Tokyo: Bijutsu shuppansha, 1971.

Yampolsky, Philip. *The Platform Sutra of the Sixth Patriarch.* New York: Columbia University Press, 1967.

Yasō (Tokyo: Peyotoru kobō; Atelier Peyotl). No. 13, "Surréalisme" (1984).

Yasō (Tokyo: Peyotoru kobō; Atelier Peyotl). No. 14, "Modan" (1985).

Yasō (Tokyo: Peyotoru kobō; Atelier Peyotl). No. 19, "Gensō no tobira" (1986).

Zeami Motokiyo. *Kadensho (Fūshikaden),* Kawase Kazuma, trans. Tokyo: Kōdansha, 1972.

Zhang Longxi. *The Tao and the Logos.* Durham, N.C.: Duke University Press, 1992.

INDEX

In this index an "f" after a number indicates a separate reference on the next page, and an "ff" indicates separate references on the next two pages. A continuous discussion over two or more pages is indicated by a span of page numbers, e.g., "57–59." *Passim* is used for a cluster of references in close but not consecutive sequence. Page numbers in italics indicate illustrations.

2